WOMEN
PHILOSOPHERS
A Bibliography of
Books through 1990

Else M. Barth

**PHILOSOPHY
DOCUMENTATION
CENTER**

BIBLIOGRAPHIES OF FAMOUS PHILOSOPHERS

The Philosophy Documentation Center publishes an ongoing series of "Bibliographies of Famous Philosophers." Published bibliographies include:

Alfred North Whitehead: A Primary-Secondary Bibliography
Edmund Husserl and His Critics: An International Bibliography (1894-1979)
Jean-Paul Sartre and His Critics: An International Bibliography (1938-1980), Second Edition
Martin Heidegger: Bibliography and Glossary
Hobbes Studies (1879-1979): A Bibliography
George Santayana: A Bibliographical Checklist (1880-1980)
Paul of Venice: A Bibliographical Guide
José Ortega y Gasset: A Bibliography of Secondary Sources
A Bibliography of Vico in English (1884-1984)
Henri Bergson: A Bibliography, Revised Edition
A Comprehensive Bibliography of the Published Works of Charles Sanders Peirce with a Bibliography of Secondary Studies
Bradley: A Research Bibliography

NEW SERIES OF BIBLIOGRAPHIES

Philosophy Books, 1982-1986
Women Philosophers: A Bibliography of Books through 1990

Published by

The Philosophy Documentation Center
Bowling Green State University
Bowling Green, Ohio 43403-0189

ISBN 0-912632-91-7

Preface

Women's works, ideas, and theories need a greater forum within the many branches of philosophy. To help provide such a forum, this bibliography was developed to meet three objectives: to incorporate women's publications in the main body of philosophical thought, increase the visibility and use of publications created by women and minorities, and indicate the variety of approaches, concepts, theories, and so on embodied in these works. The classification and selection systems used to create this bibliography are described in light of these three objectives.

1o *Incorporation*. Women's work, and women's voices, are not to be tucked away into separate corners of the academic world. They are to be put where they belong, right in the heart of each academic field and (sub)discipline. There is every reason to bring women's books out of the ghetto, i.e., to incorporate them in the general discussion, to make it possible for the ideas contained in them to penetrate that discussion at the highest possible speed and to become part and parcel of the world of ideas. Philosophical anthropologists, epistemologists, and historians of philosophy, of both sexes, should be made aware of books—in all their variety—written by women in their own field. This bibliography attempts to show within which topic areas they belong in each discipline, as far as could be seen from their titles.

For example, philosophical feminist books that deal with the images of "man," love and sex, or motherhood are found here under *AI. Theoretical Philosophy*, in the section *Philosophical Anthropology*; those concerning abortion and procreation, under *AII. Practical Philosophy*, in the section *Ethics*. Books on feminist ideology and theory, patriarchy, sexual and gender oppression, and politics are listed under *Political Philosophy*; on gender and role, home, family, or work, under *Social Philosophy*. Books that have as their main object the feminist tradition in human thought are found under *B. History of Philosophy*, in the section *Philosophical Traditions*.

This is not to say that feminist books are found mainly under these headings. Practically all sections and subsections will contain feminist masterpieces, because they are as a rule here put under the usual, not explicitly feminist (or otherwise gender-oriented) headings *whenever the subject makes this natural*. Thus a book with the title *The Troublesome Helpmate—A History of Misogyny in Liter-*

ature is listed here under *History of Philosophical Anthropology*. Feminist books on individual philosophers are listed together with other works on individual philosophers.

2o *Visibility and use.* It seems that most teachers in most philosophy departments offer programs featuring no book at all written by a woman. This means that women philosophers have little or no access to the cultural 'meme pool'.

Books by women should figure more prominently in normal programs of philosophy departments in universities and colleges. As well, in the future they should appear in these programs with (an even) higher frequency than that dictated by their numerical ratio among the total of publications on philosophy. The voices of women, minorities, and representatives of other cultures should be heard, and their works read carefully—by men and women doing research, as well as by all students.

3o *Variety.* Both among staunchly misogynical authors and in some contemporary feminist schools, the *variety* of women's (and men's) ideas and forms of expression are underestimated. As a result, theories about a specific "voice" and a specific "writing" by authors of the female sex are described and treated as truth, with little or no empirical backing. "Masculine" and "Feminine" modes of thought are distinguished with but scant respect for historical and cultural pressures.

This bibliography, in all its imperfection, is offered as a contribution to the *empirical study* of the variety of women's current intellectual activities and interests in philosophy. Similar bibliographies are needed in other academic fields, from political science to mathematics.

Criteria. A book that is listed in this bibliography satisfies *one or more* of the following conditions:

1. It has been listed as philosophical in a brochure from a publishing house, an advertisement, or a review.

2. It is written by a person who holds a university position in a philosophy department.

3. The topic and/or the way it is dealt with satisfies one or more of the several current definitions of "philosophy." There are many such definitions, from those that involve the idea of a *philosophia perennis*, to the definition that classifies a problem, or field of interest, as falling under philosophy as long as it has not yet reached a stage of development that warrants the use of the word "scientific." This means that a book on, say, mental problems may be, and often is, accepted on this list provided it is *not* the case that

psychologists would deem it a scientific rather than philosophical work within their science.

As befits a bibliography, quality of the referenced document has not been a criterion for inclusion. All books we found to satisfy one or more of the criteria listed above are included.

It is easy to explain why contributions to philosophical journals have not been considered as well: their number would make the task impossible.

Classification. It goes almost without saying that the classificatory system applied here is only one among many possible ones. It has been taken (with adaptations) from the classificatory habits in philosophy in the Netherlands.

The distinction between *A. Systematical Philosophy* (AI. Theoretical, AII. Practical) and *B. History of Philosophy* is common in the Netherlands in the basic classifications of philosophical disciplines, and has been followed here. However, it should be used with some care. Thus, if you are interested in publications on logic, refer to the section *Logic* under *AI. Theoretical Philosophy* but also consult the section *Logic, History of* under *B. History of Philosophy— History of specific philosophical disciplines*. Otherwise you will miss out on extremely important contributions to logical analysis. The same holds true of gender analysis.

Wrong slots. That a number of authors find themselves put in what they feel are the wrong slots is regrettable but rather unavoidable. In order to counteract this problem, some cross references have been inserted. An Index of Names should also help.

Completeness. Understandably, not all works from each country can be referenced in a single bibliography. For example, it has not been possible to cover Eastern Europe, or non-English speaking countries outside Europe. We have of course included everything we did find.

Doctoral theses (dissertations), even when they have remained unpublished, were included whenever possible. Recently Jacob Bouwman has contributed a great number of new titles extracted from national bibliographies of philosophical dissertations. Unfortunately, not all countries offer such lists, so here our bibliography is stronger on what has been written in Austria, the Nordic countries of Europe, and the U.S.A. In any case, the titles he has submitted allow for some interesting reflections.

A number of bordering fields are less well covered.

A bibliography of philosophical publications by men who *expressis verbis* have argued for women's inclusion, liberation, ideas, etc., covering the whole philosophical past up to the end of 1990 is being prepared. There are many such men. Some are famous, others are not, but all of them deserve to be.

In the meantime, the present bibliography is gratefully dedicated to these men.

October 1991
Else M. Barth
Department of Logic and Analytic Philosophy,
Groningen University
Groningen, The Netherlands

Acknowledgments

The work on this bibliography started as a hobby in 1976. In that year the Women's Group at the Philosophy Department of the Catholic University at Nijmegen invited me to give a talk on women and philosophy, in which I pointed out that one could—if one so wanted—set up a complete *doctoraalprogramma* in any of the current kinds of philosophy, featuring only books and articles published by women, and that this could be done without lowering (in fact, if one so wanted, while raising) the scientific level of the practically all-male programs that were and are taken for granted in our country. The nature of their response, and that of later women's or mixed groups in the Netherlands, Finland, and Sweden with whom I have discussed this topic, encouraged me to pursue the idea and to demonstrate its validity in writing. Now that this bibliography goes into print, sixteen years later, I think of them all again with warmth. I want to add that although in 1976 I had realized the existence of a lot of unrecognized philosophical work done by women, the number and quality of books that were available at that time (to say nothing of the number available now) by far surpasses even my expectations. I feel towards this collection of titles from every field of philosophy much as I felt when I saw Germaine Greer's book on women painters—a kind of incredulity, and a sense that I wish I could have known about them earlier.

Recently I have been able to profit from Kari Elisabeth Brresen's (Oslo) survey of literature by and about medieval women philosophers, Dagfinn Fllesdal's (Oslo and Stanford) survey of Scandinavian philosophers, the three published volumes of *A History of Women Philosophers*, edited by Mary-Ellen Waithe, and at an earlier stage from research on German women philosophers from earlier centuries done by Hannelore Schrder (Amsterdam). Inga Movitz (Kvinnohistoriska Samlingarna, Gothenburg), Ystein Skar (Oslo), and the philosophers Ulla Holm (Gothenburg), Elina Juusola-Halonen (Siitama, Finland), Rob van Nues (Amsterdam) and Angela Rothaan (Amsterdam), Jeanne A.M. Peijnenburg, Walfred P.A. Haans, and John D. North (Groningen) have volunteered names and titles, and I am grateful to all.

During the last weeks of the bibliography's preparation, Rene Jos Dalitz, lecturer in Feminist Philosophy; Pier A. Smit, lecturer in Analytical Philosophy; the assistant instructors Jacob Bowman, Ronald Hnneman, and Else de Jonge, all of our Department, have carried out—and extended—considerable research tasks which they delved into with enormous seriousness and gusto. I thank them all warmly for their spirited and inspiring cooperation. I also want to thank Jon and Tone Schou Wetlesen, Oslo University, for encouraging me to approach the Philosophy Documentation Center concerning this bibliography, as well as the Center for publishing it.

E.M.B.

CONTENTS

01 DIRECTORIES

Betham, Matilda
    A Biographical Dictionary of the Celebrated Women of
    Every Age and Country. London: Crosby, 1804
Cormier, Ramona, and Richard H. Lineback
    International Directory of Philosophy and Philosophers
    Vol. VII: 1990-92.
    Bowling Green, OH: Philosophy Documentation Center, 1990
Hale, Sarah Josepha
    Women's Record: or Sketches of All Distinguished Women
    from the Creation to A.D. 1854.
    New York: Harper and Brothers, 1860
Kersey, Ethel M.
    Women Philosophers: A Bio-Critical Source Book.
    New York, Westport, CT, London: Greenwood Press, 1989
Whitbeck, Caroline, and Deanne Barousse
    A Directory of Women in Philosophy 1979-1980.
    Bowling Green, OH: Philosophy Documentation Center, 1990

02 GUIDEBOOKS

Yudkin, Marcia, and Janice Moulton
    Guidebook for Publishing Philosophy
    American Philosophical Association, University of
    Delaware, 1986

03 HANDBOOKS

Ströker, Elisabeth, and Wolfgang Wieland (eds.)
    Handbuch Philosophie. 18 Vols.
    Freiburg, etc.: Alber, 1981

04 JOURNALS ESTABLISHED OR (CO-)EDITED BY WOMEN

Bioethics
    Eds.: Helga Kuhse and Peter Singer
    Oxford: Basil Blackwell, Ltd.
Business Ethics (1987)
    Ed.: Marjorie Kelly
    P.O. Box 3473, Madison, WI 53704, USA
Ethics and Advocacy (1985)
    Ed.: Nina Cunningham
    643 North Elmwood Avenue, Oak Park, IL 60302, USA
Feminist Studies (1969)
    Ed. and manager: Claire G. Moses
    University of Maryland, College Park, MD 20742, USA
    Purpose: To encourage analytic responses to feminist
    issues (etc.)

The Hastings Center Report (1971)
    Ed.: Margaret Fletcher Stack
    255 Elm Road, Briarcliff, NY 10510, USA
    Purpose: - interdisciplinary audience - ethical issues
    in biology, medicine, science, social sciences
Hypatia: A Journal of Feminist Philosophy (1982)
    Established by The Society of Women in Philosophy.
    Ed.: Margaret A. Simmons
    Bloomington: Indiana Univ. Press
    Oxford: Pergamon Press Ltd., Headington Hill Hall,
    Oxford OX3 OBW, UK
The International Journal of Philosophy and Psychotherapy (1985)
    Eds.: Sandra A. Wawrytko and James W. Kidd
    Dept. of Philosophy, San Diego State Univ., San Diego, CA, USA

Newsletters issued by the American Philosophical Association
Feminism and Philosophy (1985)
    Issued by the Committee on the Status of Women.
    Ed.: Nancy Tuana, Philosophy Dept., Univ. of Texas at Dallas
    Richardson, TX 75083-0688, USA
Medicine and Philosophy
    Ed.: Rosamond Rhodes, The Mount Sinai Medical Center
    Box 1193, One Gustave Levy Place, New York, NY 10029, USA
Teaching Philosophy
    Ed.: Tziporah Kasachkoff, The Graduate Center, CUNY
    Philosophy Dept., 33 West 42nd Street, New York, NY 10036, USA
Phenomenological Inquiry:
A Review Of Philosophical Ideas And Trends (1977)
    Ed-in-Chief: Anna-Teresa Tymieniecka
    Managing ed.: Marie Lynch, 348 Payson Road,
    Belmont, MA 02178, USA
Die Philosophin - Forum für feministische Theorie und Philosophie
    Eds.: Astrid Deuber-Mankowsky and Ursula Konnertz
    Tübingen: Edition Diskord.
Praxis International
    Eds.: Seyla Benhabib and Svetozar Stojanovic
    Oxford: Basil Blackwell, Ltd.
Proceedings Of the Far Western Philosophy Of Education Society (1971)
    Ed.: Evelina Orteza y Miranda, Dept. of Educational Policy
    and Administrative Studies, Univ. of Calgary, Calgary,
    Alberta, Canada T2N 1N4
Religious Humanism (1963)
    Eds.: Paul and Lucinda Beattie (Co-editors), First
    Unitarian Church, Ellswood and Morewood Avenue,
    Pittsburgh, PA 15213, USA

Resources for Feminist Research/Documentation sur la
Recherche Feministe. Toronto.

Social Philosophy and Policy
Ed.: Ellen Frankel Paul
Oxford: Basil Blackwell, Ltd.

Southern Journal of Philosophy
Ed.: Nancy Simcoe, Dept. of Philos., Memphis State Univ.,
Memphis, TN 38152, USA

A   **Systematic Disciplines**
         (I: Theoretical Philosophy and II: Practical Philosophy)

AI   **Theoretical Philosophy**

AI.1   **General Theoretical Philosophy**

AI.1a   **Introductions**

Calkins, Mary Whiton
An Introduction to Philosophy. 1905

AI.1b   **Other Works**

Agnesi, Maria
Propositiones philosophicae. Milan, 1738
Analytical Institutions. (Trans. J. Colson.)
London: Taylor & Wilkes, 1801

Anscombe, G.E.M.
The Collected Philosophical Papers of G.E.M. Anscombe.
Vol. I: From Parmenides to Wittgenstein.
Vol. II: Metaphysics and the Mind.
Vol. III: Ethics, Religion and the Philosophy of Mind.
Oxford: Blackwell, 1981
Minneapolis: Univ. of Minnesota Press, 1981

Bacinetti-Florenzi Waddington, Marianna
Lettere filosofiche. Paris: 1848

Beardsley, Elizabeth L., and Monroe C. Beardsley
Invitation to Philosophical Thinking.
New York, etc.: Harcourt Brace Jovanovich, 1972

Blackwell, Antoinette Brown
The Physical Basis of Immortality.
New York: G.P. Putnam, 1876

Chatterjee, Margaret
Philosophical Enquiries.
Calcutta: New Age Publishers, 1968

Conway, Anne
The Principles of the Most Ancient and Modern
Philosophy. c. 1675. New ed. by Peter Lopston
The Hague: Nijhoff, 1982

Cruz, Sor Juana Inés de la
    Carta atenagórica. Mexico, 1690
    In: Obras completas, Mexico City: Porrua, 1975
    (with a biography by Alfonso Méndez Plancarte)
Govier, Trudy
    God, the Devil, and the Perfect Pizza -
    Ten Philosophical Questions.
    Peterborough, Ontario: Broadview Press, 1989
Hursthouse, Rosalind
    Introduction to Philosophy.
    Buckinghamshire: Open Univ. Press, 1978
Langer, Susanne K.
    The Practice of Philosophy. New York: Holt, 1930
    Philosophical sketches.
    New York: New American Library, 1964

Philosophy in a New Key - A Study in the Symbolism of Reason, Rite,
    and Art. Harvard: Univ. Press, 1942; New York: Mentor Books,
    1954 [1948]
Filosofische vernieuwins: een studie over de symboliek. Utrecht, etc.:
    Spectrum, 1965
Filosofia em nova chave (trans. J. Meiches and J. Gainsberg). Sao
    Paulo: Perspective, 1971
Parain-Vial, Jeanne
    Tendances nouvelles de la philosophie.
    Paris: Centurion, 1978

   series:

Edgington, Dorothy
    Proceedings of the Aristotelian Society.
    Published by the Aristotelian Society
    Oxford: Blackwell.

AI.2   **Action, Philosophy of** *see also* Phenomenology; Medieval
        Philosophy; General Ethics and Morality; Democracy;
        Thoreau

Heidemann, Ingeborg
    Der Begriff des Spieles. Berlin: De Gruyter, 1968
Held, Virginia
    Rights and Goods: Justifying Social Action.
    New York: Macmillan, Free Press, 1984
Held, Virginia, Kai Nielsen, and Charles Parsons
    Philosophy and Political Action.
    New York: Oxford Univ. Press, 1972

Hornsby, Jennifer
    Actions. London: Routledge and Kegan Paul, 1980

LeMoncheck, Linda
    Dehumanizing Women: Treating Persons as Sex Objects.
    Totowa, NJ: Rowman & Allanheld, 1985

Lenssen, Margrit; Stefan Aufenanger and -
    Handlung und Sinnstruktur. Munich: Kindt, 1986

Nowakowska, Maria
    Language of Motivation and Language of Actions.
    The Hague: Mouton, 1973

Owens, Kathleen Marie
    Rational Action: a Study in Epistemology.
    Pittsburgh, PA: Univ. of Pittsburgh, diss., 1977

Tannen, Deborah
    You Just Don't Understand. Women and Men in Conversation.
    New York: William Morrow & Comp., 1990

Thomson, Ruth Jarvis
    Acts and Other Events. Ithaca, NY: Cornell Univ. Press, 1977

Winslett, Marianne Southall
    Reasoning About Action Using a Possible Models Approach.
    Urbana: Univ. of Illinois at Urbana-Champaign, 1988

Yaguello, Marina
    Les Mots et les Femmes: essai d'approche socio-
    linguistique de la condition féminine.
    Paris: Payot, 1987

    collections: see Phenomenology

AI.3   **Analytic Philosophy** *see also* sub Action; Epistemology;
    Logic; Mind; History of Logic; Individual Philosophers:
    Frege; Quine; Russell; Wittgenstein; a.o.

AI.3a   **General Analytic Philosophy**

Ambrose, Alice
    Essays in Analysis. London: Allen & Unwin, 1966

Ambrose, Alice, Morris Lazerowitz, and -
    Necessity and Language.
    London: Croom-Helm, 1985
    New York: St. Martin's Press, 1986

Anscombe, G.E.M.
    From Parmenides to Wittgenstein.
    Ontario: Oxford U.P., 1981

Barth, E.M.
    Perspectives on Analytic Philosophy.
    Meded. der Kon. Ned. Akad. v. Wet., afd. Letterkunde,
    N.R. 42 No. 2. Amsterdam, etc.: North-Holland, 1979

Camps, Victoria
   Pragmàtica del lenguaje y filosofìa anàlitica.
   Barcelona: Crìtica, 1976
Dach, Gertrud
   Die "regulative" Bedeutung philosophischer Ideen im
   Zusammenhang mit den Universalienproblematik.
   Vienna: diss., 1938
Ganz, Joan Safran
   Rules: A Systematic Study. The Hague: Mouton, 1971
Holmström, Ghita
   Formell viljeteori. Helsinki: Dept. of Philosophy, 1984
MacDonald, Margaret
   Philosophy and Analysis. Oxford: Blackwell, 1954, 1966
Richards, Janet Radcliffe
   The Sceptical Feminist - A Philosophical Inquiry.
   London, etc.: Routledge and Kegan Paul, 1980
Stebbing, L. Susan
   Ideals and Illusions.
   Watts, 1943, 1948 in Thinker's Library
Teichman, Jenny
   Illegitimacy - A Philosophical Examination.
   Oxford: Basil Blackwell, 1982

   collections:
Leinfellner, Elisabeth et al.
   Ethics, Foundations, Problems and Applications -
   Proc. of the 5th Internat. Wittgenstein Symposion.
   Vienna: Hölder Pichler Tempsky, 1980

AI.3b   Analytic Ontology
Bradford, Dennise E.
   The Concept of Existence -
   A Study of Non-Existent Particulars.
   Lanham: Univ. Press of America, 1980
Gosselin, Mia
   Nominalism and Contemporary Nominalism - Ontological
   and Epistemological Implications of the Work of W.V.O.
   Quine and of N. Goodman.
   Dordrecht: Kluwer, 1990
Heal, Jane
   Fact and Meaning. Oxford: Blackwell, 1989
Hesse, Mary, Michael A. Arbib, and -The Construction of Reality.
   New York: Cambridge Univ. Press, 1987
Prior, Elizabeth
   Dispositions. Aberdeen: Aberdeen Univ. Press, 1985

Seibt, Johanna
Properties as Processes:
A Synoptic Study of Wilfred Sellars' Nominalism.
Ridgeway: Ridgeway Publication Company, 1990
Steinhardt, Käthe
Zur logischen Analyse der Lehrmeinungen des
amerikanischen Neureralismus. Vienna: diss., 1935

AI.4   **Anthropology, Philosophical** *see also* Culture; Mind;
Phenomenology; Political Philosophy and History of;
Psychology and Psychoanalysis

AI.4a   **General Philosophical Anthropology**
Andreas-Salomé, Lou
Correspondence avec Sigmund Freud.
Paris: Gallimard, 1970
Bacinetti-Florenzi Waddington, Marianna
Della immortalitá dell'anima umana. Florence, 1864
Continenza, Barbara, and Vittorio Somenzi
L'etologia. Turin: Loescher, 1979
Devor, Holly
Gender Blending. Confronting the Limits of Duality.
Bloomington: Indiana Univ. Press, 1989
Didier, Julia
La question de l'homme et le fondement de la
philosophie. Paris: Aubier-Montaigne, 1965
Dölling, Irene
Naturwesen - Individuum - Persönlichkeit.
Berlin: VEB, 1979
Eisler, Riane
The Chalice of the Blade - Our History, Our Future.
San Fransisco, CA/Cambridge, MA: Harper & Row, 1987
Ferguson, Kathy E.
Self, Society and Womankind. Westport, CT: Greenwood, 1980
Friedan, Betty
Neste fase (trans. Marit Notaker, preface by Astrid
Bekken). Oslo: Universitetsforlaget, 1982
Giard, Luce
L'invention du quotidien, Vol. 2.
Paris: Union Générale d'Éditions, 1980
Giordano, Maria
Le senne tra spiritualismo e caratterologia.
Cassano: Ecumenica, 1975

Gössmann, Elisabeth
Die Frau und ihr Auftrag. Gestalten und Lebens-
formen. Freiburg, etc.: Herder, 1965
De vrouw en haar levensopdracht: levensvormen
van vrouwelijke persoonlijkheden. [Trans. from the
German]. Heerlen, etc.: Roosenboom, 1967

Griffin, Susan
Woman and Nature: The Roaring Inside Her.
New York: Harper & Row, 1978

Heinämaa, Sara, and Esa Saarinen
Olennainen nainen. Helsinki: Werner Söderström, 1983

Irigaray, Luce
Et l'une se bouge pas sans l'autre.
Paris: Editions de Minuit, 1979
La croyance même. Paris: Galilée, 1983
Sexes et parentés. Paris: Editions de Minuit, 1987

Jardine, Alice
Gynesis - Configurations of Woman and Modernity.
Ithaca, NY/London: Cornell Univ. Press, 1985

Keller, Catherine
From a Broken Web: Separation, Sexism, and Self.
Boston: Beacon Press, 1987

Kofman, Sarah
Autobiogriffures. Paris: Galilée, 1984
Le respect des femmes. Paris: Galilée, 1982

Korte, Irma
Nainen ja myytinen nainen. Helsinki, 1988

Le Doeuff, Michèle
L'étude et le rouet. 1. Des femmes, de la philosophie
Paris: Seuil, 1989

List, Elisabeth, Thomas Macho, - , and Ludwig Nagl
Philosophische Psychologie. Hannover: Schroedel, 1983

Marcil-Lacoste, Louise
La thématique contemporaine de l'égalité.
Montreal: Presses de l'Université de Montréal, 1984
La raison en procès: Essais sur la philosophie et le
sexisme. Paris:A.G. Nizet, 1986

McCall, Catherine
Concepts of a Person: An Analysis of Concepts of Person,
Self, and Human Being. Avebury: Avebury Publications, 1990

Meese, Elizabeth, and Alice Parker
The Difference Within: Feminism and Critical Theory.
Amsterdam/Philadelphia: John Benjamins, 1988

Mills, Patricia Jagentowicz
Woman, Nature, and Psyche.
New Haven, etc.: Yale Univ. Press, 1987

Nye, Andrea
    Feminist Theory and the Philosophies of Man.
    London, etc.: Croom Helm, 1987
Osborne, Martha Lee
    Genuine Risk: A Dialogue on Woman.
    Indianapolis: Hackett, 1981
Pardo Bazán, Emilia Condesa de
    La cuestiòn palpitante. 1883
Perrot, Maryvonne
    L'Homme et la métamorphose. Paris: Univ. de Dijon Press, 1979
Préclaire, Madeleine
    Une poétique de l'homme. Montreal: Tournat, 1971
Riley, Denise
    Am I that Name? Feminism and the Category of 'Women' in
    History.
    Minneapolis: Univ. of Minnesota Press, 1988
Rovighi, Sofia Vanni
    Uomo e natura: Appunti per una antropologia filosofica.
    Milan: Pensiero, 1980
Sabuco de Nantes Barrera, Oliva
    Oliva Sabuco de Nantes Barreras. Obras.
    Ed. R. Fè. Madrid, 1888
    Nueva filosofia de la naturaleza del hombre, no
    conocida ni alcancada de los grandes filosofos antiguos:
    la qual mejora la vida y salud humana.
    Madrid: Madrigal, 1587
    [idem]: Con las addiciones de la segunda impressi y,
    (en esta tercera) expurgada.
    Braga: Fructuoso Lourezo de Basto, 1622
    Reprinted Madrid 1728, 1847, Paris 1866, Biblioteca de
    Autores Españoles 1973 and 1929
Shelley, Mary
    Frankenstein - several editions, 1818, London: AMS Press
Skura, Meredith Anne
    The Literary Use of the Psychoanalytic Process.
    New Haven: Yale Univ. Press, 1981
Ströker, Elisabeth
    Ich und die Anderen: die Frage der Mitverantwortung.
    Frankfurt a.M.: Klostermann, 1984
Tanner, Nancy
    On Becoming Human. New York: Cambridge Univ. Press, 1981
Telfer, Elizabeth, Downie, R.S., and -
    Respect for Persons. London: Allen & Unwin, 1969
Westkott, Marcia
    The Feminist Legacy of Karen Horney.
    New Haven: Yale Univ. Press, c. 1980

White, Patricia
    Beyond Domination. London: Routledge & Kegan Paul, 1983
Wilkes, Kathleen V.
    Real People: Personal Identity without Thought Experiments.
    Oxford: Oxford Univ. Press, 1988
Zarri, Adriana
    L'impatience d'Adam. Toulouse: Privat, 1968

collections:

Ardener, Shirley (ed.)
    Defining Females: The Nature of Women in Society.
    New York: Wiley, 1978
Bock, Mette, Hanna Hvidtfeldt, and Lone Kalstrup (eds.)
    Kvindespin - Könsfilosofiske essays.
    Århus: Philosophia (Institut for filosofi), 1987
Eisenstein, Hester, and Alice Jardine
    The Future of Difference.
    New Brunswick, NJ: Rutgers Univ. Press, 1988
Heinämaa, Sara (ed.)
    Naisen tieto. Helsinki: Art House, 1989
Hubbard, Ruth, Mary Sue Henifin, and Barbara Fried (eds.)
    Biological Woman: The Convenient Myth.
    Cambridge, MA: Schenkman, 1982
Klinger, Cornelia, and Ruthard Stäblein (eds.)
    Identitätskrise und Surrogatidentitäten:
    Zur Wiederkehr einer romantischen Konstellation.
    Frankfurt am Main and New York: Campus Verlag, 1989
Reiter, Rayna R. (ed.)
    Toward an Anthropology of Women.
    New York: Monthly Review Press, 1975
Rorty, Amélie Oksenberg (ed.)
    The Identities of Persons.
    Berkeley: Univ. of California Press, 1976
Tymieniecka, Anna-Teresa (ed.)
    The Philosophical Reflection on Man in Literature.
    Dordrecht: Reidel, 1982

AI.4b   **Body** *see also* Mind-Body Problem; Political Philosophy
Brumberg, Joan Jacobs
    Fasting Girls. The History of Anorexia Nervosa.
    New York: New American Library, 1989
Spitzak, Carole
    Confessing Excess: Women and the Politics of Body.
    Reduction. New York: State Univ. of New York Press, 1990

Thomas, Carolyn
    Sport in a Philosophical Context.
    Philadelphia: Lea & Febiger, 1983

collections:

Gerber, Ellen W. (ed.)
    Sport and the Body: A Philosophical Symposium.
    Philadelphia: Lea & Febiger, 1972
Lynn, Joanne (ed.)
    By No Extraordinary Means:
    The Choice to Forgo Life-sustaining Food and Water.
    Bloomington: Indiana Univ. Press, 1986
Postow, Betsy C. (ed.)
    Women, Philosophy and Sport: A Collection of New Essays.
    Metuchen: Scarecrow Press, 1983
Suleiman, Susan (ed.)
    The Female Body in Western Culture - Contemporary
    Perspectives. Cambridge: Harvard Univ. Press, 1986

AI.4c   Consciousness, Creativity, Rationality *see also* Mind
Bacinetti-Florenzi Waddington, Marianna
    Saggio sulla filosofia dello spirito.
    Florence: Successori Le Monnieri, 1867
Bailin, Sharon
    Achieving Extraordinary Ends: An Essay of Creativity.
    Dordrecht: Kluwer Academic Publishers, 1988
Bowes, Pratima
    Consciousness and Freedom: Three Views.
    New York: Barnes & Noble, 1971
Le Doeuff, Michèle
    Recherches sur l'imaginaire philosophique.
    Paris: Payot, 1980
Holm, Ulla
    Medvetande och praxis - Feministfilosofiska forsök.
    Göteborg: Institutionen för filosofi, Filosofiska
    meddelanden, Gröna serien no. 36, 1990
Kassowitz, Julie
    Teleologie als Denkform. Vienna: diss., 1907
Kessler, Elisabeth
    Über die Einhet des Bewusstseins. Vienna: diss., 1925
Kohli-Kunz, Alice
    Erinnern und Vergessen. Berlin: Duncker & Humblot, 1973
Leroy, Cathérine
    Sens anthropologique et éthique du mythe Navaho de l'émergence.
    Louvain-la-Neuve: Univ. Catholic de Louvain, 1982

Lilienfeld, Irene
    Über die Erinnerung, das Wiedererkennen und die
    Phantasie. Vienna: diss., 1917
Lotringer, Ida
    Der Willensvorgang. Vienna: diss., 1917
Radden, Jennifer
    Madness and Reason. London: Allen & Unwin, 1985
Rowbotham, Sheila
    Woman's Consciousness, Man's World.
    Baltimore: Penguin, 1973; Harmondsworth: Penguin, 1977
Smith, Hilda
    Reason's Disciples.
    Urbana-Champaign: Univ. of Illinois Press, 1982

   collections:
Gibson, Mary (ed.)
    To Breathe Freely: Risk, Consent, and Air.
    Totowa: Rowman & Allanheld, 1985
List, Elisabeth, and Herlinde Studer (eds.)
    Denkverhältnisse. Feminismus und Kritik.
    Frankfurt am Main: Suhrkamp, 1989

AI.4d   Emotions and Feeling *see also* Existence, Philosophy of
Bacinetti-Florenzi Waddington, Marianna
    La Facolta di Sentire. Montepulciano, 1869
Braidotti, Rosi
    Beelden van de Leegte. Kampen: Kok Angora, 1990
Cameron, Deborah, and Elizabeth Frazer
    The Lust to Kill. A Feminist Investigation of Sexual Murder.
    Cambridge, MA: Polity Press, 1987
Coward, Rosalind
    Female Desire. London: Granada, 1984
Heller, Agnes
    Instinkt, Aggression, Charakter:
    Einleitung zu einer marxistischen Social-Anthropologie.
    Hamburg [etc]: VSA, 1977
    Az érzelmek elmélete. Eng. trans.:
    A Theory of Feelings. Assen: Van Gorcum, 1979
    Theorie der Gefühle. Hamburg: VSA-Verlag, 1980
    The Power of Shame. A Rational Perspective.
    London: Routledge & Kegan Paul, 1985
Irigaray, Luce
    Passions élémentaires. Paris: Ed. de Minuit, 1982
Kristeva, Julia
    Powers of Horror. New York: Columbia Press, 1982

Langer, Susanne K.
    Mind: An Essay on Human Feeling I-III.
    Baltimore: Johns Hopkins Univ., 1967, 1972, 1982, 1988

Michielsens, Magda
    Beschrijving van het verloop van het emotief proces
    uitgaande van een analyse van het concept "emotie" en
    van een onderzoek naar de relaties tussen emotieve en
    perceptief-cognitieve processen. Reëvaluatie van
    emotiviteit en oriëntatie naar een wetenschappelijk
    verantwoord mensbeeld. Gent: Univ. of Gent, 1973

Reich, Louise
    Die Lust. Versuch einer psychologischen und
    ästhetiscihen Analyse der Lust. Vienna: diss., 1921

Rorty, Amélie Oksenberg
    Explaining Emotions. Berkeley: Univ. of California Press, 1980

Russier, Jeanne
    La souffrance. Paris: Initiation Philosophique, 1963

Schäfer, Gisela
    Versuch einer kritischen Darstellung neuerer Theorien
    über das Wesen der Affekte. Vienna: diss., 1902

Scudéry, Madeleine de
    Discours pur et contre l'amitié tendre. 1653

Taylor, Gabriele
    Pride, Shame and Guilt: Emotions of Self-Assessment.
    Oxford: Oxford Univ. Press, 1985

Telfer, Elizabeth
    Happiness. New York: St. Martin's Press, 1980

    collections:

Craemer-Ruegenberg, Ingrid (ed.)
    Pathos, Affekt, Gefühl. Freiburg: Alber, 1981

AI.4e   Images of "Man"

Andersen, Margaret
    Thinking About Women. New York: Macmillan, 1983

Badinter, Elisabeth
    L'un est l'autre. Paris: O. Jacob, 1986
    De een is de ander: de relaties tussen mannen en
    vrouwen. Amsterdam: Contact, 1988
    The Unopposite Sex. The End of the Gender Battle.
    New York: Harper & Row, 1989

Bovenschen, Silvia
    Die imaginierte Weiblichkeit: Exemplarische Untersuchungen
    zur Kulturgeschichtlichen und literarischen Présentationsform
    des Weiblichen. Frankfurt: Suhrkamp, 1979

Butler, Judith P.
Gender Trouble. Feminism and the Subversion of Identity.
New York: Routledge, 1990

Dessaur, C.I.
De droom der rede: het mensbeeld in de sociale
wetenschappen. Een poging tot criminosofie.
The Hague: Nijhoff, 1982. Amsterdam: Querido, 21984
De achtste scheppingsdag. Arnhem: Gouda Quint BV, 1988

Dinnerstein, Dorothy
The Mermaid and the Minotaur:
Sexual Arrangements and Human Malaise.
New York: Harper & Row, 1976

Ekenvall, Asta
Mannligt-Kvinnligt. Idéhistoriska Studier.
Göteborg, 1966

Elshtain, Jean Bethke
Public Man, Private Woman:
Women in Social and Political Thought.
Princeton, NJ: Princeton Univ. Press, 1981

Farganis, Sondra
The Social Reconstruction of the Feminine Character.
Totowa, NJ: Rowman and Littlefield, 1987

Friedan, Betty
The Feminine Mystique.
New York: W.W. Norton and Company, 1963

Gaarder, Pia A.
Patriarkalske forutsetninger for skillet mellom det private og
det politiske, mennesket og makten. En kritisk analyse
av menneskebildet i nyere tid.
Oslo: Institutt for Filosofi, 1987

Gössmann, Elisabeth
Das Bild der Frau heute.
Düsseldorf: Haus d. Kath. Frauen, 1962

Greer, Germaine
The Female Eunuch.
London: Paladin/(USA): MacGibbon & Kee, 1971

Haegen, Rina van der
In het spoor van sexuele differentie.
Nijmegen: SUN, 1989

d'Héricourt, Jenny
A Woman's Philosophy of Woman.
New York: Carleton, 1846
Facsimile reprinted. Westport, CT: Hyperion Press, 1981

Herschberger, Ruth
Adam's Rib. New York: Harper & Row, 1970

Hooks, B.
    Ain't I a Woman? Black Women And Feminism.
    London: Pluto Press, 1982
    Feminist Theory. From Margin to Center.
    Boston: South End Press, 1984
Horney, Karen
    Neurosis and Human Growth. New York: Norton, 1950
Hörz, Hela E.
    Blickpunkt Persönlichkeit.
    Berlin: VEB Deutscher Wissenschaften, 1975
Irigaray, Luce
    Speculum de l'autre femme.
    Paris: Editions Minuit, 1974
    Speculum: Spiegel des anderen Geschlechts.
    Frankfurt am Main: Suhrkamp, 1980
    Speculum of the Other Woman (trans. Gillian C. Gill)
    Ithaca, NY/London: Cornell Univ. Press, 1985
    Ce sexe qui n'est pas un.
    Paris: Editions de Minuit, 1977 (1983)
    Das Geschlecht, das nicht eins ist.
    Trans. from the French. Berlin: Merve Verlag, 1979
    Dit geslacht dat niet (een) is. Tr. by Jeanne Buntinx
    et al. Amsterdam: Hölderlin, 1981
    This Sex Which Is Not One. Trans. Catherine Porter and
    Carolyn Burke. Ithaca, NY/London: Cornell Univ. Press, 1984
Klein, Viola
    The Feminine Character - History of an Ideology (1946) with a
    preface by Karl Mannheim, and an introd. to the American ed. by
    Janet Zollinger Giele. Urbana, etc.: Univ. of Illinois Press, 1972
Leacock, Eleanor B.
    Myths of Male Dominance.
    New York: Monthly Review Press, 1982
Lilar, Suzanne
    Le malentendu du deuxième sexe.
    Paris: Presses Univ. de France, 1969
Lloyd, Genevieve
    The Man of Reason -
    Male and Female in Western Philosophy.
    London: Methuen, 1982
Lundgren, Eva, and Kristin Eriksen
    Hva er kjönn? Analyser av kjönnsdikotomisering.
    Oslo: Universitetsforlaget, 1990
Marinella, Lucretia
    Le Nobilita et Eccelenze delle Donne: et i Diffetti e
    Mancamenti de gli Huomini. Venice: 1600
Massey, Marilyn Chapin
    Feminine Soul: The Fate of an Ideal. Boston: Beacon Press, 1985

McMillan, Carol
    Women, Reason and Nature - Some Philosophical Problems
    With Feminism. Oxford: Basil Blackwell, 1982
Monsen, Nina Karin
    Jomfru, mor eller menneske? Feministisk filosofi.
    Oslo: 1984
    Det kjempende mennesket - maktens etikk.
    Oslo: 1990
Morgan, Elaine
    The Descent of Woman.
    London: Souvenir Press; New York: Stein & Day, 1972

collections:

Bell, Linda A. (ed.)
    Visions of Women: A Philosophical Chronicle.
    Clifton, NJ: The Humana Press, 1983
Lowe, Marian, and Ruth Hubbard (eds.)
    Woman's Nature: Rationalizations of Inequality.
    New York: Pergamon Press, 1983
Mahowald, Mary Briody (ed.)
    Philosophy of Woman: Classical to Current Concepts.
    Indianapolis: Hackett, 1978, 21983
Sanday, Peggy Reeves, and Ruth Gallager Goodenough (eds.)
    Beyond the Second Sex. New Directions in the
    Anthropology of Gender.
    Baltimore, MD: Pennsylvania Univ. Press, 1990
Vetterling-Braggin, Mary (ed.)
    "Femininity", "Masculinity", and "Andragony" -
    A Modern Philosophical Discussion.
    Totowa, NJ: Littlefield, Adams & Co., 1982
Warren, Mary Anne
    The Nature of Woman. An Encyclopedia & Guide to the
    Literature. Inverness, CA: Edgepress, 1980

AI.4f   Love and Sex

Aragona, Tullia d'
    Dell'infinite di amore. c. 1550
Blackwell, Elizabeth
    The Human Element in Sex. London, 1884
Coveney, Lal, Margaret Jackson, Sheila Jeffreys, Leslie Kay,
    and Pat Mahoney
    The Sexuality Papers - Male Sexuality and the Social
    Control of Women.
    London/Melbourne, etc.: Hutchinson, in assoc. with The
    Explorations in Feminism Collective, 1984

Grosz, Elizabeth
>   Sexual Subversions. Three French feminists.
>   Sydney, etc.: Allen and Unwin, 1989
>   London: Unwin & Hyman, 1990

Heloïse
>   Epistolae Heloisae. In Migne, Patrologia Latina, 176
>   The Letters of Abelard and Heloïse. Trans. by C.K. Scott
>   Moncrieff. New York: Knopf, 1926

Kofman, Sarah
>   Séductions: de Sartre à Héraclite. Paris: Galilée, 1990

Kristeva, Julia
>   Abjection, Melancholia and Love. The Work of Julia
>   Kristeva. (Eds. John Fletcher and Andrew Benjamin.)
>   London and New York: Routledge, 1990

Sherfey, Mary Jane
>   The Nature and Evolution of Female Sexuality.
>   New York: Random House, 1966

collections:

Alanen, Lilli, Leila Haaparanta, and Terhi Lumme (eds.)
>   Nainen, järki ja ihmisarvo:
>   Esseitä filosofian klassikoiden naiskäsityksistä.
>   Helsinki: Werner Söderström, 1985

English, Jane (ed.)
>   Sex Equality. Englewood Cliffs, NJ: Prentice-Hall, 1977

Mariaux, Veronika, a.o. (eds.)
>   Diotima, il pensiero della differenza sessuale.
>   Milano: La Tartaruga, 1987

AI.4g   Motherhood

Chodorow, Nancy
>   The Reproduction of Mothering.
>   Berkeley, CA, etc.: Univ. of California Press, 1979

Irigaray, Luce
>   Le corps-à-corps avec la mère.
>   Montréal: Éditions de la plaine lune, 1981

Oakley, Ann
>   Becoming a Mother. Martin Robertson, 1979

Rich, Adrienne
>   Of Woman Born -
>   Motherhood as Experience and Institution.
>   London: Virago/New York: W.W. Norton, 1976

Welldon, Estela
>   Mother Madonna, Whore:
>   The Idealisation and Denigration of Motherhood.
>   New York: Free Association, Columbia Univ. Press, 1988

collections:

Arditti, Rita, et al. (eds.)
　　Test-Tube Women: What Future for Motherhood.
　　London: Pandora Press, 1984

Trebilcot, J. (ed.)
　　Mothering: Essays in Feminist Theory.
　　Totowa, NJ: Rowman and Allanheld, 1984

AI.4h　　Old Age and Death

Beauvoir, Simone de
　　De ouderdom. Utrecht: Bijleveld, 1975

Cormier, Ramona, and Janis Pollister
　　Waiting for Death. University: Univ. of Alabama Press, 1979

Dinage, Rosemary
　　The Ruffian on the Stair: Reflections on Death.
　　New York: Viking, 1990

Gervais, Karen Grandstrand
　　Redefining Death. New Haven: Yale Univ. Press, 1987

Grisé, Yolande
　　Le suicide dans la Rome antique.
　　Montreal: Bellarmin, 1982

Hockey, Jennifer Lorna
　　Experiences of death: An Anthropological Account.
　　Edinburgh: Edinburgh Univ. Press, 1990

Schuurman (or Schurman), Anna Maria van
　　De vitae humanae termino. 1639. Trans. as:
　　Pael-steen van den tyt onses levens.
　　Dordrecht and Amsterdam, 1639

AI.5　　Cosmology

Bacinetti-Florenzi Waddington, Marianna
　　Filosofemeni di cosmologia e di antologia. Perugia, 1863

Blackwell, Antoinette Brown
　　The Philosophy of Individuality.
　　New York: G. P. Putnam, 1893

Hildegard of Bingen
　　Symphonia armonie celestium revelationum. 12th cent.
　　St. Hildegard of Bingen. Symphonia. Ed. Barbara Newman.
　　A critical edition of the above.
　　Ithaca, NY: Cornell Univ. Press, 1988

Somerville, Mary
　　The Mechanism of the Heavens. London, 1831
　　Preliminary Dissertation to the "Mechanism of the
　　Heavens" by Mrs. Somerville. London, 1931
　　A Preliminary Dissertation on the Mechanism of the
　　Heavens. Philadelphia, 1832

AI.6   Empirical Sciences, Philosophy and Foundations of Special -
see also Language; Mathematics; Science, History of

AI.6a   Biology, Evolution, and Medicine

Arber, Agnes
    The Mind and the Eye: a Study of the Biologist's
    Standpoint. Cambridge: Cambridge Univ. Press, 1954
Birke, Lynda
    Women, Feminism and Biology: The Feminist Challenge.
    Brighton: Harvester (Wheatsheaf Books), 1986
Blackwell, Antoinette Brown
    The Sexes Throughout Nature.
    New York: G.P. Putnam, 1869. Hyperion Press, 1976
Bleier, Ruth
    Science and Gender: A Critique of Biology and Its
    Theories on Women. New York: Pergamon Press, 1984
Fausto-Sterling, Anne
    Myths of Gender. Biological Theories about Women and
    Men. New York: Basic Books, Inc., 1985
Grene, Marjorie
    Approaches to a Philosophical Biology.
    New York: Basic Books, 1968
    The Understanding of Nature: Essays in the Philosophy
    of Biology. Dordrecht: Reidel, 1974
Haraway, Donna
    Primate Visions: Gender, Race and Nature in the World
    of Modern Science. New York: Routledge, 1990
    Simians, Cyborgs and Women. The Reinvention of Nature.
    New York: Routledge, 1989
Hildegard of Bingen
    Causae et Curae. 12th cent.
    Trans. and ed. by Henrich Schipperges as:
    Hildegard von Bingen. Heilkunde "Cause et Curae."
    Leipzig: Paulus Kaiser, 1903
    Salzburg: Otto Müller, 41981
Hodanova, D., Cizek, F. and -
    Evolution als Selbstregulation. Jena: Fischer, 1971
Hrdy, Sarah Blaffer
    The Woman that Never Evolved.
    Cambridge, MA: Harvard Univ. Press, 1982
Keller, Evelyn Fox
    Reflections on Gender and Science.
    New Haven: Yale Univ. Press, 1985
Kevles, Bettyann
    Females of the Species. Sex and Survival in the Animal
    Kingdom. Cambridge, MA: Harvard Univ. Press, 1986

Lloyd, Elisabeth
 The Structure and Confirmation of Evolutionary Theory.
 New York: Greenwood Press, 1988
Midgley, Mary
 Evolution as Religion: Strange Hopes and Strange Fears.
 London: Methuen, 1985
 Beast and Man: the Roots of the Human Race.
 Ithaca, NY: Cornell Univ. Press, 1978
Parain-Vial, Jeanne
 Philosophie des sciences de la Nature -
 Tendances Nouvelles. Paris: Klincksieck, 1983
Teumer, Elfriede
 Philosophische Probleme der Wechselbeziehung von
 Struktur und Funktion in Biologie.
 Jena: VEB Gustav Fischer, 1969
Wappler, Sigrid
 Philosophische Studien zum Problemkreis Genetik und
 Evolution. Jena: VED Fischer, 1973
Warren, Mary Anne
 Gendercide: The Implications of Sex Selection.
 Totowa, NJ: Rowman and Allanheld, 1985

 collections:

Conry, Yvette (ed.)
 De Darwin au Darwinisme: Science et ideologie.
 Paris: Vrin, 1983
Fagot, Anne (ed.)
 Médecine et probabilités.
 Paris: Didier Erudition, 1982
Grene, Marjorie (ed.)
 Dimensions of Darwinism.
 Cambridge: Cambridge Univ. Press, 1983
Grene, Marjorie, and Everett Mendelssohn (eds.)
 Topics in the Philosophy of Biology
 (Boston Studies in the Philosophy of Science, Vol. XXVII).
 Dordrecht: Redial, 1976

AI.6b   Criminology
Dessaur, C.I.
 Foundations of Theory-Formation in Criminology -
 A Methodological Analysis.
 The Hague: Mouton, 1971
Naffine, Ngaire
 Female Crime: The Construction of Women in
 Criminology.
 Winchester, MA: Unwin Hyman, 1988

AI.6c   Economics

Bergmann, Barbara R.
   The Economic Emergence of Women.
   New York: Basic Books, 1986

Dow, Sheila
   Macroeconomic Thought:
   A Methodological Approach.
   Oxford: Blackwell, 1985

Gilman, Charlotte (Perkins)
   Women and Economics, 1898
   New ed. by Carl N. Degler, New York: Harper & Row, 1966

Gould, Carol C.
   Rethinking Democracy: Freedom and Social Co-operation
   in Politics, Economy and Society.
   Cambridge: Cambridge Univ. Press, 1988

Held, Virginia
   The Public Interest and Individual Interests.
   New York: Basic Books, 1970

Roland Holst-van der Schalk, Henriëtte
   Kapitaal en arbeid in Nederland. Amsterdam: Soep, 1902

Martineau, Harriet
   Illustrations of Political Economy I-IX.
   London: C. Fox, 1834

Waring, Marilyn
   If Women Counted - A New Feminist Economics.
   San Francisco: Harper, 1988

   collections:

Jones, Aubrey (ed.)
   Economics and Equality. London: Allen, 1976

AI.6d   Education *see also* Culture: Academy; Political
           Philosophy: Sex/Gender Oppression

AI.6da   -Education in general

Beecher, Catharine
   Woman's Profession as Mother and Educator with Views in
   Opposition to Woman's Suffrage.
   Philadelphia: Maclean, 1872
   An Essay on the Education of Female Teachers.
   New York: Van Nostrand and Dwight, 1835

Bisseret-Moreau, Noëlle
   Class, Language and Ideology.
   London: Routledge and Kegan Paul, 1979

Brann, Eva T.H.
  Paradoxes of Education in a Republic.
  Chicago: Univ. of Chicago Press, 1979

Bremer, Anne, and John Bremer
  Open Education: A Beginning.
  New York: Holt, Rinehart & Winston, 1972

Cohen, Brenda
  Education and the Individual. London: Allen & Unwin, 1981

Frostig, Marianne
  Education for Dignity: Approaches to Education in Our
  Time. New York: Grune & Stratton, 1976

Gerlach, Helen M.
  Individual Schema Development in Solving Mathematical
  Word Problems.
  Lawrence: Kansas State Univ., diss., 1986

Graham, Patricia A.
  Progressive Education: From Arcady to Academe.
  New York: Columbia Teachers College Press, 1967

Greene, Maxine
  Teacher as Stranger: Educational Philosophy for the
  Modern Age. Belmont, CA: Wadsworth, 1973
  Landscapes of Learning.
  New York: Teachers' College Press, 1978

Griffin, Christine
  Typical Girls? - Young Women from School to the Job Market.
  London: Routledge & Kegan Paul, 1985

Kehoe, Mary, and J.V. D'Cruz
  Values: Education and Society.
  Melbourne: Twentieth Century, 1978

Macaulay-Graham, Catherine
  Letters on Education. London, 1787
  Reprinted London and New York: Garland Press, 1974

Makin, Bathsua Pell
  An Essay to Revive the Ancient Education
  of Gentlewomen, 1673.
  Los Angeles: Univ. of California/W.A. Clark Library, 1980

Maria, Amalia de
  L'educazione della persona. Turin: Giappichelli, 1974

Martin, Jane Roland
  Explaining, Understanding and Teaching.
  New York: McGraw-Hill, 1970
  Reclaiming a Conversation: The Ideal of the Educated Woman.
  New Haven: Yale Univ. Press, 1985

Montessori, Maria
  Education For a New World. 1946

Roland, Madame
  Discours de Besançon: comment l'éducation des femmes
  pourrait contribuer à rendre les hommes meilleurs. 1777
Schlichter, Lea
  Der sittlich starke Charakter als oberster Zweck der
  Erziehung. Vienna: diss., 1916
Schubart-Fikentscher, Gertrud
  Studienreform: Fragen von Leibniz bis Goethe.
  Berlin: Akademie, 1973
Sharp, Rachel, and Anthony Green
  Education and Social Control.
  Boston: Routledge & Kegan Paul, 1975
Spender, Dale
  Invisible Women: the Schooling Scandal.
  London: Writers and Readers, 1982
Steiner, Elizabeth
  Educology of the Free. New York: Philosophy Library, 1981
Wollstonecraft, Mary
  Thoughts on the Education of Daughters. 1788

  collections:

Burleigh, Anne Husted (ed.)
  Education in a Free Society.
  Indianapolis: Liberty Press, 1973
Durka, Gloria, and Joanmarie Smith (eds.)
  Emerging Issues in Religious Education.
  New York: Paulist Press, 1976
Spender, Dale, and Elizabeth Sarah (eds.)
  Learning to Lose: Sexism and Education.
  London: The Women's Press, 1980

AI.6db -Critical and Creative Thinking *see also* Informal
  Logic and Logical Argumentation
Brisby, Linda-Sue et al.
  Logic: A "Hands On" Approach to Teaching.
  Hand On, CA, 1987
Drews, Ursula
  Zum dialektischen Charakter des Unterrichtsprozesses.
  Berlin: Volk und Wissen, 1983
Halpern, Diane F.
  Thought and Knowledge: An Introduction to Critical
  Thinking. Hillsdale, NJ: Lawrence Erlbaum, 1984
Needels, Margaret
  The Role of Logic in the Teacher's Facilitation of
  Student Achievement.
  Stanford: Stanford Univ., diss., 1984

Patrick, Catharine
What is Creative Thinking? New York: Philosophical Library, 1955
Reyes, Reina
Los métodos Lógicos y su aplicacion a la didáctica.
[S.L.]: Apuntes Sur, 1970

collections:
La Bar, Carol, Ian Wright, and - (eds.)
Critical Thinking and Social Studies.
Toronto: The History of Social Science Teacher, 1986

AI.6e   Historiography and Archaeology
Heller, Agnes
A Theory of History. Don Mills: Oxford U.P., 1982
London, etc.: Routledge and Kegan Paul, 1982
Kelly, Joan
Women, History and Theory - The Essays of Joan Kelly.
Chicago: Univ. of Chicago Press, 1984
Archeology and the Methodology of Science.
Albuquerque: Univ. of New Mexico Press, 1988
Löw, Elisabeth von
Zur Logik der Geschichtsphilosophie. Vienna: diss., 1938
Nagl-Docekal, Herta
Die Objektivität der Geschichtswissenschaft:
Systematische Untersuchungen zum wissenschaftlichen
Status der Historie. Vienna, etc.: Oldenbourg, 1982
Neue Ansätze in der Geschichtswissenschaft.
Vienna: VWGÖ, 1984
Salmon, Merrilee H.
Philosophy and Archeology. New York: Academic Press, 1982
Scott, Joan Wallach
Gender and the Politics of History.
New York: Columbia Univ. Press, 1989

AI.6f   Linguistics *see also* Language; Logic
Bartsch, Renate
Grundzüge einer empiristischen Bedeutungstheorie
[S.l.]. Heidelberg: Univ. Heidelberg, diss., 1969
Adverbialsemantik: die Konstitution logisch-
semantischer Repräsentationen von Adverbial-
konstruktionen. Frankfurt a.M.: Athenäum, 1972
The Grammar of Adverbials - A Study in the Semantics
and Syntax of Adverbial Constructions.
Amsterdam, etc.: North-Holland, 1976
Sprachnormen: Theorie und Praxis.
Tübingen: Niemeyer, 1985

Bartsch, Renate, and Theo Venneman
  Semantic Structures: A Study in the Relation between
  Semantics and Syntax. Frankfurt a.M.: Athenäum, 1972
Cameron, Deborah
  Feminism and Linguistic Theory.
  London/Hampshire: Macmillan, 1985, 21987
Kristeva, Julia
  Language: The Unknown - An Initiation into Linguistics.
  London, etc.: Harvester Wheatsheaf, 1989
Partee, Barbara Hall
  Fundamentals of Mathematics for Linguistics.
  Dordrecht, etc.: Reidel; Stanford, CT: Greylock, 1978
Partee, Barbara Hall, and Alice B. ter Meulen
  Mathematical Methods in Linguistics.
  (Studies in Linguistics and Philosophy 30)
  Norwell: Kluwer, 1990

  bibliographies:
Partee, Barbara Hall et al.
  Bibliography: Logic and Language.
  Bloomington: Indiana Univ. Linguistics Club, 1971

  collections:
Bartsch, Renate, and Theo Venneman (ed.)
  Linguistik und Nachbarwissenschaften.
  Kronberg/Ts.: Scriptor, 1973
Cameron, Deborah (ed.)
  The Feminist Critique of Language: A Reader.
  London, etc.: Routledge (World and Word series), 1990

AI.6g   Literature, The study of
Felman, Shoshana
  The Literary Speech Act. (Trans. Catherine Porter)
  Ithaca, NY: Cornell Univ. Press, 1983
  Writing and Madness: Literature/Philosophy/Psychoanalysis.
  Ithaca, NY: Cornell Univ. Press, 1985
Göttner, Heide, and Joachim Jakobs
  Der logische Bau von Literaturtheorien. München: Fink, 1979
Maitre, Doreen
  Literature and Possible Worlds.
  London: Middlesex Polytechnic Press, 1983
Nussbaum, Martha
  Essays on Philosophy and Literature.
  Oxford: Clarendon Press, 1977
  Love's Knowledge: Essays on Philosophy and Literature.
  Oxford: Oxford Univ. Press, 1990

Pratt, Mary Louise
Toward a Speech Act Theory of Literary Discourse.
Bloomington: Indiana Univ. Press, 1977

AI.6h   Physical Sciences *see also* Science, History of
Cartwright, Nancy
How the Laws of Physics Lie.
London, etc.: Oxford University Press, 1982
Nature's Capacities and their Measurement.
Oxford: Clarendon Press, 1989
Châtelet-de Breteuil, Gabrielle Emilie le Tonnelier, du
Institutions de physique. Paris: Prault fils, 1740
Response de Madame *** à la lettre que M. de Mairan, Sécrétaire
perpétuel de l'Académie Royale des Sciences, lui a écrite le
18 février sur la question des forces vives. Brussels, 1741
Dissertation sur la nature et la propagation du feu.
Paris: Académie Française, 1744
First French translation of Isaac Newton's
Philosophiae Naturalis Principia Mathematica
"Principes Mathématiques de la Philosophie Naturelle."
Paris: Desaint & Saillant, 1759
Destouches-Février, Paulette
La structure des théories physiques.
Paris: P.U.F., 1951
Fairfax-Somerville, Mary
The Connection of the Physical Sciences. c. 1820
Hager, Nina
Modelle in der Physik, erkenntnistheoretisch betrachtet.
Berlin: Akademie Verlag
Hesse, Mary
Forces and Fields. London: Nelson, 1961
Hildegard of Bingen
Physica. 12th cent.
Hildegard von Bingen. Naturkunde. "Physica."
Ed. P. Riethe. Salzburg: Otto Müller Verlag, 1980
Hildegard von Bingen. Das Buch von den Steinen.
Ed. P. Riethe. Salzburg: Otto Müller Verlag, 1986
Nersessian, Nancy
Faraday to Einstein -
Constructing Meaning in Scientific Theories.
Dordrecht: Nijhoff, 1984
Parain-Vial, Jeanne
Les difficultés de la quantification et de la
mesure. Paris: Maloine, 1981
Philosophie des sciences de la nature: tendances.
Nouvelles. Paris: Klincksieck, 1983

Somerville, Mary
> On the Connection of the Physical Sciences. London: 1834, 1846.
> London and New York: Harper & Bros., 1846
> De la connexion des sciences physiques où expose et
> rapide de tous les principaux phenomènes astronomiques,
> chimigues, géologiques, et météorologiques, accompagné
> des découvertes modernes, tant français qu'étrangers.
> Trans. de l'Anglais, sous l'auspices de M. Arago, par Mme
> T. Meulien. Paris, 1839

Ströker, Elisabeth, and Rainald Hahn
> Denkwege der Chemie:
> Elemente ihrer Wissenschaftstheorie.
> Freiburg, etc.: Alber, 1967
> Wissenschaftstheorie der Naturwissenschaften.
> Grundzügen ihrer Sachproblematik und Modelle für den
> Unterricht. Freiburg: Alber, 1981

editions:
Riethe, P. *see* Hildegard von Bingen

AI.6i **Political Science** *see also* Political Philosophy

Cocks, Joan
> The Oppositional Imagination - Feminism, Critique and
> Political Theory. New York: Routledge, 1989

Coole, Diana
> Women in Political Theory:
> From Ancient Misogyny to Contemporary Feminism.
> Brighton: Harvester (Wheatsheaf Books), 1987

AI.6j **Psychology and Psychoanalysis** *see also* Freud;
Psychoanalytical Tradition

Amado Levy-Valensi, Eliane
> Les voies et les pièges de la psychanalyse.
> Paris: Universitaires, 1971

Benjamin, Jessica
> The Bonds of Love: Psychoanalysis, Feminism, and the
> Problem of Domination. New York: Pantheon, 1988

Boden, Margaret A.
> Purposive Explanation in Psychology.
> Cambridge: Harvard Univ. Press, 1972

Gilligan, Carol
> In a Different Voice -
> Psychological Theory and Women's Development.
> Cambridge, MA/London: Harvard Univ. Press, 1982

Hollway, Wendy
    Subjectivity and Method in Psychology: Gender, Meaning,
    and Science. London: Sage, 1989
Irigaray, Luce
    Unbewusstes, Frauen, Psychoanalyse.
    Berlin: Merve Verlag, 1977
Mitchell, Juliet
    Psychoanalysis and Feminism: Freud, Reich, Laing and
    Women. New York: Pantheon, 1974
    Psicoanàlysis y feminismo: Freud, Reich, Laing y las
    mujeres. Barcelona: Anagrama, 1976
Penfold, P. Susan, and Gillian Walker
    Women and the Psychiatric Paradox. Montreal: Eden, 1983
Piesch, Hermine
    Beiträge zur Methodologie der geistigen Vererbungslehre.
    Vienna: diss., 1918
Sayers, Janet
    Sexual Contradictions: Psychology, Psychoanalysis and
    Feminism. London: Tavistock, 1986

collections:

Hare-Mustin, Rachel, and Jeanne Marecek (eds.)
    Making a Difference. Psychology and the Construction of
    Gender. New Haven: Yale Univ. Press, 1990
Brennan, Teresa (ed.)
    Between Feminism and Psychoanalysis.
    London, etc.: Routledge, 1989

AI.6k   Social Sciences

Adam, Barbara
    Time and Social Theory
    Philadelphia: Temple Univ. Press, 1990
Brodbeck, May
    Readings in the Philosophy of the Social Sciences.
    New York: Macmillan, 1968
Eichler, Margrit
    The Double Standard - A Feminist Critique of Feminist
    Social Science. London: Croom Helm, 1980
    Nonsexist Research Methods: A Practical Guide.
    (London and) Winchester, MA: Allen & Unwin, 1988
Emmet, Dorothy
    Rules, Roles and Relations. London: Macmillan, 1966
Goodwin, Barbara
    Social Science and Utopia. Brighton: Harvester, 1978

Hekman, Susan J.
  Weber, The Ideal Type and Contemporary Social Theory.
  Univ. of Notre Dame, 1983
Mayntz, Renate
  Formalisierte Modelle in der Soziologie.
  Berlin: Hermann Luchterhard, 1967
Michl, Emilie
  Ist Soziologie als Wissenschaft möglich?
  Vienna: diss., 1914
Roure, Francine, and Alain Butury
  Mathématiques pour les sciences sociales.
  Paris: P.U.F., 1970
Schneider, Ulrike
  Sozialwissenschaftliche Methodenkrise und
  Handlungsforschung.
  Frankfurt: Campus, 1980
Sydie, Rosalind A.
  Natural Women, Cultured Men. A Feminist Perspective
  on Sociological Theory.
  Milton Keynes: Open Univ. Press, 1987

  collections:

Emmet, Dorothy and Alasdair MacIntyre (eds.)
  Sociological Theory and Philosophical Analysis.
  New York: Macmillan, 1970
Harding, Sandra (ed.)
  Feminism and Methodology: Social Science Issues.
  Bloomington: Indiana Univ. Press, 1987
Hockey, Susan, and Nancy Ide
  Research in Humanities Computing (annual).
  Oxford: Clarendon Press, 1990
Stanley, Liz (ed.)
  Feminist Praxis: Research, Theory and Epistemology
  in Feminist Sociology.
  London: Routledge, 1990

AI.7   **Epistemology** *see also* Anthropology: Consciousness,
            Creativity, Rationality; Empirical Sciences, Foundations
            of the Special; Logic; Mind; Philosophy of Science

AI.7a   Introductions
Trusted, Jennifer
  An Introduction to the Philosophy of Knowledge.
  London: Macmillan, 1982

AI.7b   General Epistemology (Theory of Knowledge)
see also General Theoretical Philosophy

Allart de Meritens, Hortense
Novum Organum, ou Sainteté Philosophique.
Paris: Garnier Frères, 1857
Lettres Inédites à Sainte-beuve, 1841-1848.
Paris: Mercure de France, 1908

Barnes, Annette
On Interpretation - A Critical Analysis.
Oxford: Blackwell, 1988

Barragan, Julia
Hipotesis metodologicasi.
Caracas: Editorial Juridica Venezoelana, 1983

Blackwell, Antoinette Brown
The Making of the Universe.
New York: The Gorham Press, 1914

Code, Lorraine
Epistemic Responsibility.
Hanover/London: University Press of New England, 1987
Feminist Theory and the Construction of Knowledge.
Ithaca, NY: Cornell Univ. Press

Mac Coll, Sylvia Hazelton
Structure and Development of Phenomenal Reality:
A Psychological Analysis.
New York: Exposition Press, 1963
Essays in the Sociology of Perception.
London: Routledge and Kegan Paul, 1982

Gardner, Helen
In Defense of the Imagination.
Cambridge: Harvard Univ. Press, 1982

Grene, Marjorie
Philosophy In and Out of Europe.
Berkeley: Univ. of California Press, 1976

Grosholz, Emily R.
Cartesian Method and the Problem of Reduction.
Oxford and New York: Oxford Univ. Press, 1990

Harding, Sandra
Feminism and Methodology.
Bloomington: Indiana Univ. Press, 1987

Johnson, Barbara
The Critical Difference.
Baltimore: Johns Hopkins Univ. Press, 1981

Klein, Ellen Ruth
Should Epistemology be Naturalized?
A Meta-epistemological Investigation.
Coral Gables, FL: Univ. of Miami, diss., 1989

Knorr-Cetina, Karin
   The Manufacture of Knowledge. Oxford: Pergamon, 1981
Kokoszynska, Marian
   Eine Widerlegung der Relativität der Wahrheit.
   Poznan, 1947
List, Elisabeth
   Alltagsrationalität und soziologischer Diskurs.
   Frankfurt: Campus, 1983
Loeck, Gisela
   Auskunft über die Gesetzesartigkeit aus ihrer
   Konstruktion.
   Osnabrück: Osnabr. Philos. Schr., 1985
   Der Cartesische Materialismus. Maschine, Gesetz,
   Simulation. Bern: Peter Lang, 1986
Luhrmann, Rosemary
   Persuasions of the Witch's Craft: Ritual Magic in Contemporary
   England. Cambridge, MA: Harvard Univ. Press, 1989
Mayberry, Katherine J.
   Christina Rosetti and the Poetry of Discovery.
   Baton Rouge: Louisiana State Univ. Press, 1989
Minnich, Elizabeth Kamarck
   Transforming Knowledge.
   Philadelphia: Temple Univ. Press, 1990
Motycka, Alina
   Ideal racjonalnosci. Szkice o filozoficznych.
   Wroclaw: Ossolineum, 1986
Niggli, Ursula
   Erkenntnis und Ernst. Bern: Lang, 1982
O'Brien, Mary
   Reproducing the World - Essays in Feminist Theory.
   Boulder, CO: Westview Press, 1989
Richter, Gudrun
   Gesetzmässigkeiten und Geschichtsprozess.
   Berlin: Dietz, 1985
Roberts, Joan
   Beyond Intellectual Sexism: A New Woman, a New Reality.
   New York: David McKay, 1976
Robles, Nilda, Rodolfo Gaeta, and -
   Nociones de epistemologia. Buenos Aires: Endeba, 1985
Schlözer, Dorothea
   philosophical thesis, 1787
Schott, Robin May
   Cognition and Eros: A Critique of the Kantian Paradigm.
   Boston: Beacon, 1988

Simson, Rosalinde Slivka
    Perspectives on the Epistemic Regress Problem.
    New Haven: Yale Univ., diss., 1979
Spender, Dale
    For the Record -
    The Making and Meaning of Feminist Knowledge.
    London: The Women's Press, 1985
Stanley, Liz, and Sue Wise
    Breaking Out: Feminist Consciousness and Feminist
    Research. London: Routledge & Kegan Paul, 1980
Stebbing, L. Susan
    Ideals and Illusions. London: Watts, 1941
Stefano, Anna Escher di
    Il radicalismo filosofico come esperienza del vissuto.
    Napels: Loffredo, 1981
Stein, Edith = Sister Teresa Benedicta
    Zum Problem der Einfühlung. Halle, 1917
    Das Einfühlungsproblem in seiner historischen
    Entwicklung und in phänomenologischer Betrachtung;
    Tl. 2, Nr. 4. Diss. Freiburg i. Br.
    On the Problem of Empathy [trans. from the
    German by Waltraut Stein. With a forew. by Erwin
    W. Straus]. The Hague: Nijhoff, 1964
    Collected Works. ISC Publ. 1989
    Vol. III: On the Problem of Empathy. Trans. by W. Stein.
    Il problema dell'empathia. Rome: Studium, 1985
Thom, Martina
    Ideologie und Erkenntnistheorie. Berlin: Deutscher, 1980
Unzer, Johanna Charlotte
    Grundriss einer Weltweisheit für das Frauenzimmer:
    mit Anmerkungen und einer Vorrede von J.G. Krügern.
    Halle: CH Hemmerde, 1767
Walsh, Dorothy
    Literature and Knowledge.
    Middletown, CT: Wesleyan Univ. Press, 1969
Warnock, Mary
    Imagination. Berkeley: Univ. of California Press, 1976
Winters, Barbara Anne
    Reasonable Believing.
    Berkeley: Univ. of California, diss., 1977

collections:

Code, Lorraine, S. Mullett, and Christine Overall (eds.)
    Feminist Perspectives: Philosophical Essays on Methods
    and Morals. Toronto: Univ. of Toronto Press, 1988

Garry, Ann, and Marilyn Pearsall (eds.)
  Women, Knowledge & Reality -
  Explorations in Feminist Philosophy.
  London: Unwin & Hyman, 1989
Gergen, Mary M. (ed.)
  Feminist Thought and the Structure of Knowledge.
  New York: New York Univ. Press, 1988
Grene, Marjorie (ed.)
  The Anatomy of Knowledge.
  Amherst: Univ. of Massachusetts Press, 1969
  Knowing and Being: Essays by Michael Polanyi.
  London: Routledge & Kegan Paul, 1969
  Toward a Unity of Knowledge.
  New York: International Univ. Press, 1969
Gunew, Sneja (ed.)
  Feminist Knowledge: Critique and Construct.
  London, etc.: Routledge, 1990
Harding, Sandra, and Merrill B. Hintikka (eds.)
  Discovering Reality - Feminist Perspectives on
  Epistemology, Methodology and Philosophy of Science.
  Dordrecht, etc.: Reidel, 1983
Hekman, Susan J.
  Gender and Knowledge. Elements of a Post-modern
  Feminism. Cambridge: Polity Press, 1990
Jaggar, Alison M., and Susan R. Bordo (eds.)
  Gender/Body/Knowledge:
  Feminist Reconstructions of Being and Knowledge.
  New Brunswick, NJ: Rutgers Univ. Press, 1989

AI.7c   Causality and Determinism

Destouches-Février, Paulette
  Déterminisme et indéterminisme (Pref. by Éduard Le Roy).
  Paris: P.U.F., 1955
Emmet, Dorothy
  Function, Purpose and Powers. London: Macmillan, 1972
  The Effectiveness of Causes. London, etc.: McMillan, 1984
Fodor, Judit
  Die Entwicklung der Determinismus-Konzeption.
  Budapest: Kiadò, 1980
Puterman, Zalma M.
  The Concept of Causal Connections I-II.
  Uppsala: Uppsala Univ. (Philosophical Studies), 1977
Zagzebski, Linda
  The Dilemma of Freedom and Foreknowledge.
  Oxford and New York: Oxford Univ. Press, 1990

Wolf, Susan
    Freedom Within Reason.
    Oxford and New York: Oxford Univ. Press., 1990

AI.7d   Knower and the Known *see also* Rhetoric

Astell, Mary
    A Serious Proposal to the Ladies for the Advancement of
    their True and Greatest Interest. By a Lover of her Sex
    Vol. I: London: Printed for R. Wilkins at the King's
    Head in St. Paul's Church Yard, 1694, 1695, 1696

Bregman, Lucy
    The Rediscovery of Inner Experience.
    Chicago: Nelson Hall, 1982

Belenky, Mary Field, Blythe McVickere Clinchy, Nancy Rule
        Goldberger, and Jill Mattuck Tarule
    Women's Ways of Knowing:
    The Development of Self, Voice, and Mind.
    New York: Basic Books, 1986

Douglas, Mary
    In the Active Voice.
    Boston: Routledge & Kegan Paul, 1982

Grene, Marjorie
    The Knower and the Known.
    Berkeley: Univ. of California Press, 1974

Harding, Sandra
    Whose Science? Whose Knowledge? Thinking From Women's
    Lives. Ithaca, NY: Cornell Univ. Press, 1990

Högemann, Brigitte
    Die Idee der Freiheit und das Subjekt.
    Königstein, 1980

Nelson, Lynn H.
    Who Knows - From Quine to a Feminist Empiricism.
    Philadalphia: Temple Univ. Press, 1990

Nagl-Docekal, Herta, and H.Vetter (eds.)
    Tod des Subjekts? Vienna, etc.: Oldenbourg, 1987

Schuurman (or Schurman), Anna Maria van
    Eucleria: seu, melioris partis electio. Tractatus
    brevem vitae ejus delineationem exhibens I-II
    Altona and Amsterdam: C. van der Meulen, 1673, 1685
    Eucleria, of uitverkiezing van het beste deel
    Amsterdam: Jacob van de Velde, 1684
    Leeuwarden: De Tille, 1978 (photomech. reprint)
    Continuatie van de Eukleria. Appended to Yvon: Oprecht
    verhael, 1754
    Opuscula hebraeca, greca, latina, gallica, prosaica et

metrica (with letters to contemporary scholars)
Leyden: Elsevir, 1642 and later; Utrecht, 1652; ext.
ed. Leipzig, 1749
Anna Maria van Schurman en J. van Beverwyck: Geleerde
brieven van de edele deugt- en konst-rycke Juffrouw,
Anna Maria van Schuurman gewisselt met de geleerde en
beroemde heeren Samuel Rachelius, Professor in de
Rechten te Kiel en Johan van Beverwyk, Med. Doct. tot
Dordrecht. Amsterdam, 1728
Lettres de la très fameuse demoiselle Anna Marie
Schurmans, académicienne de la fameuse Université
Utrecht. Tr. from Dutch by J.D. van Zoutelande
Lindenaer. Paris: 1730

AI.7e   Knowledge Representation

Brodsky, Claudia J.
The Imposition of Form. Studies in Narrative
Representations and Knowledge.
Princeton, NJ: Princeton Univ. Press, 1987

Calvet de Magalhaes, Theresa
Un, deux, trois: catégories fondamentales.
Joâo Pessoa, Brasil: Editora universitaria, 1980
Louvain-La-Neuve: Cabay, 1981

Egidi, Rosaria
Il languaggio delle teorie scientifiche. Esperianza ed
ipotesi nell'epistemologia contemporanea.
Naples: Guida editori, 1979

Emerton, Norma E.
The Scientific Representation of Form.
Ithaca, NY: Cornell Univ. Press, 1984

Goodisoor, Lucy
Symbols of Sexuality & Spirituality.

Hogan, Melinda Ann
The Concept of Thought:
Logical Form in the Account of Mental Representation.
Madison: Univ. of Wisconsin, diss., 1989

Jaggar, Alison M., and Paula Rothenberg Struhl
Feminist Frameworks.
New York: McGraw-Hill, 1978

Judge, Brenda
Thinking about Things -
A Philosophical Study of Representation.
Edinburgh: Scottish Academic Press, 1985

Kappeler, Susanne
The Pornography of Representation.
Minneapolis: Univ. of Minnesota Press, 1986

Kempson, Ruth M.
    Mental Representations. The Interface between Language
    and Reality. Cambridge: Cambridge Univ. Press, 1989
Markova, Ivana
    Paradigms, Thought and Language. New York: Wiley, 1982
Pavlova, Vera Todorova
    Logiko-istoricheskii analiz metodologii i metodov
    nauchnogo predvideniia.
    Sofia: idz-vo Bolgarskoi akademii nauk, 1984
Pitkin, Hanna Fenichel
    The Concept of Representation.
    Berkeley: Univ. of California Press, 1972

collections:

Bresnan, Joan (ed.)
    The Mental Representation of Grammatical Relations.
    Cambridge, MA: MIT Press, 1982
Craig, Colette (ed.)
    Categorization and Noun Classification.
    Amsterdam and Philadelphia: John Benjamins, 1986
Gelder, B. de (ed.)
    Knowledge and Representation. Proc. of Conf. at the
    Neth. Inst. Advanced Studies, Wassenaar, March 1979.
    London: Routledge & Kegan Paul, 1981
Jacobson, Pauline, and Geoffrey K. Pullum - (eds.)
    The Nature of Syntactic Representation.
    Dordrecht: Reidel, 1982
Nichols, Johanna, Wallace Chafe, and (eds.)
    Evidentiality. The Linguistic Coding of Epistemology.
    Norwood, NJ: Ablex Publishing Co., 1986
Rosch, Eleanor, and B.B. Lloyd (eds.)
    Cognition and Categorization. Hillsdale, NJ: Erlbaum, 1978

AI.7f   Objectivity

Bello, Angela Ales
    L'oggetività come pregiudizio.
    Rome: La Goliarda, 1982
Bordo, Susan R.
    The Flight to Objectivity:
    Essays on Cartesianism and Culture.
    Albany: State Univ. of New York Press, 1987
Heldke, Lisa Maree
    Coresponsible Inquiry:
    Objectivity from Dewey to Feminist Epistemology.
    Evanston, IL: Northwestern Univ., diss., 1987

Longino, Helen E.
    Science as Social Knowledge. Values and Objectivity.
    in Scientific Inquiry.
    Princeton, NJ: Princeton Univ. Press, 1990
Vawter, Dorothy E.
    The Truth and Objectivity of Practical Propositions:
    Contemporary Arguments in Moral Epistemology.
    Washington, DC: Georgetown Univ., diss., 1987

AI.7g   Paradoxes, Epistemic
Belgum, Eunice
    Knowing Better. An Account of Acrasia.
    New York: Garland Publishing, 1990, diss., 1976)
Wolgast, Elizabeth Hankins
    Paradoxes of Knowledge.
    Ithaca, NY: Cornell Univ. Press, 1977

AI.7h   Physicalism
Baker, Lynne R.
    Saving Belief: A Critique of Physicalism.
    Princeton, NJ: Princeton Univ. Press, 1988
Stebbing, L. Susan
    Philosophy and the Physicists. London, 1937
Traweek, Sharon
    Particle Physics Culture: Buying Time and Taking Space. 1987
Wilkes, Kathleen V.
    Physicalism. Atlantic Highlands: Humanities Press, 1978

AI.7i   Positivism
Andrei, Marga
    Cunoastere si sens:
    Perspective critice asupra pozitivismului.
    Bucharest: Editura Politica, 1984
Mannlicher, Gertrud
    Die Kausalkritik Hume's und ihre Auswirkung im
    Positivismus. Vienna: diss., 1933
Rischmüller, Marie, and Burkhard Tuschling
    Kritik des logischen Empirismus.
    Berlin: Duncker und Humblot, 1983
Schüssler, Ingeborg
    Philosophie und Wissenschaftspositivismus.
    Frankfurt: Klosterman, 1979
Serebrenik, Erna
    Das Erkenntnistheoretische Fundamentalbestand der
    positivistischen Philosophie. Vienna: diss., 1926

Stebbing, L. Susan
  Logical Positivism and Analysis. Annual Philosophical
  Lecture, British Academy, 1933

AI.7j   Pragmatism
Mahowald, Mary Briody
  An Idealistic Pragmatism. The Hague: Nijhoff, 1972
Rosenthal, Sandra B.
  Speculative Pragmatism.
  Amherst: Univ. of Massachusetts Press, 1986
Rosenthal, Sandra B., and Patrick L. Bourgeois
  Pragmatism and Phenomenology.
  Atlantic Highlands: Humanities Press, 1980

AI.7k   Skepticism
Annas, Julia, and Jonathan Barnes
  The Modes of Skepticism.
  Cambridge: Cambridge U.P., 1985
Freiin von Reicher, Franziska
  Das Nichtreale als Fiktion. Vienna: diss., 1919
Hnidey, Ludmilla
  Zur Frage der philosophischen Skepsis.
  Vienna: diss., 1917
McGinn, Marie
  Sense and Certainty: The Dissolution of Scepticism.
  Oxford: Blackwell, 1989
Moreux, Colette
  La conviction ideologique.
  Montreal: Presses Univ. de Québec, 1978

AI.8   Language, Philosophy of
  see also Action; Analytic Philosophy; Logic: Semantics;
  Linguistics, Foundations of; Mind

AI.8a   "Language in General" *see also* Religion; Aesthetics
Avramides, Anita
  Meaning of Mind: An Examination of a Gricean Account of
  Language. Cambridge, MA: MIT Press, 1989
Berger, Gertrude, and Beatrice Kachuk
  Sexism, Language and Social Change.
  Washington, DC (USA): US Dept. of Health, Education and
  Welfare, National Institute of Education, 1977
Bolton, Martha
  Humorous Monologues. New York: Sterling, 1989

Bruggen, Carry van
  Hedendaagsch Fetischisme. Amsterdam: Querido, 1925
Cixous, Hélène
  Entre l'écriture. Paris: des Femmes, 1986
Cook, Vivian
  Chomsky's Universal Grammar - An Introduction.
  Oxford: Blackwell, 1988
Dahlgren, Kathleen
  The Nature of Linguistic Stereotypes.
  Chicago: Chicago Linguistic Society, 1978
Harvey, Irene E.
  Derrida and the Economy of Difference.
  Bloomington: Indiana Univ. Press, 1986
Herzler, Joyce D.
  A Sociology of Language. New York: Random House, 1965
Irigaray, Luce
  Parler n'est jamais neutre.
  Paris: Editions de Minuit, 1985
Johnson, Barbara
  A World of Difference.
  Baltimore and London: Johns Hopkins Univ. Press, 1989
Kramarae, Cheris
  Women and Men Speaking. Rowley, MA: Newbury House, 1981
Kremer-Marietti, Angèle
  La symbolicité. Paris: P.U.F., 1982
Kristeva, Julia
  Desire in Language (ed. and trans. by L. S. Roudiez).
  New York: Columbia Univ. Press, 1980
  The Kristeva Reader (ed. Toril Moi).
  New York: Urizen Books, 1986
Lakoff, Robin
  Language and Woman's Place.
  New York: Harper & Row, 1975
Nowakowska, Maria
  Educational Variables.
  Dordrecht: Kluwer Academic Publishers, 1988
Penn, Julia M.
  Linguistic Relativity Versus Innate Ideas.
  The Hague: Mouton, 1972
Sänger, Monika
  Die Kategoriale Systematik. Berlin: De Gruyter, 1982
Schober, Rita
  "Im Banne der Sprache."
  Halle: Mitteldeutscher, 1968

Smith, Barbara Herrnstein
    On the Margins of Discourse.
    Chicago: Univ. of Chicago Press, 1978
Spender, Dale
    Man Made Language.
    London/Boston/Henley: Routledge and Kegan Paul, 1980, 1985
Wierzbicka, Anna
    Lingua mentalis. Sydney: Academic Press, 1980
Yaguello, Marina
    Les mots et les femmes: essai d'approche socio-
    linguistique de la condition féminine.
    Paris: Payot, 1978 (reprinted: 1982, 1987)
    Les Fous du language: des langues imaginaires et de
    leurs inventeurs. Paris: Seuil, 1984

    collections:

Barr, Marleen S., and Richard Feldstein (eds.)
    Discontented Discourses:
    Feminism/Textual Intervention/Psychoanalysis.
    Ithaca, N.Y.: Univ. of Illinois Press, 1989
Henley, Nancy, Barrie Thorne, and (eds.)
    Language and Sex: Difference and Dominance.
    Rowley, MA: Newbury House, 1975
Seidel, Gill (ed.)
    The Nature of the Right: Feminist analysis of order
    patterns (Critical Theory Series).
    Amsterdam: John Benjamins, 1988
Suleiman, Susan, and Inge Crosman (eds.)
    The Reader in the Text -
    Essays on Audience and Interpretation.
    Princeton, NJ: Princeton Univ. Press, 1980
Vetterling-Braggin, Mary (ed.)
    Sexist Language: A Modern Philosophical Analysis.
    Totowa, NJ: Littlefield, Adams, 1981

AI.8b   Communication *see also* Informal Logic and Logical
    Argumentation
Akhmanova, Olga Sergeevna
    Optimization of Natural Communication Systems.
    The Hague: Mouton, 1977
Bavelas, Janet Beavin, Alex Black, Nicole Chovil, and
    Jennifer Mullett
    Equivocal Communication.
    London: Sage, 1990

Corradi Fiumara, Gemma
Filosofia dell'ascolto.
Milan: Jaca Book spa (Le Editioni Universitarie), 1985
The Other Side of Language: A Philosophy of Listening
(trans. of (1985)). London: Routledge

De Fossard, Esta
For Argument's Sake - A First Course in Argument.
Evaluation. Melbourne: L&S Publications, 1981

Levy-Valensi, Eliane Amado
La communication. Paris: Presses Univ. de France, 1967

Shimanoff, Susan B.
Communication Rules: Theory and Research.
Beverly Hills: Sage, 1980

Wilson, Deirdre, Dan Sperber, and -
Relevance: Communication and Cognition.
Oxford: Blackwell, 1986

AI.8c   **Meaning** *see also* Knowledge Representation

Akhmanova, Olga Sergeevna
Meaning Equivalence and Linguistic Expression.
Moscow: MGU, 1973

Corradi Fiumara, Gemma
Funzione simbolica e filosofia del linguaggio.
Turin: Boringhieri, 1980
The Symbolic Function and Philosophy of Language.
Oxford: Blackwell, 1990

Elgin, Catherine Z.
With Reference to Reference.
Indianapolis: Hackett, 1983

Gumpel, Liselotte
Metaphor Reexamined - A Non-Aristotelian Perspective.
Bloomington: Indiana Univ. Press, 1985

Kempson, Ruth M.
Presupposition and the Delimitation of Semantics.
New York: Cambridge Univ. Press, 1975
Semantic Theory. Cambridge: Cambridge U.P., 1977

Kerbrat-Orrechioni, Catherine
La connotation. Lyon: Univ. de Lyon Press, 1977

Kittay, Eva Feder
Metaphor: Its Cognitive Force and Linguistic Structure.
Oxford: Clarendon Press, 1989

Lehrer, Adrienne, and Keith Lehrer
Theory of Meaning. Englewood Cliffs, NJ: Prentice-Hall, 1970

Lorraine, T.E.
Gender, Identity, and the Production of Meaning. c. 1986

Meulen, Alice B. ter
  Substances, Quantities and Individuals -
  A study in the formal semantics of mass terms.
  Stanford University, diss., 1980
Pusch, Luise F., and Christoph Schwarz
  Probleme einer Semantiksprache für den Sprachvergleich.
  Trier: Linguistic Agency Univ. of Trier, 1974
Reis, Marga
  Präsuppositionen und Syntax. Tübingen: Niemeyer, 1977
Röska-Hardy, Louise
  Die "Bedeutung" in natürlichen Sprachen.
  Frankfurt a/M: Athenäum, 1988
Sweetser, Eve Eliot
  Semantic Structure and Semantic Change.
  Berkeley: Univ. of California, diss., 1984
Wilson, Deirdre
  Presuppositions and Non-Truth-Conditional Semantics.
  London: Academic Press, 1975

collections:
Partee, Barbara Hall (ed.)
  Montague Grammar. New York: Academic Press, 1976

AI.8d   Pragmatics
Armegaud, Françoise
  La pragmatique. Paris: P.U.F., 1985
Diller, Anne-Marie
  La pragmatique des questions et des réponses.
  Tübingen: Narr, 1984
Hajicová, Eva, Peter Sgall, and Jamilla Panevová (eds.)
  The Meaning of the Sentence in its Semantic and
  Pragmatic Aspects. Dordrecht: Reidel, 1986
Kates, Carol
  Pragmatics and Semantics: An Empirical Theory.
  Ithaca, NY: Cornell Univ. Press, 1980
Michard-Marchal, Claire, and Claudine Ribery
  Sexisme et sciences humaines:
  Pratique linguistique du rapport de sexage.
  Lille: Presse Univ. de Lille, 1982
Schlieben-Lange, Brigitte
  Linguistische Pragmatik. Stuttgart: Kohlhammer, 1975

AI.8e   Rhetoric
Arnold, Carroll C.
  Criticism of Oral Rhetoric. Columbus, OH: Merrill, 1974

Fahnenstock, Jeanne, and Marie Secor
    A Rhetoric of Argument. New York: Random House, 1982
    McGraw-Hill, 1990
Foss, Sonja K., Karen A. Foss, and Robert Trapp
    Contemporary Perspectives on Rhetoric.
    Prospect Heights, IL: Waveland Press
Olbrechts-Tyteca, Lucie
    Le comique du discours.
    Brussels: Editions de l'Université 1974
Olbrechts-Tyteca, Lucie, Ch. Perelmans, and
    Rhétorique et philosophie.
    Presses Universitaires de France, 1952
    La nouvelle rhétorique. Traité de l'argumentation.
    Brussels: Institut de Sociologie, 1970
    (Presses Universitaires de France, 1958),
    [It. trans. Turin, 1962]
    The New Rhetoric: A Treatise on Argumentation.
    Notre Dame: Univ. Press, 1958, 1969
Russow, Lilly-Marlene
    Principles of Reasoning.
    New York: St. Martin's Press, c. 1989
Steiner, Wendy
    The Colors of Rhetoric. Chicago: Univ. of Chicago Press, 1982

AI.8f Semiotics, General

AI.8fa -Introductions

Walther, Elizabeth
    Allgemeine Zeichenlehre: Einführung in die Grundlagen
    der Semiotik. Stuttgart: Deutsche Verlags-Anstalt, 1974

AI.8fb -Other works

Akhmanova, Olga Sergeevna
    Linguistics and Semiotics.
    Moscow: Moscow Univ. Press, 1979
Coward, Rosalind, and Jon Ellis
    Language and Materialism -
    Developments in Semiology and the Theory of the Subject.
    London: Routledge & Kegan Paul, 1977
Fischer-Lichte, Erika
    Bedeutung: Probleme einer semiotischen Hermeneutik und
    Aesthetik. Munich: Beck, 1979
Klarfeld, Maria
    Über das Problem der inneren Sprache.
    Vienna: diss., 1919

Ramos, Alice
Signum: de la semiotica universal a la metafisica del
signo. Pamplona: EUNSA, 1987
Welby, Victoria Lady
Links and Clues. London: Macmillan, 1881, 1983
The Use of the "Inner" and "Outer" in Psychology: Does
the Metaphor Help or Hinder? Grantham: W. Clarke (Late
L. Ridge). For private circulation. 1892
A Selection of Passages from "Mind" (1876-1889)
"Nature" (1879, 1888, 1892) "Natural Science" (1892)
bearing on the changes and defects in the significance
of terms and in the theory and practice of logic.
Grantham: W. Clarke, 1893
Grains of Sense. London: J.M. Dent & Co., 1897
The Witness of Science to Linguistic Anarchy.
Grantham: W. Clarke, 1898
What is Meaning? Studies in the Development of
Significance (with an Introductory essay by Gerrit Mannoury
and a Preface by Achim Eschbach). London: Macmillan, 1903
Reprinted Amsterdam/Philadelphia: John Benjamins
(Foundations of Semiotics Series vol. 2), 1983
Significs and Language - The Articulate Form of our
Expressive and Interpretative Resources.
London: Macmillan, 1911
Reprinted of (1911) and two articles, ed. and introd. H.
Walter Schmitz. Amsterdam/Philadelphia: John Benjamins
(Foundations of Semiotics Series vol. 5), 1985
Significato, metafora e interpretazione (transl. Susan Petrilli).
Bari: Segni di Segni, Quaderni di Filosofia del linguaggio e
Antropologica culturale dell'Universitá di Bari, 1986

collections:

Kristeva, Julia et al. (eds.)
Semeiotike. Recherches pour une sémanalyse.
Paris: Éditions de Seuil, 1969
Essays in Semiotics. The Hague: Mouton, 1971
Lange-Seidl, Annemarie (ed.)
Zeichen und Magie
Akten des Koll. der Bereiche Kultur und Recht der
Deutschen Ges. für Semiotik 5.9.1986, TU Munich
Tübingen: Stauffenberg, 1988

AI.8g   Special Language Forms *see also* Philosophy of Language,
History of
Alscher, Helga
Die Vervendung der Gelenkwörter als Stilkriterium in
deutschen Texten gebundener Rede in der Zeit von Opitz
bis Kästner. Vienna: diss., 1938

Blum, Carol
    Rousseau and the Republic of Virtue:
    The Language of Politics in the French Revolution.
    Ithaca, NY: Cornell Univ. Press, 1989

Chatterjee, Margaret
    The Language of Philosophy. Delhi: Allied, 1981

Disterheft, Dorothy
    The Syntactic Development of the Infinitive in Indo-
    European. Columbus, OH: Slavica, 1980

Frank, Francine Wattman, and Paula A. Treichler
    Language, Gender, and Professional Writing: Theoretical
    Approaches and Guidelines for Nonsexist Usage.
    New York: Commission of the Status of Women in the
    Profession, Modern Language Assoc. of America, 1989

Freed, Alice F.
    The Semantics of English Aspectual Complementation.
    Dordrecht: Reidel, 1979

Goodman, Dena
    Criticism in Action:
    Enlightenment Experiments in Political Writing.
    Ithaca, NY: Cornell Univ. Press, 1989

Irigaray, Luce
    Le language des déments. The Hague: Mouton, 1973

Key, Mary Ritchie
    Male/Female Language.
    Metuchen, NJ: Scarecrow Press, 1975

Luersch, Greta
    Die Sprache der Deutschen Mystik des mittelalters im
    Werke der Mechtild von Magdeburg.
    Munich: Ernest Reinhardt, 1926

Pusch, Luise F.
    Die Substantivierung von Verben mit Satzkomplementen im
    Englischen und im Deutschen.
    Frankfurt a.M., 1972
    Das Deutsche als Männersprache - Aufsätze und Glossen
    zur feministischen Linguistik.
    Frankfurt am Main: Suhrkamp, 1984

Traugott, Elizabeth Closs
    A History of English Syntax.
    New York: Holt Rinehart & Winston, 1972

Trömel-Plötz, Senta
    Frauensprache in unserer Welt der Männer.
    Konstanz: Universitätsverlag Konstanz, 1979
    Frauensprache: Sprache der Veränderung.
    Frankfurt am Main: Fisher, 1982

collections:
Wodak, Ruth (ed.)
Language, Power and Ideology: Studies in Political
Discourse (Critical Theory Series).
Amsterdam: John Benjamins, 1988

AI.9   Logic
Argumentation Theory
see Informal Logic and Logical Argumentation
Dialogue Logic, *see* Philosophical Logic

AI.9a   Dictionaries
Greenstein, Carol Horn
Dictionary of Logical Terms and Symbols.
New York, etc.: Van Nostrand Reinhold, 1978

Empirical Logic, *see* Philosophical Logic

AI.9b   Introductions

AI.9ba   -to Informal Logic and Logical Argumentation
Astell, Mary
A serious Proposal to the Ladies for the Advancement of
their True and Greatest Interest. By a Lover of her Sex
Vol. II. London, 1697
Govier, Trudy
A Practical Study of Argument.
Belmont, CA: Wadsworth, 1985, 21988
La Bar, Carol, and Jerrold Coombs
First Steps in Practical Reasoning.
Vancouver: Univ. of British Columbia,
Faculty of Education, 1986
Mechanic, Janevive Jean
The Logic of Decision Making: An Introduction to
Critical Thinking. New York: Lang, 1988
Missimer, Connie A.
Good Arguments: An Introduction to Critical Thinking.
Englewood Cliffs, NJ: Prentice-Hall, 1986
Pizarra, Fina
Apprender a razonar.
Madrid: Alhambra, 1986
Rottenberg, Anette T.
Elements of Arguments. A Text and Reader.
New York: St. Martin's Press, 1985

Salmon, Merrilee H.
  Introduction to Logic and Critical Thinking.
  San Diego, etc.: Harcourt Brace Jovanovich, 1984, 1989
Stebbing, L. Susan
  Logic in Practice. New York: Methuen, 1934, 1945, 1952, 1954
  Thinking to Some Purpose.
  Harmondsworth: Penguin Books, 1952 [1939]

AI.9bb   -to Philosophical Logic

Wolfram, Sybil
  Philosophical Logic: An Introduction.
  London, etc.: Routledge, 1989

AI.9bc   -to Symbolic and Mathematical Logic

Cobb, Vicki
  Logic. New York: F. Wath, 1969 [Ill. by Ellie Haines]
Galli, Elisabetta, Giorgio Fiora, and -
  Lezioni di Logica matematica.
  Soncino: Arti Grafiche, Filli Binda, 1982
Giovannoni, Laura
  Lingua e logica. Milan: F. Angeli, 1986
Hill, Shirley, Patrick Suppes, and -
  First Course in Mathematical Logic.
  Waltham, MA, etc.: Blaisdel, 1964
  Dubuque, IA: W.C. Brown Co., 1956
James, Patricia, James Dickoff, and -
  Symbolic Logic and Language - A Programmed Text.
  New York, etc.: McGraw-Hill, 1965
Kegley, Jacquelyn Ann, Charles W. Kegley, and -
  Introduction to Logic.
  Lanham, MD, etc.: Univ. Press of America, 1984
Klenk, Virginia H.
  Understanding Symbolic Logic.
  Englewood Cliffs, NJ: Prentice-Hall, 1983, 1989
Langer, Susanne K.
  An Introduction to Symbolic Logic,
  Revised edition, New York: Dover, 1953 [1937]
Risby, Bonnie, Dianne Draze, and Sousie Conroy (eds.)
  Logic Countdown.
  Logic Lift Off.
  Orbiting with Logic.
  San Luis Obispo, CA: Dandy Lion, 1987
Roure, Marie-Louise
  Éléments de logique contemporaine.
  Paris: Presses Universitaires de France, 1967

Schipper, Edith Watson
  A First Course in Modern Logic.
  London: Routledge & Kegan Paul, 1960
Schipper, Edith Watson, and Edward Schuh
  Principles of Applied Logic. Dubuque, IA: W.C. Brown, 1956
Sergant, M.
  Geformaliseerde logica. Leuven: Acco, 1980
  Logisch redeneren - een inleiding in de logica.
  Leuven: Kruk, Amersfoort: Acco, 1986
Simco, Nancy D.
  Elementary Logic. Belmont, CA: Wadsworth, 1983
Simco, Nancy D., and Gene G. James
  Elementary Logic. Encino and Belmont, CA: Dickenson, 1976
Stebbing, L. Susan
  A Modern Introduction to Logic.
  New York: Methuen, 1933 [1930 or 1931];
  Atlantic Highlands: Humanities Press, 1950;
  New York: Harper & Bros., 1961
  A Modern Elementary Logic.
  London/New York: Methuen, 1963 [1943]
Trusted, Jennifer
  Logic of Scientific Inference - An Introduction.
  London: Macmillan/Atlantic Highlands: Humanities Press, 1980
Virieux-Reymond, Antoinette
  La logique formelle. Paris: P.U.F., 1962
Yren, Maria Teresa
  Lógica formal. Mexico: Cultural, 1982
  Lógica simbolica. Mexico: Cultural, 1984

AI.9c   Informal Logic and Logical Argumentation
  see also Education: Critical and Creative Thinking;
  Language: Rhetoric. (NB.: Some titles below may belong
  here.)
Andree, Josephine, and Richard Andree
  Logic Unlocks.
  Norman: Mu Alpha Theta, Univ. of Oklahoma, 1979
Barker, Evelyn M.
  Everyday Reasoning.
  Englewood Cliffs, NJ: Prentice-Hall, 1981
Borel, Marie-Jeanne
  Discours de la logique et logique du discours.
  Lausanne: L'Age d'homme, 1978
Ceasar, Lisbeth D.
  Making Inferences.
  Belmont, CA: Lake Publications, 1986

Casey, Helen, and Mary Clarke
   Logic, A Practical Approach. Chicago: Regnery, c. 1963
Eads, Sandra, and Beverly Post
   Digging Into Logic.
   Belmont, CA: Lake Publications, 1987
   Logic in the Round.
   Belmont, CA: Lake Publications, 1989
Govier, Trudy
   Selected Issues in Logic and Communication.
   Belmont, CA: Wadsworth, 1988
   Problems in Argument Analysis and Evaluation.
   Dordrecht: Foris, 1987
Hakkenberg, Anneke
   Logica en beslissen. Amsterdam: Kobra, 1979
Hample, Dale, and Judith M. Dallinger
   Argument-as-Procedure and the Art of Controversy.
   Seattle, WA: Wester Speech Community Association, 1984
Harnadek, Anita E.
   Inductive Thinking Skills.
   Pacific Grove, CA: Midwest Publications, 1964
   Mind Benders.
   Pacific Grove, CA: Midwest Publications, 1978, 1982
Kulka, Olga
   Zur Theorie der Begründugen. Vienna: diss., 1934
La Bar, Carol, and Ian Wright
   Reasoning: Individual and Social Decision Making.
   Vancouver: Univ. of British Columbia,
   Faculty of Education, 1983
Leimbach, Judy, Dianne Draze, and Mary Williver (eds.)
   Primarily Logic. San Luis Obispo, CA: Dandy Lion, 1986
Lieber, Lillian Rosanoff
   Mits, Wits and Logic. New York: W.W. Norton, 1947
Makau, Josina M.
   Reasoning and Communication: Thinking Critically About
   Arguments. Belmont, CA: Wadsworth, 1990
Mayberry, Katherine J.
   For Arguments' Sake.
   Glenview, IL: Scott Foresman/Little Brown, c. 1990
Meichsner, Irene
   Die Logik von Gemeinplätzen -
   Vorgeführt an Steuermannstopos und Schiffmetapher.
   Bonn: Bouvier/VVA, 1983
Moore, Kathleen Dean
   A Field Guide to Inductive Arguments.
   Dubuque, IA: Kendall Hunt Publishing Co., 1987

Pieraut-Le Bonniec, Gilberte, and Jean-Blaise Grize
La contradiction: Essai sur les opérations de la pensée.
Paris: P.U.F., 1983

Ratizza, Rita
Cateoria delle transformazioni inferenziali ed il
futuro. Trieste: Svevo, 1986

Russow, Lilly-Marlene
Principles of Reasoning.
New York: St. Martin's Press, 1989

Schian, Ruth
Untersuchungen über das 'argument e consensus omnium'.
Hildesheim/Zürich/New York: George Olms, 1973

Seubert, Karen M.
Bare Bones Logic.
Lanham, MD: Univ. Press of America, c. 1986

Walberg, Franette
Puzzle Thinking.
Philadelphia: Franklin Institute Press, 1980

Warnick, Barbara, and Edward S. Inch
Critical Thinking and Communication:
The Use of Reason in Argument.
New York: Macmillan, 1989

Wilson, Barbara, and Edward S. Inch
Critical Thinking and Communication: the Uses of Reason
in Argument. New York: Macmillan, 1989

collections:

Borel, Marie-Jeanne (ed.)
Argumentation and Logic.
Dordrecht: Kluwer Academic Publishers, 1989

Goody, Esther (ed.)
Questions and Answers. Cambridge: Cambridge Univ. Press, 1978

Govier, Trudy (ed.)
Selected Issues in Logic and Communication.
Belmont, CA: Wadsworth, 1983, 1988

Moore, Rosalind (ed.)
The Dell Book of Logic Problems. New York: Dell, 1984

Schuetz, Janice, Robert Trapp, and - (eds.)
Perspectives on Argumentation. Essays in Honor of Wayne
Brockriede. Prospect Heights, IL: Waveland Press, 1990

AI.9d   Mathematical Logic and Metalogic
see also Model Theory, Recursive Functions

Ferrante, Jeanne, and Charles W. Rackoff
The Computational Complexity of Logical Theories.
Berlin, etc.: Springer, 1979

Franklin, Christine (Ladd)
Thesis (Ph.D.).
Baltimore: Johns Hopkins Univ., diss., 1926

Gersting, Judith, and Joseph E. Kuczkowski
Yes-No, Stop-Go: Some Patterns of Mathematical Logic.
New York: Crowell, 1977

Guessarian, Irène, and José Meseguer
On the Axiomatization of "if-then-else."
Stanford, CA: CSLI Publications CSLI 8522

Hahn, Olga
Über die Koeffizienten einer logischen Gleichung und
ihre Beziehungen zur Lehre von den Schlüssen.
Vienna: diss., 1911

James, Patricia
Decidability in the Logic of Subordinate Proofs.
New Haven, CT: Yale Univ. (diss.), 1962

Leeson, Marjorie M.
Programming Logic. Chicago, 1988

Mirkowska-Salwicka, Grazyna, and A. Salwicki
Algorithmic Logic.
Dordrecht and Boston: Reidel/Warszaw: PWN-Polish
Scientific Publishers/Norwell, MA/
sold and distributed in the USA and Canada by
Kluwer Academic Publishers, 1987

Noto, Maria Giulia
Matematica e logica intuizioniste.
Trapani: Celebes, 1970

Rasiowa, Helena
An Algebraic Approach to Non-Classical Logics.
Amsterdam: North-Holland/New York: Elsevier Publishers, 1974
[Studies in logic and the foundations of mathematics; vol. 78]
A Generalization of a Formalized Theory of Fields
of Sets on Non-classical Logics.
Warszawa : Pa/nstwowe Wydawnictwo Naukowe, 1964
[Rozprawy matematyczne; 42]

Rasiowa, Helena, and Roman Sikorski
The Mathematics of Metamathematics.
Warzawa: Pa/nstwowe Wydawnicto Naukowe, 1963

Rosenblüth, Amalie
Über das sogenannte disjunktive Urteil in der neueren
Logik. Vienna: diss., 1916

Roure, Marie-Louise
Logique et metalogique: Essai sur la structure et les
frontières de la pensée.
Paris: Flammarion, 1957

AI.9e   Model Theory

Bridge, Jane
   Beginning Model Theory -
   The Completeness Theorem and Some Consequences.
   Oxford: Clarendon Press, 1977

Scabia, Maria Luisa dalla Chiara
   Modelli sintattici e semantici delle teorie elementari.
   Milan: Feltrinelli, 1968

AI.9f   Philosophical Logic *see also* Semantics, Pragmatics, Paradoxes

Bachner-Cohen, Cynthia
   The Logic and Ontology of Ian Ramsey's Theory of
   Religious Language.
   New York: Columbia Univ., diss., 1970

Barth, E.M.
   The Logic of the Articles in Traditional Philosophy:
   A Contribution to the Study of Conceptual Structures.
   Dordrecht/New York: Reidel, 1974. Paper 1980.
   Transl. by the author and T.C. Potts of:
   De logica van de lidwoorden in de traditionele
   filosofie. Leiden: U.P./Stenfert Kroese, 1971.

Barth, E.M., and E.C.W. Krabbe
   From Axiom to Dialogue -
   A philosophical study of logics and argumentation.
   Berlin/New York: Walter de Gruyter, 1982

Britt, Patricia Marie
   A Logical Analysis of Subjunctive Conditionals.
   Los Angeles: U.C.L.A., diss., 1960

Campbell, Jean Alice
   Status and Necessity of Logical Categories.
   New York: New School for Social Research, 1981

Chandler, Marthe Atwater
   Philosophical Issues in Tense Logic.
   Ann Arbor, MI, etc.: Univ. Microfilms International, 1980
   Chicago: Univ. of Illinois at Chicago Circle, 1980

Citro, Olga
   Axiome und ihre Verhältnisse zu den Definitionen.
   Vienna: diss., 1916

Cohen, Mary Elizabeth
   Vagueness Logic and Truth.
   Columbus: Ohio State Univ., diss., 1987

Corradini, Antonella
   Appunti sul problema degli universali nella logica
   moderna. Trento: Università, 1984

Crane, Esther
   The Place of Hypothesis in Logic.
   Chicago: Univ. of Chicago, diss., 1917
Davidson, Lee Merril
   A System of Arithmetic in Modal Logic.
   New Haven, CT: Yale Univ., diss., 1981
Fimiani, Mariapaola
   Futuro logico e tempo storico. Napels: Guida (n.d.).
Franks, Vicky Ruth Vicklund
   The Definite Description and Quine's Formal Attack on
   Quantified Modal Logic.
   An Arbor, MI: UMI, diss., 1982
Garden, Rachel Wallace
   Modern Logic and Quantum Mechanics.
   Bristol: Hilger, 1984
Griffin-Collart, Evelyne
   Philosohie morale et politique, y compris notions de
   logique formelle.
   Brussels: Presses Univ. de Bruxelles, 1980
Larson, Sue Howard
   Practical Implication. Some Problems in the Logic of
   Assertion. Stanford, CA: Stanford Univ., diss., 1962
Lothringer, Rachaela
   Induktion und transcendentallogik.
   Vienna: diss., 1917
Morgenstern, Leora
   Preliminary Studies Towards a Logic of Knowledge,
   Action, and Communication.
   New York: New York University Technical Note, 1986
Pieraut-le Bonniec, Gilberte
   Le raisonnement modal. Etude génétique.
   Hawthorne: Mouton-De Gruyter, 1975
Popper, Lilli
   Wesen und Bedeutung der Analogie. Vienna: diss., 1928
Rossitto, Christina
   Riflessioni sulla struttura logica della filosofia.
   Padova: Libreria editrice Gregoriana, 1982
Sher, Gila
   Generalized Logic: A Philosophical Perspective with
   Linguistic Applications.
   New York: Columbia Univ., diss., 1989
Vosniadou, Stella, and Andrew Ortony
   Similarity and Analogical Reasoning.
   Cambridge, etc.: Cambridge Univ. Press, 1989

Wallace, Rachel Carys
A Logic for Mechanics: a Generalized Logic for Mechanical
Theories with Applications to Modalities and Probabilities.
London, Ontario: Univ. of Western Ontario, diss., 1979

Wolf, Ursula
Möglichkeit und Notwendigkeit bei Aristoteles und heute.
Munich: Fink, 1979

Wu, Kathleen Gibbs Johnson
A New Formalization of the Logic of Knowledge and Belief.
New Haven, CT: Yale Univ. diss., 1970

collections:

Barth, E.M., and J. van Dormael (eds.)
Empirical Logic.
Ghent: Cognition & Communication (special issue), 1990

Barth, E.M., and J.L. Martens (eds.)
Argumentation: Approaches to Theory Formation.
Proceedings of the 1978 Groningen Conference on the
Theory of Argumentation. Amsterdam: John Benjamins, 1982

AI.9g   Philosophy of Logic

Ayres, Edith
Some Ethical Factors in Logical Theory.
Chicago: Chicago Univ., diss., 1921

Bacinetti-Florenzi Waddington, Marianna
Saggi di psicologia e di logica. Florence, 1868

Barth, E.M.
Evaluaties. Assen: Van Gorcum, 1972
Empiristische en empirische logica
Meded. der Kon. Ned. Akad. v. Wet., Afd. Letterkunde,
N.R. 50 No. 3. Amsterdam, etc.: North-Holland, 1987

Borel, Marie-Jeanne
Essai sur le problème du sujet dans le language et la
logique. Lausanne: L'Age d'homme, 1978

Cavaliere, Fania
Logica formale in Unione Sovietica: Gli anni del debattito
Casellina di Scandini: La Nuova Italia, 1990

Creed, Isabel P.
A Critical Study of the Philosophy of Logic and Theory
of Meaning of Recent Positivism.
Univ. of California, 1936

Echave, Delia Teresa
Logica, proposición y norma.
Buenos Aires: Editorial Astrea, 1980

Fiaccadori, Anna
  Appunti di logica simbolica. Unicoli, 1981
Formigari, Lia
  La logica del pensiero vivente.
  Bari: Bibl. di Cult. Mod., 1977
Gutzmann, Gabriele
  Logik als Erfahrungswissenschaft:
  Der Kalkülismus und Wege zu seiner Überwindung.
  Berlin: Duncker & Humblot, 1980
Haack, Susan
  Deviant Logic - Some Philosophical Issues.
  London: Cambridge Univ. Press, 1974
  Philosophy of Logics.
  Cambridge/London: Cambridge Univ. Press, 1978
  Filosofia delle logiche. Angelli, 1983
Havas, Katalin G.
  Logic and Dialectic - Essays in the Philosophy of Logic.
  Budapest: Hungarian Academy of Sciences, 1989
Kalokerinou, Helen
  Logic and Morality: The Ambiguities of Universal
  Prescriptivism. Exeter: Univ. of Exeter, diss., 1988
Kumbruck, Christel
  Die binäre Herr-schaft. Intuition und logisches Prinzip.
  Munich: 'Profil Mchn' Profil Verlag, 1990
Massey, Barbara Delp
  Relativism in Logic.
  Pittsburgh: Univ. of Pittsburgh, diss., 1986
Moncta, Giuseppina Chiara
  The Identity of the Logical Proposition: a Study in
  Genetic Phenomenology.
  New York: New School for Social Research, diss., 1969
Pankhurst, Helen Huss
  Recent Logical Realism.
  Bryn Mawr, PA: Bryn Mawr College, diss., 1917
Sergant, M.C.
  Taal en Logica. Baarn: Het Wereldvenster, 1971
Spangler, Mary Michael
  Logic: An Aristotelian Approach.
  Lanham, MD: Univ. Press of America, 1986
Stebbius, Sarah Ann
  Logical Form.
  Berkeley: Univ. of California, diss., 1977
Swabey, Marie Collins
  Logic and Nature.
  New York: New York Univ. Press, 1955

collections:

Salmon, Merrilee H.
> The Philosophy of Logical Mechanism.
> Essays in Honor of Arthur W. Burks.
> Dordrecht, Boston, London: Kluwer, 1990

Zarnecka-Biaty, Ewa (ed.)
> Logic Counts.
> Dorecht, etc.: Kluwer, 1990

AI.9h   Recursive Functions

Peter, Ròsza
> Rekursive Funktionen. Budapest, 1950.
> Second enlarged ed. Budapest, 1957.
> There exists an English translation of this classical work.

AI.9i   Semantics, Pragmatics, Paradoxes *see also*
Epistemology: Paradoxes; Foundations of Linguistics

Barth, E.M., and R.T.P. Wiche
> Problems, Functions, and Semantic Roles -
> A pragmatists' analysis of Montague's theory of
> sentence meaning.
> Berlin/New York: Walter de Gruyter, 1986

Blakemore, Diane
> Semantic Constraints on Relevance.
> Oxford: Blackwell, 1987

Elliott, Lisa
> The Paradoxes of Fiction: A Study in the Logic of
> Fictional Language.
> New York: Columbia Univ., diss., 1979

Heim, Irene Roswitha
> The Semantics of Definite and Indefinite Noun Phrases.
> Ann Arbor, MI: UMI, 1982

Peterson, Sandra Lynne
> The Masker Paradox.
> Princeton, NJ: Princeton Univ., diss., 1969
> Ann Arbor, MI: University Microfilms, 1978

Rivetti Bardò, Francesca
> l'Antinomia del mentori. Da Peirce a Tarski.
> Milano: Jaca Book, 1986

Wagner, Catherine
> On Martin's Conjecture.
> Cornell Univ., diss., 1979

Walther-Klaus, Ellen
> Inhalt und Umfang: Untersuchungen zur Geltung und zur
> Geschichte der Reziprozität von Extension und Intension.
> Hildesheim/Zürich/New York: Olms, 1987

AI.9j Set Theory

Hasse, Maria
    Grundbegriffe der Mengenlehre und Logik.
    Frankfurt: 'Deutsch H./BRO', (1970), 1989

Lindström, Ingrid
    Trees in Set Theory. Stanford, CA: Stanford Univ. 1979

Rubin, Jean E., Herman Rubin and -
    Equivalents of the Axiom of Choice, II.
    Amsterdam: North-Holland, 1985

Tiles, Mary
    The Philosophy of Set Theory:
    An Historical Introduction to Cantor's Paradise.
    Oxford: Blackwell, 1989

AI.10 Mathematics, Philosophy of *see also* Mathematical Logic, Recursive Functions; Hilbert; Peirce; Wittgenstein

AI.10a Introductions

Sullivan, Helen
    An Introduction to the Philosophy of the Natural and
    Mathematical Sciences.
    New York: Vantage Press, 1952

AI.10b Other works

Franz, Marie-Louise von
    Zahl und Zeit. Stuttgart: Klett, 1970

Furinghetti, Fulvia, and Mario Borga
    Il problema dei fondamenti della matematica.
    Genova: ECIG, 1986

Maddy, Penelope
    Realism in Mathematics.
    Oxford and New York: Oxford Univ. Press, 1990

Rheinwald, Rosemarie
    Der Formalismus und seine Grenzen.
    Königstein: Hain, 1984

Ströker, Elisabeth
    Investigations in Philosophy of Space.
    (Trans. Algis Mickunas.)
    Athens: Ohio Univ. Press, 1987

Yanovskaya (Janovskaja), S.A.
    Sborni statei po filosofii matematiki
    (Collected Articles on the Philosophy of Mathematics).
    Moscow, 1936

AI.11 **Metaphilosophy** *see also* General Theoretical Philosophy;
Analytical Philosophy; Metaphysics; Mind; Phenomenology

Addelson, Kathryn Pyne
Impure Thoughts:
Essays on Philosophy, Feminism, and Ethics.
Philadelphia: Temple Univ. Press, 1990

Almond, Brenda
The Philosophical Quest. New York: Penguin, 1991

Bruton, Leone
Gender and Mathematics.
London: Cassell, 1990

Culpepper, Emily
Philosophia in a Feminist Key: Revolt of the Symbols.
Cambridge, MA: Harvard Univ., diss., 1983

Elgin, Catherine Z., Nelson Goodman, and -
Reconceptions in Philosophy and Other Arts and Sciences.
London: Routledge, 1988

Grimshaw, Jean
Philosophy and Feminist Thinking.
Minneapolis: Univ. of Minnesota Press, 1986

Hartle, Ann
Death and the Disinterested Spectator -
An Inquiry into the Nature of Philosophy.
New York: State Univ. of New York Press, 1986

Holland, Nancy
Is Women's Philosophy Possible?
Totowa, NJ: Rowman & Littlefield, 1990

collections:

Bishop, S., and M. Weinzweig (eds.)
Philosophy and Women. Belmont, CA: Wadsworth, 1979

Gould, Carol C., and Marx W. Wartowsky (eds.)
Women and Philosophy: Toward a Theory of Liberation.
New York: Putnam, 1976

Griffiths, Morwenna, and Margaret Whitford (eds.)
Feminist Perspectives in Philosophy.
Bloomington: Indiana Univ. Press, 1988; London: Macmillan

Keohane, Nancy O., Michelle Z. Rosaldo, and Barbara C. Gelpi (eds.)
Feminist Theory: A Critique of Ideology.
Chicago: Univ. of Chicago Press, 1982, 1990
Brighton: Harvester Press (Wheatsheaf Books)

Schröder, Hannelore (ed.)
Intellekt kent geen sekse.
Deel I: Grote vrouwen van de 20e eeuw.
Kampen: Kok Agora, 1988

Vetterling-Braggin, Mary, Frederick A. Elliston, and Jane English (eds.)
Feminism and Philosophy.
Totowa, NJ: Littlefield Adams (Rowman & Littlefield), 1977

AI.12   **Metaphysics** *see also* General Theoretical Philosophy;
Mind; Leibniz; Whitehead

AI.12a   Introductions

Calkins, Mary Whiton
The Persistent Problems of Philosophy: An Introduction
to Metaphysics Through the Study of Modern Systems.
New York: Macmillan, 1907, 1925
New York: AMS Press, 1979

AI.12b   General Metaphysics

Barthélémy-Madaule, Madeleine
L'ideologie du hasard et de la nécessité.
Paris: Seuil, 1972

Bender, Helene
Zur Lösung des metaphysischen Problems. Kritische
Untersuchungen über den metaphysischen Wert des
Transzendental-Idealismus und der atomistischen Theorie.
Berlin, diss., 1886
Philosophische Metaphysik und Einzelforschung.
Leipzig, 1897

Benedetto-Porone, M. Grazia
Metastruttura ed esistenza. Pompei: Morano, 1972

Benincasa, Carmine
La svolta dell'interpretazione: Memoria e profezia.
Rome: Caruccu, 1972

Christian, Petra
Einheit und Zwiespalt. Berlin: Duncker & Humblot, 1978

Conrad-Martius, Hedwig
Naturwissenschaftlich-metaphysische Perspektiven.
Hamburg, 1948

Dufour-Kowalska, Gabrielle
L'origine. Paris: Beauchesne, 1973

Emmet, Dorothy
The Nature of Metaphysical Thinking.
London, etc.: Macmillan, 1966 [1945]

Forest, Aimé
Essai sur les formes du lien spirituel.
Paris: Beauchesne, 1981

Grene, Marjorie
Approaches to a Philosophical Being.
New York: Basic Books, 1968

Grandi, Gabriella
    Misurazione e valutazione.
    Florence: Nuova Italia, 1977

Jahoda, Emma
    Metaphysik als Wissen und Glaube.
    Vienna: diss., 1921

Lecourt, Dominique
    La philosophie sans feinte. Paris: Albin, 1982

Stambaugh, Joan
    The Real is not the Rational.
    New York: State Univ. of New York Press, 1986

Tymieniecka, Anna-Teresa
    Warum nicht nichts? Assen: Van Gorcum, 1966
    Why Is There Something Rather Than Nothing?
    Assen: Van Gorcum, 1966

Voogd, Stephanie de
    The Matter of Form: Three Conversations.
    Amsterdam: Multicopy, 1986

Wagner, Malinda Bollar
    Metaphysics in Mid-Western America.
    Columbus: Ohio State Univ. Press (n.d.).

Wahsner, Renate
    Das Aktive und das Passive. Berlin: Akademie, 1981

Weisshaupt, Brigitte
    Der Geist als Grund der Zeit, Freiburg i. Br. 1967

AI.13   **Mind, Philosophy of**
        see also General Theoretical Philosophy; Analytical Philosophy,
        Epistemology: Knowledge Representation; Phenomenology

AI.13a   **Introductions**

Teichman, Jenny
    The Mind and the Soul -
    An Introduction to the Philosophy of Mind.
    London: Routledge & Kegan Paul, 1974

AI.13b   **General Philosophy of Mind** *see also* General Philosophy
        of Religion

Aitchinson, Jean
    Words in the Mind: An Introduction to the Mental
    Lexicon. Oxford, etc.: Blackwell, paper, 1987

Anscombe, G.E.M.
    Metaphysics and the Philosophy of Mind.
    Ontario: Oxford Univ. Press, 1981

Arendt, Hannah
    The Life of the Mind I-II. Vol.I: Thinking. Vol. II:
    Willing. London: Secker & Warburg/
    New York: Harcourt Brace Jovanovich, 1978
Baier, Annette
    Postures of the Mind: Essays on Mind and Morals.
    London: Methuen, 1985
    Minneapolis: Univ. of Minnesota Press, 1985
Calkins, Mary Whiton
    Association. An Essay Analytical and Experimental.
    New York: Charles Scribner's Sons, 1986
Donaldson, Margaret
    Children's Minds. New York: Norton, 1978
Grene, Marjorie
    Interpretations of Life and Mind - Essays around the
    Problem of Reduction.
    London: Routledge & Kegan Paul, 1971
Haight, Mary R.
    A Study of Self-Deception.
    Atlantic Highlands, NJ: Humanities Press, 1980
John-Steiner, Vera
    Notebooks of the Mind: Explorations of Thinking.
    New York: Harper & Row, 1987
Midgley, Mary
    Wisdom, Information and Wonder.
    London: Routledge, 1989
Millikan, Ruth Garret
    Language, Thought and Other Biological Categories.
    Cambridge, MA: MIT Press, 1984
Reeves, Joan Wynn
    Thinking About Thinking: Studies in the Background of
    Some Psychological Approaches.
    London: Methuen, 1969
Rorty, Amélie Oksenberg
    Mind in Action - Essays in the Philosophy of Mind.
    Boston: Beacon, 1989
Sheets-Johnstone, Maxine
    The Roots of Thinking.
    Philadelphia: Temple Univ. Press, 1990
Sommese, Rebecca Rooze
    Cartesian Categories in Twentieth Century Philosophy of
    Mind. New Haven, CT: Yale Univ., diss., 1973
Teichman, Jenny
    Philosophy and the Mind.
    Oxford: Blackwell, 1988

Tymieniecka, Anna-Teresa
  Logos and Life: Creative Experience and the Critique of
  Reason. Analecta Husserliana 14
  Dordrecht, etc.: Kluwer Academic Publishers, 1987
  Logos and Life: The Three Movements of the Soul,
  or, The Spontaneous and the Creative in Man's Self-
  Interpretation-in-the-Sacred. Analecta Husserliana 25
  Dordrecht, etc.: Kluwer Academic Publishers, 1988

  collections:

Astington, Janet W., and others (eds.)
  Developing Theories of Mind.
  New York: Cambridge Univ. Press, 1988
Brion-Guerry, Liliane (dir.)
  L'Esprit et les formes. Paris: Klincksieck, 1985
Devaney, Shella Greeve (ed.)
  Feminism and Process Thought. Lewiston: Mellon Press, 1981
Greenfield, Susan, and Colin Blakemore (eds.)
  Mindwaves. Thoughts on Intelligence, Identity and
  Consciousness. Oxford: Blackwell, 1989

AI.13c   Artificial Intelligence *see also* Mathematics, History of
Boden, Margaret A.
  Minds and Mechanisms: Philosophical Psychology and
  Computational Models.
  Ithaca, NY: Cornell Univ. Press, 1981
  Artificial Intelligence and Natural Man,
  Expanded ed., Cambridge, MA: MIT Press, 1987 [1977]
  The Creative Mind - Myths and Mechanisms.
  New York: Basic Books (Harper Collins), 1990
Böe, Solveig
  Intensjonalitet i mennesker og maskiner.
  Trondheim: Filosofisk Institutts Publ.serie, 1989
Davis, Ruth E.
  Truth, Deduction, and Computation.
  New York: Computer Science Press, c. 1989
  (Principles of Computer Science Series)
Duran, Jane
  Epistemics: Epistemic Justification Theory Naturalized
  and the Computational Model of Mind.
  Lanham, MD: Univ. Press of America, 1989
  Toward a Feminist Epistemology.
  Totowa, NJ: Rowman & Littlefield, 1990
Gopnik, Myrna, I. Gopnik and -
  From Models to Modules. [Theoretical Issues on Cognitive Science
  Series: vol. 2] Norwood, NJ: Ablex Publishing Co., 1986

Johansson, Anna-Lena
  Prolog versus You. Berlin, New York: Springer-verlag, 1989
McCorduck, Pamela
  Machines Who Think. San Francisco: Freeman, 1979
Morik, Katharina
  Überzeugungssysteme der künstlichen Intelligenz.
  Tübingen: Niemeyer, 1982
Rich, Elaine
  Artificial Intelligence. New York: McGraw-Hill, 1988 [1983]
Rosen, Deborah Ann
  Two Transcendental Arguments for the Logical Notion of
  a Memory Trace.
  Stanford, CA: Stanford Univ., diss., 1970
Tabossi, Patrizia
  Intelligenza naturale e intelligenza artificiale.
  Bologna: Il Mulino, 1988

  collections:
Boden, Margaret A. (ed.)
  The Philosophy of Artificial Intelligence.
  Oxford: Clarendon Press, 1990 (Oxford readings in philosophy)

AI.13d Intentionality
Anscombe, G.E.M.
  Intention. Oxford: Blackwell, 21963
Harney, Maurita J.
  Intentionality, Sense and the Mind.
  The Hague: Nijhoff, 1984

  collections:
Diamond, Cora, and Jenny Teichman (eds.)
  Intentions and Intentionality. Sussex: Harvester, 1979

AI.13e Mind-Body Problem *see also* AI; Neurophilosophy;
      Anthropology, History of Philosophical
Goldstein, Rebecca
  The Mind-Body Problem. New York: Random House, 1983
Macdonald, Cynthia
  Mind-Body Identity Theories. London: Routledge, 1989
Meijsing, Monica
  Mens of machine? Het lichaam-geest probleem in de
  cognitieve psychologie. Lisse: Swets & Zeitlinger, 1986
Scarry, Elaine
  The Body in Pain: The Making and Unmaking of the World.
  Oxford: Oxford Univ. Press, 1988 (also paper)

AI.13f   Neurophilosophy

Churchland, Patricia Smith
Neurophilosophy -
Toward a Unified Science of the Mind-Brain.
Cambridge, MA: The MIT Press, 1986, 1989

Gelder, Beatrice de
Hersenschimmen. (Inaugural lecture, Cath. Univ. Tilburg)
Amsterdam: John Benjamins, 1981

collections:

Vaina, Lucia M. (ed.)
Matters of Intelligence - Conceptual Structures in
Cognitive Neuroscience. Dordrecht: Kluwer, 1987

AI.14   Mysticism and Spirituality

AI.14a   Medieval Works

Birgitta Sueccica
Revelationes Extravagantes. 14th cent. Ed. L. Hollman:
Uppsala, 1956
Revelationes S. Birgittae. 14th cent. Ed. Elias
Wessin. Corpus Codicum Suecicorum Medii Aevi. Auspisis
Regis Sueciae. Vol. XIII.
Gustav Adolphi, ed. Hafniae: Munksgaard, 1952

Catherine of Siena
S. Caterina da Siena. Le Orazioni.
Ed. Giuliana Cavallini.
Rome: Edizioni Catheriniane, 1968, 1980
Santa Caterina da Siena. Il Dialogo della divina
Provvidenzia ovvero Libro della divina dottrina.
Ed. Giuliana Cavallini.
Rome: Edizioni Catheriniane, 1968
Catherine of Siena. The Dialogue. Ed. Suzanne Noffke.
London and New York: Paulist Press
(The Classics of Western Spirituality), 1980
The Letters of Catherine of Siena 1: Letters 1-88.
Ed. Suzanne Noffke. Binghampton, NY: Center for
Medieval and Renaissance Studies, 1988
The Orchards of Sydon.
Eds. P. Hodgson and G.M. Liegez. n.p.d.
Catherina of Siena. Letters. Ed. V.D. Scudder, n.p.d.

Gertrud of Hefta
Exercitia spiritualia septem. c. 1296
Legatio divine pietatis. c. 1296
Gertrude d'Hefta. Oeuvres spirituelles.
1. Les exercises. Eds. J. Hourlier and A. Schmitt.
Paris: Les Éditions du Cerf, 1967

Hadewych of Antwerp
  Hadewych. The Complete Works. Ed. C. Hart.
  New York: Paulist Press (The Classics of Western
  Spirituality), 1980
  Visionen. Ed. J. van Mierloo. Leuven, 1924-1962
Hildegard of Bingen
  Opera omnia.
  In: Migne, Patrologiae cursus completus, series Graeca,
  series Latina.
  Paris: Garnieri Fratres, 1844-1890
  Analecta Sanctae Hildegardis Opera.
  Ed. Johannes B. Pitra. Monte Cassino, 1882
  Scivias. Written 1141-1151
  Hildegard von Bingen. Wisse die Wege. Scivias
  Ed. Maura Böckeler. German trans. from the original.
  Salzburg, 1954
  Hildegard von Bingen. Briefwechsel. Ed. A. Führkötter.
  Salzburg: Otto Müller Verlag, 1965
Roswitha (Hrotsvitha)
  Hrotsvithae opera. (10th cent.) Ed. Helene Hohmeyer.
  Munich: Ferdinand Schöningh, 1970
  Hrotswith von Gandersheim. Werke in deutscher
  Übertragung. Ed. Helene Hohmeyer.
  Paderborn: Ferdinand Schöningh, 1973
Julian of Norwich
  Revelations of Divine Love. 14th cent. Trans. Clifton Wolters.
  Harmondsworth: Penguin, 1966, 1985
  London: Buns and Oaks, 1961
  Trans. M.L. del Maestro.
  Garden City, NY: Image, 1977
  Julian of Norwich, Showings.
  New York: Paulist Press, 1978
Mechthild of Magdeburg
  Das fliessende Licht der Gottheit. (13 cent.)
  New edition with introd. by M. Schmidt and study by H.U.
von Balthasar, Einsiedeln: Benzinger Verlag, 1955
  Revelationes Gertrudianae ac Mechtildianae I-II. Ed.
  Benedictines of Solesmes.
  Paris: Henricum Oudin, 1875
Revelations of Mechthild of Magdeburg (1210-1297) or,
  The Flowing Light of the Godhead (trans. Lucy Menzies)
  New York: Longmans, Green and Co., 1953
Teresa of Avila (Teresa of Jesus)
  The Complete Works of St. Teresa of Jesus.
  Ed. and trans. by E. Allison Peers.
  London, 1946

AI.14b   Other works
Besant, Annie
The Law of Population.
London: Freethought Publishing, 1877
Theosophy and the Law of Population.
London: Theosophical Publishing, 1904
Esoterisch Christendom (trans. from Eng. by H.J. van Ginkel).
Amsterdam, 1904
In den Buitenhof (trans. J.W. Boissevain)
Amsterdam, 1904
Een studie over het bewustzijn (trans. J.A.W. Schuurman).
Amsterdam: Theosofische Uitgeversmaatschappij, 1905
Het bouwen van den kosmos.
Amsterdam, 1908
De Wijsheid der Upanishads.
Amsterdam, 1908
Het levensraadsel en hoe de theosofie dit oplost.
Amsterdam, 1947, and many other works
(Lectures in London, 1907)
Man: Whence, How and Wither: A Record of Clairvoyant
Investigation. Adyar etc.: (without publication), 1913

Blavatsky, Helena Petrovna
Isis Unveiled, 1877
The Secret Doctrine, 1888
The Key to Theosophy, 1889
The Voice of Silence, 1889
A Glossary of Theosophical Terms, 1890-91

Coxhead, Nona
The Relevance of Bliss - A Contemporary Exploration of
Mystic Experience. Hounslow: Wildwood, 1985
New York: St. Martin's Press, 1986

King, Ursula
Towards a New Mysticism. London: Collins, 1980
Women and Spirituality.
Basingstoke: Macmillan, 1988

Schimmel, Annemarie
Mystical Dimensions of Islam.
Chapel Hill: Univ. of North Carolina Press, 1975

Schuurman (or Schurman), Anna Maria van
Nysterium magnum, oder: grosses Geheimnüs. Das ist: ein sehr
herrliches und im heiligen Wort Gottes wohlgegründetes
Redeneren uber die Zukunft des Reichs Christi. Trans. from Latin.
Wezel, Duisburg, Frankfurt, 1699
Uitbreiding over de drie eerste capitels van Genesis
beneffens een vertoog van het geestelijk huwelijk van
Christus met de gelovigen. Groningen, 1732

Weil, Simone, posthumous editions
  La pesanteur et la grâce. Paris, 1946
  Gravity and Grace (trans. Emma Craufurd).
  London: Routledge and Kegan Paul, 1952
  L'Enracinement. Paris, 1949
  The Need for Roots (trans. Arthur F. Wills).
  London/New York, 1952
  Attente de Dieu. Paris, 1950
  Waiting for God (trans. Emma Craufurd).
  London/New York, 1951
  La connaissance surnaturelle. Paris, 1950
  Lettre à un religieux. Paris, 1951
  Letter to a Priest (trans. Arthur F. Wills).
  London/New York, 1953
  Leçons de philosophie. Paris: Plon, 1959
  Intuitions pré-chrétiennes. Paris, 1951
  Intimations of Christianity Among the Ancient Greeks
  (trans. Elisabeth Geissbühler). London/New York, 1957
  Cahiers I-III. Paris, 1951, 1953, 1956
  The Notebooks of Simone Weil I-II (trans. Arthur F. Wills).
  London/New York, 1956
  La source grecque. Paris, 1953
  Écrits de Londres. Paris, 1957
  First and Last Notebooks (trans. R. Rees).
  London: Oxford Univ. Press, 1970
  Formative Writings, 1929-1941 (ed. and trans. by
  Dorothy Tuck McFarland and Wilhelmina van Ness).
  Amherst: The Univ. of Massachusetts Press, 1988

AI.15   Natural Philosophy

Blackwell, Antoinette Brown
  Studies in General Science. New York: G.P. Putnam, 1869

Cavendish, Margaret
  Philosophical and Physical Opinions. London, 1662
  Philosophical Letters; or, Modest Reflections upon some
  Opinions in Natural Philosophy, maintained by several
  famous and learned Authors of this Age. London, 1664
  Observations on Experimental Philosophy.
  London, 1666, 1668
  Grounds of Natural Philosophy. London, 1668

AI.16   Phenomenology   see also Anthropology; Metaphilosophy; Mind: Intentionality; Husserl

Bishop, Anne H., and John R. Scudder, Jr.
  The Practical Sense of Nursing: A Phenomenological Philosophy
  of Practice. New York: State Univ. of New York Press, 1990

Conrad-Martius, Hedwig
  Der Selbstaufbau der Natur. Hamburg, 1944
  Die Zeit. Munich, 1954
  Das Sein. Munich, 1957
  Der Raum. Munich: Köselverlag, 1958
Eckfeld, Alice
  Studie zur Phänomenologie des Psychischen. Vienna: diss., 1927
Motroshilova, N.V. (Nelli Vasilevna)
  Principles and Contradictions of Phenomenological
  Philosophy. Moscow: Univ. of Moscow Publication House, 1968
  Kritika fenomenologicheskogo napravleniia sovremennoi
  burzhuaznoi filosofii. Riga: "Zinatne", 1981
Ströker, Elisabeth, and Paul Janssen
  Phänomenologische Philosophie. Freiburg, etc.: Alber, 1989
Tymieniecka, Anna-Teresa
  Beyond Ingarden's Idealism/Realism Controversy with
  Husserl. Dordrecht: Reidel, 1976
  The Phenomenology of Man and of the Human Condition.
  Dordrecht: Reidel, 1983
  Logos and Life - Creative Experience and the Critique of Reason.
  Analecta Husserliana 24. Deventer: Kluwer, 1987

  collections:
Tymieniecka, Anna-Teresa (ed.)
  For Roman Ingarden: nine essays in phenomenology.
  The Hague: Nijhoff, 1959
  Analecta Husserliana:
  The Yearbook of Phenomenological Research. 1971-
  Vols. 1-7, 11, 13-24, 26-28, 32. Dordrecht, etc.:
  Reidel, from vol. 24: Kluwer Academic Publishers.
  The phenomenological realism of the possible worlds:
  the "a priori", activity and passivity of
  consciousness, phenomenology and nature. 1974
  Ingardeniana. I. A spectrum of specialised studies
  establishing the field of research. With a bibliography
  concerning Roman Ingarden. 1976
  The Crisis of Culture: steps to reopen the
  phenomenological investigation of man. The modalities
  of human life, the irreducible in values and their
  fluctuating framework of reference, from reason to
  action, alienation and belonging. 1976
  The self and the other: the irreducible element in
  man. I. The 'Crisis of Man'. 1977
  The human being in action: the irreducible element in man. 1978
  The teleologies in Husserlian phenomenology: the
  irreducible element in man. 1979

Tymieniecka, Anna-Teresa, Wojtyla, Karol, and -
     The acting Person
     [Definite text established in collaboration
     with the author by Anna-Teresa Tymieniecka.
     Trans. from the Polish by Andrzej Potocki]. 1979
     The philosophic reflection of man in literature. 1982
     The phenomenology of man and of the human condition:
     individualisation of nature and the human being.
     2 vols.: 14, 21, 1983-1986:
     I. Plotting the territory for interdisciplinary communication
     II. The meeting point between Occidental and Oriental
     Philosophies. (with Calvin O. Schrag)
     Foundations of morality, human rights, and the human
     sciences: phenomenology in a foundational dialogue with
     the human sciences. 1983
     Soul and body in Husserlian phenomenology: man
     and nature. 1983
     Phenomenology of life in a dialogue between Chinese
     and Occidental philosophy. 1984
     The existential coordinates of the human
     condition: poetic, epic, tragic: the literary genre. 1984
     Poetics of the elements in the human condition.
     3 vols. 1985-1990
     I. The sea: from elemental stirrings to symbolic
     inspiration, language, and life-significance in
     literary interpretation and theory.
     II. The airy elements in poetic imagination: breath,
     breeze, wind, thunder, snow, flame, fire, volcano.
     III. The elemental passions of the soul.
     The moral sense in the communal significance of
     life: investigations in phenomenological praxeology:
     psychiatric therapeutics, medical ethics and social
     praxis within the life- and communal world. 1986
     Morality within the life- and social world:
     Interdisciplinary Phenomenology of Authentic Life
     in the Moral Sense. 1987
     Logos and Life.
     2 vols. 1988
     Man within his life-world: contributions to
     phenomenology by scholars from East-Central Europe. 1989
     Man's self-interpretation-in-existence: phenomenology
     and philosophy of life - introducing the Spanish perspective.
     The moral sense and its foundational significance:
     self, person, historicity, community: phenomenological
     praxeology and psychiatry. 1990
Tymieniecka, Anna-Teresa, and Calvin Schrag (eds.)
     Analecta Husserliana 14. Dordrecht: Reidel, 1983

AI.17   **Religion, Philosophy of**   *see also* Mysticism; Ethics and Morality

AI.17a   **General Philosophy of Religion and Theology**

Astell, Mary
Letters Concerning the Love of God Between the Author of the
Proposal to the Ladies and Mr. John Norris, wherein his
Discourse shewing That it ought to be entire and exclusive of all
other Loves, is further cleared and justified. London: J. Norris,
1695

Bal, Mieke
Lethal Love: Feminist Literary Readings of Biblical
Love Stories. Bloomington: Indiana Univ. Press, 1987

Becher, Jeanne
Women, Religion and Sexuality:
Studies of the Impact of Religious Teachings on Women.
Geneva: WCC Publications, 1990

Beecher, Catharine
Letters on the Difficulties of Religion.
Hartford: Belknap & Hammersley, 1836
An Address to the Protestant Clergy of the United States.
New York: Harper & Bros., 1846
Common Sense Applied to Religion, or the Bible and the People.
Harper & Brothers, 1846
An Appeal to the People on Behalf of their Rights as
Authorized Interpreters of the Bible.
New York: Harper & Brothers, 1860

Bry, Ilse
Über zwei Grundformen des Erlösungsgedankens.
Vienna: diss., 1929

Chalres-Saget, Annick
L'architecture du Divin. Paris: Belles, 1982

Cloyes, Shirley A., *see* Sölle, Dorothee, and - [1968]

Damaris Cudworth Masham, *see* Masham

Daly, Mary
The Church and the Second Sex: With a New Feminist
Postchristian Introduction by the Author.
New York: Harper & Row, Harper Colophon Books, 1975
Beyond God the Father -
Toward a Philosophy of Women's Liberation.
Boston: Beacon's Press, 1973

Davis, Caroline Franks
The Evidential Force of Religious Experience.
Oxford: Clarendon Press, 1989

Evans, Gillian R.
Old Arts and New Theology.
Oxford: Clarendon Press, 1980

Fulbrook, Mary
Piety and Politics. Cambridge: Cambridge Univ. Press, 1983

Gerhart, Mary, and Allan Russell
Metaphoric Process.
Forth Worth: Christian Univ. Press, 1984

Gössmann, Elisabeth
Die streitbare Schwestern: was will die
feministische Theologie? Freiburg, etc.: Herder, 1981

Halkes, C.H.
Feminisme en spiritualiteit. Baarn: Ten Have, 1986

Haughton, Rosemary
The Passionate God. London: Darton Longman & Todd, 1981

Jantzen, Grace
God's World, God's Body.
Philadelphia: Westminster Press, 1984

Jay, Elisabeth
The Religion of the Heart. London: Oxford Univ. Press, 1979

King, Ursula
Women and Spirituality. London: Macmillan, 1988

Langley, Myrtle
Equal Woman: A Christian Feminist Perspective.
Basingstoke: Marshalls, 1983

Maclaren, Elizabeth
The Nature of Belief. London: Sheldon Press, 1976

Martineau, Harriet
Miscellanies. I-II
Boston: Hillard, Gray and Company, 1836

Masham, Damaris Cudworth
A Discourse Concerning the Love of God.
London: For A. and J. Churchill at the Black-Swan in
Paternoster-Row, 1696

McFague, Sallie
Metaphorical Theology -
Models of God in Religious Language.
London: SMC Press, 1983

Metzger, H.
Théologie naturelle et gravitation universelle.
Paris, 1937

Monaghan, Patricia
The Book of Goddesses and Heroines.
New York: Dutton, 1981

Murphy, Nancy
Theology in the Age of Scientific Reasoning.
Ithaca, NY: Cornell Univ. Press, 1990

Nogarola, Isotta
    De pari aut impari Evae atque Adae peccato. 1451
    Oratio in laudem beati Hieronymus. 1453
Ochs, Carol
    Women and Spirituality. Totowa, NJ: Rowman & Allanheld, 1983
    Adam, Eve, and the Serpent.
    New York: Vintage Books, 1988
Oppenheimer, Helen
    The Hope of Happiness. London: SCM, 1983
Re-Bartlett, Lucy
    Sex and Sanctity. London: Longmans, 1912
Radford-Ruether, Rosemary
    Sexism and God Talk: Towards a Feminist Theology.
    Boston: Beacon Press, 1983
Singer, Beth J.
    Ordinal Naturalism. East Brunswick, NJ: Bucknell U.P., 1983
Sölle, Dorothee, and Shirley A. Cloyes
    To Work and to Love. Philadelphia: Fortress Press, 1984
Soskice, Janet Martin
    Metaphor and Religious Language.
    Oxford: Clarendon Press, 1985
Stone, Merlin
    When God Was a Woman.
    New York: Harcourt Brace Jovanovich, Harvest Books, 1976
    Simon and Shuster, Wallaby Books, 1978

collections:

Bynum, Caroline Walker, S. Harrell and P. Richman (eds.)
    Gender and Religion: On the Complexity of Symbols.
    Boston: Beacon Press, 1986
Frazier, Allie M. (ed.)
    Issues in Religion: A Book of Readings.
    New York: Van Nostrand, 1975
Gössmann, Elisabeth, Engelbert Neuhäusler, and - (eds.)
    Was ist Theologie? Munchen: Hueber, 1966
Hageman, Alice (ed.)
    Sexist Religion and Women in the Church: No More Silence!
    New York: Association Press, 1974
Holden, Pat (ed.)
    Women's Religious Experience.
    Totowa, NJ: Rowman & Littlefield, 1983
Lundgren, Eva (ed.)
    Den bortkomne datter.
    Kvinneteologi - kvinnefrigjöring - teologikritikk.
    Oslo: Universitetsforlaget, 1981

Moltmann-Wendel, Elisabeth, Elisabeth Gössmann et al. (ed.)
    Weiblichkeit in der Theologie: Verdrängung und
    Wiederkehr. Gütersloh: Mohn, 1988
Spretnak, Charlene (ed.)
    The Politics of Women's Spirituality: Essays on the
    Rise of Spiritual Power Within the Feminist Movement.
    Garden City, NY: Doubleday and Company, Inc., 1982
Tessier, Linda J. (ed.)
    Concepts of the Ultimate - Philosophical Perspectives
    on the Nature of the Divine. Oxford: Blackwell, 1990

AI.17b   Special Religions and Churches, Philosophy of

Astell Mary
    The Christian Religion as Profess'd by a Daughter Of
    The Church of England. London, 1705
Barnes, Hazel E.
    The Meddling Gods: Four Essays On Classical Themes.
    Lincoln: Univ. of Nebraska Press, 1974
Chatterjee, Margaret
    Gandhi's Religious Thought. London: Macmillan, 1984
Ching, Julia
    Confucianism and Christianity: A Comparative Study.
    Tokyo: Kodansha, 1978
Fiorenza, Elisabeth Schüssler
    In Memory of Her: A Feminist Theological Reconstruction
    of Christian Origins. London: SCM Press, 1983
Gössmann, Elisabeth
    Religiöse Herkunft, profane Zukunft: das Christentum in
    Japan. Munich: Heuber, 1965
Harrison, Jane Ellen
    Themis: A Study of the Social Origins of Greek Religion.
    Cambridge: University Press, 1912, 1927
Ivékovic, Rada
    Rana budistica misao. Sarajevo: Veselin Maslesa, 1977
Lualdi, Maria
    Il problema della philia. Milan: Celuc, 1976
Macy, Joanna
    Dharma and Development - Religion as Resource in the
    Sarvodaya Self-help Movement.
    West Hartford, CT: Kumarian Press, 1985
Miles, Margaret R.
    Carnal Knowing: Female Nakedness and Religious Meaning
    in the Christian West. Boston: Beacon Press, 1989
Paul, Diana
    Women in Buddhism. Berkeley, CA: Asian Humanities Press, 1979

Plaskow, Judith
> Standing Again at Sinai. Judaism from a Feminist
> Perspective. San Francisco: Harper, 1990

Rodinson, Maxime
> Mohammed. Lucern: Bucher, 1975

Ross, Nancy Wilson
> Buddhism: A Way of Life and Thought.
> London: Collins, 1981

Smith, Jane Idleman, and Yvonne Yazbeck Haddad
> The Islamic Resurrection of Death and Understanding.
> Albany: State Univ. of New York Press, 1981

Tanner, Kathryn E.
> God and Creation in Christian Theology.
> Oxford: Blackwell, 1988

Vogel, C.J. de
> De laatste ernst. Zutphen: G.J.A. Ruys, 1931
> Wijsgerige aspecten van het vroeg-christelijk denken.
> Baarn: Het Wereldvenster, 1970
> De grondslag van onze zekerheid - Over de problemen van
> de kerk heden. Assen: Van Gorcum, 1977

Warner, Marina
> Alone of All her Sex:
> The Myth and the Cult of the Virgin Mary.
> New York: Alfred A. Knopf, 1976

collections:

Frazier, Allie M (ed.)
> Buddhism: Readings in Eastern Religious Thought, Vol. 2.
> Philadelphia: Westminster Press, 1969

AI.17c   Various other themes

Cary, Mary
> A New and More exact Mappe or Description of the New
> Jerusalem's Glory. 1651

Fredriksen, Paula
> From Jesus to Christ - The Origins of the New Testament.
> London: Yale Univ. Press, 1988

Nelkin, Dorothy
> The Creation Controversy: Science or Scripture in the
> Schools. New York: Norton, 1982

Pazilova, V.P.
> A Critical Analysis of the Religious and Philosophical
> Doctrines of N.F. Fodorov.
> Moscow: Moscow Univ., 1985

AI.18   **Science, Philosophy of**
see also Empirical Sciences, Foundations and Philosophy
of the Special; Epistemology, especially Objectivity

AI.18a   **Introductions**

Ströker, Elisabeth
Einführung in die Wissenschaftstheorie.
Darmstadt: Wissenschaftliche Buchgesellschaft, 1973

Trusted, Jennifer
Inquiry and Understanding. An Introduction to
Explanation in the Physical and Human Sciences.
Atlantic Highlands, NJ: Humanities Press, 1987

AI.18b   **General Philosophy of Science**

Adam, Barbara
Time and Social Theory. Philadelphia: Temple Univ. Press, 1990

Bannett, Eve Tavor
Structuralism and the Logic of Dissent - Barthes,
Derrida, Foucault, Lacan. London: Macmillan, 1989

Brighton Women and Science Group
Alice Through the Microscope. London: Virago, 1980

Diaz, Esther, and Mario Heler
El conociemento cientifico. Hacia una visión critica de
la ciencia. Buenos Aires: Eudeba, 1988

Dohm, Hedwig
Die Wissenschaftliche Emanzipation der Frau.
Berlin: Wedekind und Schweiger, 1874

Feldman, Jacqueline
Voyage mal poli à travers le savoir et la science.
Paris: Editions Tierce, 1980

Germain, Sophie
Considérations générales sur l'État des Sciences et des
Lettres aux différentes Époques de leur Culture
Oeuvres posthumes, publ. par L'Herbette
Paris, 1833; German trans. Jena, 1910
Oeuvres philosophiques
(ed. and with preface by H. Stupuy). Paris, 1879

Harding, Sandra
The Science Question in Feminism.
Ithaca, NY and London: Cornell Univ. Press, 1986

Jacobus, Mary, Evelyn Fox Keller, and Sally Shuttleworth
Body/Politics: Women and the Discourses of Science.
London and New York: Routledge, 1990

Kurzweil, Edith
The Age of Structuralism. New York: Columbia Univ. Press, 1980

Ladd-Franklin, Christine
    Color and Color Theories. London: Reprinted by Ayer Co.,
    1929 edition, 1932
Lazari-Pawlowska, Ija
    [Concept Formation in the Humanities]. Lodz: Univ. Press, 1958
Metzger, Hélène
    La science, l'appel de la religion et la volonté
    humaine. Paris: E. de Boccard, 1954
Metzger-Bruhl, Hélène
    Les concepts scientifiques. 1925
Nelkin, Dorothy
    Science as Intellectual Property. Cambridge: Macmillan, 1984
Parain-Vial, Jeanne
    La Nature du fait dans les sciences humaines.
    Paris: P.U.F., 1966
Redman, Deborah A.
    Economics and the Philosophy of Science.
    Oxford: Oxford Univ. Press, 1990
Sheehan, Helena
    Marxism and the Philosophy of Science.
    Atlantic Highlands, NJ: Humanities Press, 1985
Schrader, Wiebke
    Die Selbstkritik der Theorie. Amsterdam: Ropodi, 1978
Shaw, Evelyn
    Strategies of Being Female.
    Brighton: Harvester (Wheatsheaf Books), 1983
Stengers, Isabelle, Ilya Prigogine, and -
    La nouvelle alliance - Métamorphose de la science.
    Paris: Gallimard, 1979
    Order Out of Chaos: Man's New Dialogue With Nature.
    Glasgow: William Collins Sons & Co., 1984
    New York: Banton Books, 1984
    Entre le temps et l'éternité. Paris: A. Fayard, 1988
Stengers, Isabelle, and Judith Schlanger
    Les concepts scientifiques: Invention et pouvoir.
    Paris and Strasbourg: La Découverte/Conseil de
    l'Europe/Unesco, 1989
Yanovskaya (Janovskaja), S.A.
    Metodologicheskie problemy nauki
    (Methodological Problems of Science). Moscow: Mysl, 1972

collections:
Bleier, Ruth (ed.)
    Feminist Approaches to Science.
    New York: Pergamon Press, 1986

Fehér, Márta, Imre Hronsky, and Balasz Dajka (eds.)
  Scientific Knowledge Socialized: Selected Readings of
  the 5th Joint International Conference on the
  History and Philosophy of Science Organized by
  the IUPHS: Veszprem, 1984.
  Dordrecht, etc.: Kluwer Academic Press, 1988
Koch, Ulla, et al. (eds.)
  Kön og videnskab. Aalborg: Aalborg Universitetsforlag
  (Serie om kvindeforskning, 270), 1989
Montinari, Maddalene (ed.)
  Sulle libertà della scienza e l'autorità delle Scritture.
  Rome: Edizioni Theoria, 1983
Signs: Journal of Women in Culture and Society 4 No. 1
  Special issue on women and science (1978)
Stafford, Barbara Maria
  Symbol and Myth.
  Newark: Univ. of Delaware Press, 1980
Tuana, Nancy (ed.)
  Feminism and Science.
  Bloomington: Indiana Univ. Press, 1989

AI.18c   Aesthetics in Science

collections:
Curtin, Deane W. (ed.)
  The Aesthetic Dimension of Science.
  New York: Philosophical Library, 1982
Wechsler, Judith (ed.)
  On Aesthetics in Science.
  Cambridge, MA: MIT Press, 1981

AI.18d   Science of Science *see also* Culture: Academy

Bertilsson, Margareta
  Towards a Social Reconstruction of Science Theory:
  Peirce's Theory of Inquiry and Beyond.
  Lund: Univ. of Lund, 1978
Egidi, Rosaria
  Studi di logica e di filosofia della scienza.
  Rome: Bulzoni, 1971
Fehér, Márta
  A tudomány fej lödes kerdöjelei.
  Budapest: Akademia Kiadó, 1983
Hausen, K., and H. Nowotny
  Wie männlich ist die Wissenschaft?
  Frankfurt am Main: Suhrkamp, 1986

Hesse, Mary
    Models and Analogies in Science.
    Notre Dame, IN: Notre Dame Univ. Press, 1966
    The Structure of Scientific Inference.
    London: Macmillan, 1974
    Revolutions and Reconstructions in the Philosophy of Science.
    Bloomington: Indiana Univ. Press, 1980

Koertge, Noretta A.
    A Study of Relations Between Scientific Theories:
    A Test of the General Correspondence Principle.
    London: London University, 1969

Michard-Marchal, Claire, and Claudine Ribéry
    Sexisme et sciences humaines: pratique linguistique du rapport
    de sexage.
    Lille: Presses Universitaires de Lille, 1982

Naukoznawstwa, Zagadnienia
    Problems of the Science of Science. Warsaw, 1970

Ullman-Margalit, Edna
    Science in Reflection. Dordrecht: Reidel, 1988

collections:

List, Elisabeth, G. Pauritsch, and B. Frakele (ed.)
    Über Frauenleben, Männerwelt und Wissenschaft.
    Vienna: Verlag für Gesellschaftskritik, 1987

Lubrano, Linda L., and Susan Gross Solomon (eds.)
    The Social Context of Soviet Science.
    Boulder, CO: Westview Press, 1980

Nersessian, Nancy (ed.)
    The Process of Science.
    Dordrecht/Boston/Lancaster: Nijhoff, 1987

Robert, Michèle (ed.)
    Fondéments et étapes de la recherche scientifique.
    Montreal: Chenelière et Stanké, 1982

AII: **Practical Philosophy**

AII.1   **General Practical Philosophy**

Cockburn (Trotter Cockburn), Catharine
    The Works of Mrs. Catharine Cockburn, Theological,
    Moral, Dramatic, and Poetical, I-II
    Ed., with biography, by Thomas Birch. London, 1751

Cruz, Sor Juana Inéz de la
    Respuesta a Sor Filotéa de la Cruz. 1691
    In: Obras completas, Mexico City: Porrua, 1975
    (with a biography by Alfonso Méndez Plancarte)

Wollstonecraft, Mary
   The Works of Mary Wollstonecraft, Vols. I-VII
   Eds. Janet Todd and Marilyn Butler.
   London: Pickering and Chatto, 1989.

AII.2   Aesthetics

AII.2a   Introductions
Saw, Ruth Lydia
   Aesthetics: An Introduction. New York: Macmillan, 1972

AII.2b   General Aesthetics *see also* Hegel; Kant; Plato
Borowicka, Silvia
   Eine Untersuchung der Begriffe des Angenehmen und des
   Schönen. Vienna: diss., 1931
Bozarth-Campbell, Alla
   The Word's Body -
   An Incarnational Aesthetic of Incarnation.
   University: Univ. of Alabama Press, 1979
Brown, Merle E.
   Neo-Idealistic Aesthetics: Croce-Gentile-Collingwood.
   Detroit: Wayne State Univ. Press, 1966
Donnell-Kotrozo, Carol
   Critical Essays on Post-Modernism.
   Philadelphia: Art Alliance Press, 1983
Golaszewka, Maria
   Swiadomosc piekna: Problematyka genezy, funkcji,
   struktury i wartosci w estetyce.
   Warszawa: Panstwowe, 1970
Haezrahi, Pepita
   The Contemplative Activity - Eight Lectures on
   Aesthetics. London: Allen & Unwin 1954
Hanna, Judith Lynne
   The Performer-Audience Connection.
   Austin: Univ. of Texas Press, 1983
Heidemann, Ingeborg
   Der Begriff des Spieles und das aesthetische Weltbild
   in der Philosophie der Gegenwart.
   Berlin: De Gruyter, 1968
Hübner, Kathinka
   Über das Schöne und das Deformierte. Köln: Mayer, 1969
Hutcheon, Linda
   A Theory of Parody. New York: Methuen, 1985
Ives, Margaret C.
   The Analogue of Harmony. Pittsburgh: Duquesne Univ. Press, 1970

Johnson, Pauline
    Marxist Aesthetics. London: Routledge & Kegan Paul, 1984
Kelley, Theresa M.
    Wordsworth's Revisionary Aesthetics.
    Cambridge: Cambridge Univ. Press, 1988
Kofman, Sarah
    Mélancolie de l'art. Paris: Galilée, 1985
    Paroles suffoquées. Paris: Galilée, 1987
Kofman, Sarah, Sylviane Agacinski, and Jacques Derrida
    Mimesis des articulations. Paris: Aubier-Flammarion
    (La philosophie en effet), 1975
Krook, Dorothea
    Elements of Tragedy. New Haven, CT: Yale Univ. Press, 1969
Langer, Susanne K.
    Feeling and Form. London: Routledge & Kegan Paul, 1953
    Problems of Art: ten philosophical Lectures.
    London: Routledge and Kegan Paul, 1957
Lauretis, Teresa de
    Technologies of Gender: Essays on Theory, Film, Fiction.
    Bloomington: Indiana Univ. Press, 1987
Martienssen, Heather
    The Shapes of Structure. Oxford: Oxford Univ. Press, 1976
Mothersill, Mary
    Beauty Restored. An Essay in Aesthetic Theory.
    Oxford: Clarendon Press, 1984
Paglia, Camille
    Sexual Personae: Art and Decdence from Nefertiti to
    Emily Dickinson. New Haven: Yale Univ. Press, 1990
Rose, Jacqueline
    Sexuality in the Field of Vision. London: Verso, 1987
Rose, Margaret A.
    Marx's Lost Aesthetic. Cambridge: Cambridge Univ. Press, 1984
Schaper, Eva
    Prelude to Aesthetics. London: Allen & Unwin, 1968
    Studies in Kant's Aesthetics.
    Edinburgh: Edinburgh Univ. Press, 1979
Seghers, Anna
    Über Kunst und Wirklichkeit. (Revised with an introd.
    by Sigrid Bock.) Berlin: Akademie, 1970
Tymieniecka, Anna-Teresa
    Roman Ingarden's Aesthetics in a New Key and the
    Independent Approaches of Others: the Performing Arts,
    the Fine Arts and Literature.
    The World Institute for Advanced Phenomenological
    Research and Learning

collections:

Langer, Susanne K. (ed.)
Reflections on Art: a Source Book of Writings by
Artists, Critics and Philosophers.
Baltimore: Johns Hopkins Press, 1958

Schaper, Eva (ed.)
Pleasure, Preference and Value -
Studies in Philosophical Aesthetics.
New York: Cambridge Univ. Press, 1983. Paperback, 1988

AII.2c   Literature and Theatre

Caws, Mary Ann
The Eye in the Text - Essays on Perception, Mannerist to Modern.
Princeton, NJ: Princeton Univ. Press, 1981

Forrest-Thomson, Veronica
Poetic Artifice.
Manchester: Manchester Univ. Press, 1978

Gilman, Margaret
The Idea of Poetry in France From Houdar de la Motte to
Baudelaire. Cambridge, MA: Harvard Univ. Press, 1958

Hungerland, Isabel C.
Poetic Discourse. Univ. of California, 1958

Orenstein, Gloria Feman
The Theater of the Marvelous: Surrealism and the
Contemporary Stage.
New York: New York Univ. Press, 1975

collections:

Heller, Agnes, and Ferenc Fehér (ed.)
Reconstructing aesthetics: writings of the Budapest School.
Oxford, etc.: Blackwell, 1986

Wheeler, Kathleen (ed.)
German Aesthetic and Literary Criticism I-III.
Cambridge: Cambridge Univ. Press, 1984

AII.2d   Music, Dance, Opera

Katz, Ruth
Divining the Powers of Music -
Aesthetic Theory and the Origins of Opera.
New York: Pendragon Press, 1986

collections:

Sheets-Johnstone, Maxine (ed.)
Illuminating Dance: Philosophical Explorations.
Lewisburg, PA: Bucknell Univ. Press, 1987

Steiner, Wendy (ed.)
  The Sign in Music and Literature.
  Austin: Univ. of Texas Press, 1981

AII.2e   Visual Arts

Dissanayake, Ellen
  What Is Art For? London: Univ. of Washington Press, 1988
Eaton, Marcia Muelder
  Art and Non-art. London: Associated Univ. Press, 1983
Gethmann-Siefert, Annemarie
  Die Funktion der Kunst in der Geschichte.
  Bonn: Bouvier, 1984
Greenfeld, Liah
  Different Worlds - A Sociological Study of Taste,
  Choice, and Success in Art.
  Cambridge: Cambridge Univ. Press, 1988
Henderson, Linda Dalrymple
  The Fourth Dimension and Non-Euclidean Geometry in
  Modern Art. Princeton, NJ: Princeton Univ. Press, 1983
Huxtable, Ada Louise
  Kicked a Building Lately. New York: Quadrangle, 1976
Kofman, Sarah
  L'enfance et l'art: Une interprétation de l'esthétique freudienne.
  Paris: Payot, 1970
Kuhn, Annette
  Women's Pictures: Feminism and Cinema.
  London: Routledge & Kegan Paul, 1982
  The Power of the Image - Essays on Representation and
  Sexuality. New York: Routledge, Chapman and Hall, 1985
Langer, Susanne K.
  Problems of Art: Ten Philosophical Lectures.
  London: Routledge & Kegan Paul, 1957
Lippard, Lucy R.
  From the Center: Feminist Essays on Women's Art.
  New York: Dutton, 1976
Nochlin, Linda
  Women, Art, and Power and other Essays.
  London: Thames and Hudson, 1989
Oberti, Elisa
  Per una fondazione fenomenologica della conoscivita
  dell'arte. Milan: Vita e Pensiero, 1968
Pointon, Marcia R.
  Milton and English Art.
  Manchester: Manchester Univ. Press, 1970

Rosenau, Helen
    The Ideal City: Its Architectural Evolution.
    London: Studio Vista, 1974
Spiel, Hilde
    Versuch einer Darstellungstheorie des Films.
    Vienna: diss., 1936
Spitz, Ellen Handler
    Art and Psyche - A Study in Psychoanalysis and Aesthetics.
    New Haven, CT: Yale Univ. Press, 1985
Tejera, Victorine
    Art and Human Intelligence. New York: Meredith, 1965
Torgovnick, Marianna
    The Visual Arts, Pictorialism, And the Novel.
    Princeton, NJ: Princeton Univ. Press (n.d.)
Werhane, Patricia H.
    Philosophical Issues in Art.
    Englewood Cliffs, NJ: Prentice-Hall, 1984
Wolff, Janet
    Hermeneutic Philosophy and the Sociology of Art.
    London: Routledge & Kegan Paul, 1975
    Aesthetics and the Sociology of Art.
    Winchester: Allen & Unwin, 1983

    collections:

Babcock, Barbara A. (ed.)
    The Reversible World: Symbolic Inversion in Art and Society.
    Ithaca, NY: Cornell Univ. Press, 1978
Balfe, Judith H., and Margaret Jane Wyszomirski
    Art, Ideology, and Politics. New York: Praeger, 1985
Henle, Mary (ed.)
    Vision and Artifact. New York: Springer, 1976
Meyer, Ursula (ed.)
    Conceptual Art. New York: Dutton, 1972

> **Applied Philosophy:** *see* type of philosophy,
> e.g., Applied Political Philosophy: cf. Political Philosophy

AII.3   **Culture, Philosophy of**
         see also Political philosophy: Sexual and Gender Politics

AII.3a   **General Philosophy of Culture** *see also* Phenomenology;
         Political Philosophy, History of: Patriarchy; Social Philosophy
Archer, Margaret S.
    Culture and Agency - The Place of Culture in Social Theory.
    Cambridge: Cambridge Univ. Press, 1988

Bennent, Heidemarie
  Galanterie und Verachtung. Eine philosophisch-geschichtliche
  Untersuchung zur Stellung der Frau in Gesellschaft und Kultur.
  Frankfurt/New York: Campus Verlag, 1985
Burnier, Andreas (C.I. Dessaur)
  De zwembadmentaliteit. Amsterdam: Querido, 1979
  Essays 1968-1985. Amsterdam: Querido, 1985
Douglas, Ann
  The Feminization of American Culture.
  New York: Alfred A. Knopf, 1977
Heller, Agnes
  Hypothese über eine marxistische Theorie der Werte.
  Frankfurt am Main: Suhrkamp, 1972
  Can Modernity Survive?
  Oxford: Blackwell, 1990
  Cambridge: Polity Press, 1990
  Berkeley: Univ. of California Press, 1990
Heller, Agnes, and Ferenc Fehér
  Diktatur über die Bedürfnisse. 1979
Monsen, Nina Karin
  Det kvinnelige mennesket. Oslo: Aschehoug, 1975
  Det elskende mennesket. Oslo: Cappelen, c. 1986
Nerheim, Hjördis, and Viggo Rossvær
  Filosofiens historie: Kulturen som virkelighet og selvbedrag.
  Oslo: Aschehoug/Tanum-Norli, 1984
Russell, Diana E.H.
  The Secret Trauma-Incest in the Lives of Girls and Women.
  New York: Basic Books, 1987
Sandbacka, Carola
  Understanding Other Cultures.
  Helsinki (Acta Philosophical Fennica), 1987
Showalter, Elaine
  The Female Malady -
  Women, Madness, and English Culture, 1830-1980.
  New York: Pantheon Books, 1985
  Harmondsworth: Penguin Books, 1987
Sochor, Zenovia A.
  Revolution and Culture: The Bogdanov-Lenin Controversy.
  Ithaca, NY: Cornell Univ. Press, 1990
Spivak, Gayatri Chakravorty
  In Other Worlds: Essays in Cultural Politics.
  New York: Methuen, 1987
Springborg, Patricia
  The Problem of Human Needs and the Critique of Civilization.
  London: Allen & Unwin, 1981

Torgovnick, Marianna
> Gone Primitive - Savage Intellects, Modern Lives.
> Chicago, etc.: The Univ. of Chicago Press, 1990

Washburn, Dorothy K., and Donald W. Crowe
> Symmetries of Culture - Theory and Practice of Plane.
> Pattern Analysis. London: Univ. of Washington Press, 1988

collections:

Andreas-Grisebach, Manon, and Brigitte Weisshaupt (eds.)
> Was Philosophinnen denken II.
> Zürich: Ammann Verlag, 1986

Bendkowski, Halina, and Brigitte Weisshaupt (eds.)
> Was Philosophinnen denken.
> Zürich: Amman Verlag, 1983

Boralevi, Lea Campos, Maurice Cranston, and - (eds.)
> Culture et Politique/Culture and Politics.
> Hawthorne: de Gruyter, 1988

MacCormack, Carol, and Marilyn Strathern (eds.)
> Nature, Culture and Gender.
> Cambridge: Cambridge Univ. Press, 1980

Maren-Grisebach, Manon, and Ursula Menzer (eds.)
> Philosophinnen. Von Wegen ins 3. Jahrtausend.
> Mainz: Tamagnini, 1982

Ortner, Sherry, and Harriet Whitehead (eds.)
> Sexual Meanings -
> The Cultural Construction of Gender and Sexuality.
> New York: Cambridge Univ. Press, 1981

Pearsall, Marilyn (ed.)
> Women and Values.
> Belmont, CA: Wadsworth, 1986

Rosaldo, Michelle Z., and Lamphere, LouiseLouise Lamphere (eds.)
> Women, Culture, and Society.
> Stanford, CA: Stanford Univ. Press, 1974

Walker, Nancy
> "A Very Serious Thing":
> Women's Humour and American Culture.
> Minneapolis: Univ. of Minnesota Press, 1988

AII.3b Academy, Philosophy of the

Aisenberg, Nadya, and Mona Harrington
> Women of Academe: Outsiders in the Sacred Grove.
> Amherst: Univ. of Massachusetts Press, 1988

Battersby, Christine
> Gender and Genius. Towards a Feminist Analysis.
> Bloomington: Indiana Univ. Press, 1989

Bisseret-Moreau, Noëlle
Les inégaux ou la sélection universitaire.
Paris: P.U.F., 1974

Chamberlain, Mariam K.
Women in Academe: Progress and Prospects.
Ithaca, NY: Russel Sage Foundation, 1989

Coignet, Clarisse
De l'enseignement public au point de vue de
l'Université, de la commune et de l'État.
Paris: Meyreis, 1886

Fraser, Antonia
The Weaker Vessel.
New York: Knopf, 1984

Fürst, Elisabeth
Kvinner i Akademia - inntrengere i en mannskultur?
Om ansettelsesprosessen ved universitet og distrikts-högskoler.
Oslo: NAVFs sekretariat for Kvinneforskning, Norges
allmennvitenskapelige forskningsråd, 1988

Hornig, Lilli S.
Climbing the Academic Ladder -
Doctoral Women Scientists in Academe.
Washington, DC: National Academy of Sciences, 1979

Leporin, Dorothea Christina (Leporin-Erxleben)
Gründliche Untersuchung der Ursachen, die das
weibliche Geschlecht vom Studiren abhalten.
With a Preface by Christian Polycarpus Leporin.
Berlin, 1742
Reprinted with the title: Vernünftige Gedanken vom
Studiren des schönen Geschlechts. Frankfurt, 1749.
Reprinted with the orig. title, with a Epilogue by
Gerda Rechenberg: Hildesheim/New York: Georg Olms, 1977
[Quod nimis cito ac jucunde curare saepius fiat caussa
minus tutae curationis (doctorate thesis in Medicine),
Halle: 1754]

Miller, Jane
Seductions: Studies in Reading and Culture.
London: Virago, 1990

Ruddick, Sara, and Pamela Daniels (eds.)
Working It Out: 23 Women Writers, Scientists, and
Scholars Talk About Their Lives.
New York: Pantheon, 1977

Warnock, Mary
A Common Policy for Education.
Oxford: Oxford Univ. Press, 1988
Universities: Knowing our Minds.
London: Chatto & Windus, 1989

collections:

Farnham, Christie (ed.)
    The Impact of Feminism in the Academy.
    Bloomington: Indiana Univ. Press, 1987

Mattfeld, Jacquelyn A., and Carol G. van Aken (eds.)
    Women and the Scientific Professions.
    Cambridge, MA: MIT Press, 1965

Murray, Penelope (ed.)
    Genius. The History of an Idea.
    Oxford: Blackwell, 1989

Shuster, Marilyn R., and Susan R. van Dyne (ed.)
    Women's Place in the Academy -
    Transforming the Liberal Arts Curriculum.
    Totowa, NJ: Rowman & Allanheld, 1985

Spender, Dale (ed.)
    Men's Studies Modified -
    The Impact of Feminism on the Academic Disciplines.
    Oxford and New York: Pergamon Press, 1981

Spender, Dale (ed.)
    Women of Ideas and What Men Have Done to Them -
    From Aphra Behn to Adrienne Rich.
    London: Routledge and Kegan Paul, 1982

AII.3c   Ecosophy (Ecological Philosophy)

Andreas-Grisebach, Manon
    Philosophie der Grünen. Munich: Olzog, 1982

Carson, Rachel
    The Sea Around Us.
    New York: New American Library, Mentor Books, 1961
    Silent Spring. New York: Fawcett, 1962

Chisholm, Anne
    Philosophers of the Earth: Conversations with Ecologists.
    New York: Dutton, 1972

Flader, Susan
    Thinking Like a Mountain: Aldo Leopold and the Evolution of
    an Ecological Attitude Toward Deer, Wolves, and Forests.
    New York: Columbia Univ. Press, 1974

Graber, Lina H.
    Wilderness as Sacred Space.
    Washington, DC: Association of American Geographers, 1976

Gray, Elizabeth Dodson
    Green Paradise Lost.
    Wellesley: Roundtable Press, 1979
    Why the Green Nigger: Re-Mything Genesis.
    Wellesley, MA: Roundtable Press, 1979

Griffin, Susan
> Pornography and Silence: Culture's Revenge Against Nature.
> London: The Women's Press, 1981

Merchant, Carolyn
> The Death of Nature -
> Women, Ecology and the Scientific Revolution.
> New York: Harper & Row, 1980
> Ecological Revolutions: Nature, Gender, and Science in
> New England. Chapel Hill: Univ. of North Carolina Press, 1989

Roberts, Catherine
> Science, Animals and Evolution.
> Westport, CT: Greenwood Press, 1980

Shiva, Vandana
> Staying Alive. Women, Ecology and Development.
> London: Zed Books Ltd., 1988

Wilkinson, Loren (ed.)
> Earthkeeping: Christian Stewardship of Natural Resources.
> Grand Rapids, MI: Eerdman, 1980

bibliographies:

Anglemyer, Mary, a.o.:
> A Search for Environmental ethics: An Initial Bibliography.
> Washington, DC: Smithsonian Institute Press, 1980

collections:

Diamond, Irene, and Gloria Feman Orenstein (eds.)
> Reweaving the World: The Emergence of Ecofeminism.
> San Fransisco: Sierra Club Books, 1990

AII.3d Technology, Philosophy of

McCorduck, Pamela
> The Universal Machine - Confessions of a
> Technological Optimist. New York: McGraw-Hill, 1985

Ormiston, Gayle, and Raphael Sassover
> Narrative Experiments: The Discursive Authority of
> Science and Technology.
> Minneapolis: Univ. of Minnesota Press, 1989

Rothschild, Joan
> Machina ex dea: Feminist Perspectives on Technology.
> New York: Pergamon Press, 1983

Russell, Dora
> The Religion of the Machine Age.
> London: Routledge abd Kegan Paul, 1983

Tavrizjanovà, G.M.
> Technika, Kultura, Celovek. Moskou: Nauka, 1986

AII.4   **Ethics and Morality** *see also* Law

AII.4a   **Introductions**
Calkins, Mary Whiton
> The Good Man and the Good: An Introduction to Ethics.
> New York: Macmillan, 1918

AII.4b   **General Ethics and Morality** *see also* General Philosophy
Almond, Brenda
> Moral Concerns.
> Atlantic Highlands, NJ: Humanities Press International, 1987

Andreas-Grisebach, Manon
> Stellung beziehen: Eine Einführung in ethische Probleme.
> Göttingen: Vandenhoek, 1981

Anscombe, G.E.M.
> Ethics, Religion and Politics.
> Ontario: Oxford Univ. Press, 1981

Augspurg, Anita
> Die ethische Seite der Frauenfrage.
> Minden and Leipzig, 1984 (1883)

Bailey, Alison
> Posterity and Strategic Policy: A Moral Assessment of
> Nuclear Policy Options.
> Lanham, MD: Univ. Press of America, 1989

Ban Zhao (Pan Chao)
> Nu Chien ("Advice to Women"). c. 85 A.D.

Barnes, Hazel E.
> An Existentialist Ethics.
> Chicago: Univ. of Chicago Press, 1978

Battin, Margaret Pabst
> Ethics in the Sanctuary. Examining the Practices of
> Organized Religion. New Haven, CT: Yale Univ. Press, 1990

Beauvoir, Simone de
> Pour une morale de l'ambiguité. Paris: Gallimard, 1948
> The Ethics of Ambiguity.
> Secaucus, NJ/New York: The Citadel Press, 1964 [1948]

Beecher, Catharine
> The Elements of Mental and Moral Philosophy, Founded
> Upon Experience, Reason, and the Bible. Hartford, 1831

Bender, Helene
> Über das Wesen der Sittlichkeit und den natürlichen
> Entwicklungsprozess des sittlichen Gedankens. Halle, 1894

Benhabib, Seyla, and Fred Dallmayr
> The Communicative Ethics Controversy.
> Cambridge, MA: MIT Press, 1990

Bok, Sissela
  Lying: Moral Choice in Public and Private Life.
  New York: Vintage Books, 1979; London: Quartet Books, 1980
  Secrets: On the Ethics of Concealment and Revelation.
  New York: Pantheon Books, 1983; Oxford: Univ. Press, 1984
Brilmayer, Lea
  Justifying International Acts.
  Ithaca, NY: Cornell Univ. Press, 1989
Cady, Duane L.
  From Warism to Pacifism: A Moral Continuum.
  Philadelphia: Temple Univ. Press, 1989
Coignet, Clarisse
  Cours de morale à l'usage des écoles laïques.
  Paris: Le Chevalier, 1874
  La Morale dans l'éducation. Paris: Delagrave, 1881
Dessaur, C.I.
  De rondgang der gevangenen: een essay over goed en
  kwaad, in de vorm van zeven brieven aan de Platoclub.
  Amsterdam: Querido, 1987
Douglas, Mary, and Baron Isherwood
  The World of Goods. New York: Basic Books, 1979
Downey, Meriel, and A.V. Kelly
  Moral Education: Theory and Practice.
  London: Harper & Row, 1978
Dupuis, Helene
  Wat is goed voor een mens: macht en onmacht van de
  moraal. Amsterdam: Balans, 1987
Emmet, Dorothy
  The Moral Prism. London: Macmillan, 1979
Fagot-Largeault, Anne
  L'Homme bioéthique. Paris: Maloine, 1985
Foot, Philippa
  Morality and Art. Annual Philosophical Lecture.
  British Academy, 1970
  Virtues and Vices, and Other Essays in Moral Philosophy.
  Oxford: Basil Blackwell, 1979
Haezrahi, Pepita
  The Price of Morality.
  London: Allen & Unwin, 1961
Hager, Nina
  Der Traum vom Kosmos. Berlin, 1988
Harrison, Beverly Wildung
  Making the Connection. Essays in Feminist Social Ethics.
  Boston: Beacon Press, 1985

Heller, Agnes
    General Ethics. Oxford: Blackwell, 1988
    A Philosophy of Morals. Oxford: Blackwell, 1989
Hildegard of Bingen
    Liber vitae meritorum. 12th cent. Trans. and ed., with
    a commentary, by H. Schipperges, as:
    Der Mensch in der Verantwortung [c. 1158-1163]. Das
    Buch der Lebensverdienste Liber Vitae Meritorum,
    c. 1903, Salzburg: Otto Müller Verlag, 1972
Hochschild, Jennifer J.
    The New American Dilemma. New Haven: Yale Univ. Press, 1984
Hopkins, Ellice J.
    A Plea for the Wider Action of the Church of England in
    the Prevention of the Degradation of Women.
    London: Hatchards, 1879
    Grave Moral Questions Addressed to the Men and Women of
    England. London: Hatchards, 1882
    The Ride of Death. London: White Cross League (n.d.)
Huby, Pamela
    Plato and Modern Morality. London: Macmillan, 1972
Irigaray, Luce
    Ethique de la différence sexuelle.
    With a Dutch trans. by Jeanne Butinx et al.
    Rotterdam: Erasmus Universiteit, 1982
    Paris: Les Éditions Minuit, 1984
Jayusi, Lena
    Categorization and the Moral Order.
    London: Routledge and Kegan Paul, 1984
Kagan, Shelly
    The Limits of Morality. Oxford: Oxford Univ. Press, 1989
Kanger, Helle
    Human Rights in the U.N. Declaration.
    Uppsala, etc.: Almquist and Wiksell, 1984
Klein, Martha
    Determinism, Blameworthiness, and Deprivation.
    Oxford: Clarendon Press, 1990
    (Oxford Philosophical Monographs)
Kremer-Marietti, Angèle
    La morale. Paris: P.U.F., 1982
Lang, Berel
    Act and Idea in the Nazi Genocide.
    Chicago: Univ. of Chicago Press
Letwin, Shirley Robin
    The Gentleman in Trollope - Individuality and Moral Conduct.
    London: Macmillan, 1982

Macklin, Ruth
   Man, Mind and Morality: The Ethics of Behavior Control.
   Englewood Cliffs, NJ: Prentice-Hall, 1982
Makai, Maria
   The Dialectics of Moral Consciousness.
   Budapest: Akadémiai Kiadò, 1972
McDonagh, Enda
   Gift and Call: Towards a Christian Theology of Morality.
   Dublin: Gill & Macmillan, 1975
Midgley, Mary
   Heart & Mind: The Varieties of Moral Experience.
   Brighton: Harvester Press, 1981
   London: Methuen (University Paperback), 1983
   Wickedness: A Philosophical Essay.
   London: Routledge and Kegan Paul, 1984
Murdoch, Iris
   The Sovereignty of Good over Other Concepts.
   London: Routledge and Kegan Paul, 1970
Newton, Lisa
   Ethics in America: A Study Guide.
   Englewood Cliffs, NJ: Prentice-Hall, 1989
Noddings, Nel
   Caring - A Feminine Approach to
   Ethics and Moral Education.
   Berkeley: Univ. of California Press, 1984
   Women and Evil.
   Berkeley, etc.: Univ. of California Press, 1989
Okin, Susan Moller
   Justice, Gender and the Family.
   New York: Basic Books, 1989
Petersson, Ingrid
   Utilitarianism, Responsibility and Punishment.
   Lund: Bokförlaget Doxa, 1976
Pisan (Pizan), Christine de
   The Moral Proverbes of Christine. (c. 1400)
   Facsimile reprinted 1977
   Christine de Pizan. Le Livre des Trois Vertus.
   Eds. C.C. Willard and E. Hicks.
   Genève: Éditions Slatkine, 1990
Rich, Adrienne
   On Lies, Secrets, and Silence.
   New York & London: W.W. Norton, 1979
Roland Holst-van der Schalk, Henriëtte
   Over leven en schoonheid. Opstellen over aesthetische
   en ethische onderwerpen.
   Arnhem: Van Loghum & Slaterus, 1925

Rosenthal, Abigail
    A Good Look at Evil. Philadelphia: Temple Univ. Press, 1987
Shklar, Judith
    Ordinary Vices. Cambridge: Harvard Univ. Press, 1984
Slattery, Mary Francis
    Hazard, Form & Value. Detroit: Wayne State Univ. Press, 1971
Sölle, Dorothee
    Phantasie und Gehorsam: Überlegungen zu einer
    künftigen christlichen Ethik. Stuttgart: n.n., 1968
Taylor, Monica
    Progress and Problems in Moral Education.
    New York: NFRER, 1975
Thomson, Judith Jarvis
    Rights, Restitution and Risk: Essays in Moral Theory.
    Cambridge: Harvard Univ. Press, 1991
Wyschogrod, Edith
    Saints and Postmodernism. Revisioning Moral Philosophy.
    Chicago: Univ. of Chicago Press, 1990

bibliographies: see Culture: Ecosophy

collections and series:
Adams, Marilyn McCord, and Robert Merrihew Adams (eds.)
    The Problem of Evil. Oxford/New York: Oxford Univ. Press
Almond, Brenda, and Bryan Wilson (eds.)
    Values: A Symposium.
    Atlantic Highlands, NJ: Humanities Press International, 1988
Andolson, Barbara Hilkert, Christine E. Gudorf, and Mary D. Pellauer
(eds.)
    Women's Consciousness Women's Conscience:
    A Reader in Feminist Ethics.
    San Francisco: Harper and Row, 1985
Asperen, G.M. van (ed.), Philosophica practica
    (series of books on ethics). Assen: Van Gorcum, 1980 -
Banu, Beatrice, and Mark Weinstein (eds.)
    The Fieldston Ethics Reader.
    Lanham, MD: Univ. Press of America, 1988
Brabeck, Mary M. (ed.)
    Who Cares: Theory Research and Educational Implications
    of the Ethic of Care. Westport, CT: Greenwood Press, 1989
Callahan, Joan C.
    Ethical Issues in Professional Life.
    Oxford/New York: Oxford Univ. Press, 1988
Gibson, Mary (ed.)
    To Breathe Freely. Totowa, NJ: Rowman & Littlefield, 1987

Gilligan, Carol, Janie Victoria Ward, Jill Taylor, and
Betty Barige (eds.)
> Mapping the Moral Domain.
> Cambridge, MA: Harvard Univ. Press, 1988

Hanen, M., and K. Nielson (eds.)
> Science, Morality and Feminist Theory.
> Calgary, Alberta: Univ. of Calgary Press, 1987

Harding, Carol Gibb (ed.)
> Moral Dilemmas: Philosophical and Psychological Issues
> in the Development of Moral Reasoning.
> Chicago: Precedent, 1985

Kittay, Eva Feder, and Diana T. Meyers (eds.)
> Women and Moral Theory.
> Totowa, NJ: Rowman and Littlefield, 1987

Overing, Joanna (ed.)
> Reason and Morality. London: Tavistock, 1985

Rosenblum, Nancy L. (ed.)
> Liberalism and the Moral Life.
> Cambridge, MA: Harvard Univ. Press, 1989

Thomson, Judith Jarvis, and Gerald Dworkin (eds.)
> Ethics. New York: Harper & Row, 1968

AII.4c   Abortion and Procreation

Harrison, Beverly Wildung
> Our Right to Choose: Toward a New Ethic of Abortion.
> Boston: Beacon Press, 1983

Hursthouse, Rosalind
> Beginning Lives. Oxford: Blackwell, 1987

Lebacqz, Karen
> Genetics, Ethics and Parenthood.
> New York: Pilgrim Press, 1983

Nicholson, Susan T.
> Abortion and the Roman Catholic Church.
> Knoxville, TN: Religious Ethics, 1978

Overall, Christine
> Ethics and Human Reproduction - A Feminist Analysis.
> London: Unwin & Hyman, 1987

Warnock, Mary
> A Question of Life. The Warnock Report on Human
> Fertilization and Embryology. Oxford: Blackwell, 1985

collections:

Chadwick, Ruth (ed.)
> Ethics, Reproduction and Genetic Control.
> Oxford: Blackwell, 1987; London, etc.: Routledge, 1990

AII.4d   Animals, Ethics of Behavior towards

Midgley, Mary
> Beast and Man: The Roots of Human Nature.
> Ithaca, NY: Cornell Univ. Press, 1978
> Animals and Why They Matter.
> Athens: Univ. of Georgia Press, 1984

Rodd, Rosemary
> Biology, Ethics, and Animals.
> Oxford: Clarendon, 1990

Sperling, Susan
> Animal Liberators - Research and Morality.
> Berkeley: Univ. of California Press, 1989

AII.4e   Computer Ethics

Johnson, Deborah G.
> Computer Ethics. Englewood Cliffs, NJ: Prentice-Hall, 1985

collections:

Gould, Carol C. (ed.)
> The Informal Web: Ethical and Social Implications of
> Computer Networking. Boulder, CO: Westview, 1988

Johnson, Deborah G., and John W. Snapper (eds.)
> Ethical Issues in the Use of Computers.
> Belmont: Wadsworth, 1985

AII.4f   Medical Ethics

Apel, Roberta J., and Susan M. Fisher
> To Do No Harm -
> DES and the Dilemma's of Modern Medicine.
> New Haven, CT: Yale Univ. Press, 1984

Battin, Margaret Pabst
> Ethical Issues in Suicide.
> Englewoord Cliffs, NJ: Prentice-Hall, 1982

Beaufort, Inez de
> Ethiek en medische experimenten met mensen.
> Assen: Van Gorcum, 1985

Collinson, Diane, Robert Campbell and -
> Ending Lives. Oxford: Blackwell, 1988

Crane, Diana
> The Sanctity of Social Life -
> Physicians' Treatment of Critically Ill Patients.
> New York: Russell Sage Foundation, 1975

Dessaur, C.I., and C.J.C. Rutenfrans
> Mag de dokter doden? Argumenten en documenten
> tegen het euthanasiasme.
> Amsterdam: Querido, 1986

Dupuis, Helene
Medische ethiek in perspectief: een onderzoek naar
normen en argumentaties in de (medische) ethiek.
Leiden: Stafleu, 1976
Goed te leven: reflecties op de moraal.
Baarn: Ten Have, 1980
Voordelen van de twijfel: een inleiding tot de
gezondheidsethiek. Alphen a.d.
Rijn etc.: Stafleu, 1983

Fromer, Margot Joan
Ethical Issues in Health Care.
St Louis: Mosby, 1982

Kuhse, Helga, and Peter Singer
Should the Baby Live - The Problem of Handicapped Infants.
Oxford: Oxford Univ. Press, 1985

Lyons, Catherine
Organ Transplants: The Moral Issues.
London: SCM Press, 1970

Mannoni, Maud
Le psychiatre, son "fou" et la psychanalyse. Paris: Seuil, 1970

McLean, Sheila, and Gerry Maher
Medicine, Morals, and the Law. Hampshire: Gower, 1983

Phillips, Melanie, and John Dawson
Doctor's Dilemmas: Medical Ethics and Contemporary
Science. New York: Methuen, 1985

Russell, Ruth
Freedom to Die. New York: Human Sciences Press, 1975

Shearer, Ann
Everybody's Ethics: What Future for Handicapped Babies.
London: Campaign for Mentally Handicapped, 1984

Thom, Susanne Hahn/Achim
Sinnvolle Lebensbewahrung - Humanes Sterben.
Berlin: VEB Deutscher, 1983

Zembaty, Jane S., Thomas A. Mappes, and -
Biomedical Ethics.
Hightstown, NJ: McGraw-Hill, 1991

collections:

Almond, Brenda (ed.)
AIDS: A Moral Issue - The Ethical, Legal and Social Aspects.
London (Basingstoke): Macmillan/New York: St. Martin, 1990

Beaufort, I.D., and H.M. Dupuis (eds.)
Handboek der gezondheidsethiek. Assen: Van Gorcum, 1988

Steinbock, Bonnie (ed.)
Killing and Letting Die.
Englewood Cliffs, NJ: Prentice-Hall, 1980

AII.4g   Meta-ethics

Asperen, G.M. van
Het ongedwongen gesprek: over de waardevrijheid van een
meta-ethische theorie (Inaugural address, Groningen
Univ.). Groningen: Wolters Noordhoff, 1977

Belaief, Lynne
Toward a Whiteheadian Ethics.
Lanham, MD: Univ. Press of America, 1984

Coignet, Clarisse
La Morale indépendante dans son principe et dans son
objet. Paris: Bailliere, 1869

Craemer-Ruegenberg, Ingrid
Moralsprache und Moralität: Zu Thesen der sprach-
analytischen Ethik. Freiburg: Alber, 1975

Foot, Philippa
Moral Relativism. Lawrence: Univ. of Kansas, 1978
Ethics and the Limits of Philosophy.
Cambridge, MA: Harvard Univ. Press, 1985

Lovibond, Sabina
Realism and Imagination in Ethics.
Oxford: Blackwell, 1983

Malmström, Anna-Karin
Motive and Obligation.
Uppsala: Uppsala Univ. (Philosophy Studies), 1980

Ossowska, Maria
Normy morale. Warszawa: PWN, 1970
Social Determinants of Moral Ideas.
London: Routledge & Kegan Paul, 1971
Moral Norms - A Tentative Systematization.
Warszawa: PWN-Polish Scientific Publishers, 1980
Amsterdam, etc.: North-Holland, 1980
Bourgeois Morality.
New York: Routledge, Chapman and Hall, 1986

Petersson, Ingrid
Utilitarianism, Responsibility and Punishment.
Lund (Lund Monographs in Practical Philosophy), 1976
Four Theories of Responsibility. Lund, 1990

Overall, Christine
Ethics and Human Reproduction. A Feminist Analysis.
(London and) Winchester, MA: Allen & Unwin, 1988

Riedinger, Monika
Das Wort "Gut" in der Angelsäksischen Metaethik.
Freiburg: Alber, 1984

Royer, Clémence Augustine
Le Bien et la Loi Morale: Éthique et Téléologie.
Paris: Guillaumin et Cie., 1881

Samsonova, Tamara
Theoretische Probleme der Ethik.
Trusted, Jennifer
Free Will and Responsibility.
Don Mills: Oxford Univ. Press, 1984
Ullmann-Margalit, Ursula E.
The Emergence of Norms.
Oxford: Oxford Univ. Press, 1978
Wolf, Ursula
Das Problem des moralischen Sollens.
Berlin: De Gruyter, 1984

collections:
Foot, Philippa (ed.)
Theories of Ethics. Oxford: Oxford Univ. Press, 1967
Ströker, Elisabeth (ed.)
Ethik der Wissenschaften. München: Fink, 1984

AII.5 **Existence, Philosophy of** *see also* Anthropology; Ethics

AII.5a **Introductions**
Grene, Marjorie
Introduction to Existentialism.
Chicago: Univ. of Chicago Press, 1976

AII.5b **Other works**
Bayer-Katte, Wanda von, Walter von Baeyer, and -
Angst. Frankfurt: Suhrkamp, 1971
Beauvoir, Simone de
L'Existentialisme et la sagesse des nations.
Paris: Éditions Nagel, 1947
Bruggen, Carry van
Prometheus. Een Bijdrage tot het begrip der
ontwikkeling van het individualisme.
Rotterdam: Nijgh & Van Dittmar, 1919
De grondgedachte van "Prometheus". Amsterdam:
Maatschappij voor goede en goedkope lectuur, 1924
Daly, Mary
Gyn-ecology: The Metaethics of Radical Feminism.
Boston: Beacon Press, 1979
London: The Women's Press, 1979
Pure Lust: Elemental Feminist Philosophy.
London: The Women's Press, 1984
Gössmann, Elisabeth, Ludolf C. Baas, C. Bronkhorst, et al.
Alleen staan. Hilversum: Brand, 1963

Guzzoni, Ute
   Wege im Denken. Versuche mit und ohne Heidegger.
   Freiburg/München: Verlag Karl Alber, 1990
Heller, Agnes
   Alltag und Geschichte.
   Neuwied and Berlin: Luchterhand, 1969
   Das Alltagsleben. Versuch einer Erklärung der
   individuellen Reproduktion. (Trans. from Hungarian;
   ed. and introduction by Hans Joas)
   Frankfurt am Main: Suhrkamp, 1978
   Everyday Life (trans. G.L. Campbell).
   London: Routledge & Kegan Paul, 1984
Kern, Edith
   Existential Thought and Fictional Technique -
   Kierkegaard, Sartre, Beckett.
   New Haven, CT: Yale Univ. Press, 1970
Kristina Wasa, Queen of Sweden
   Les sentiments héroiques. c. 1670/1680
   L'Ouvrage de loisir: Les sentiments Raisonnables.
   c. 1670/1680. Stockholm: Kungliga Bibioteket
Kruks, Sonia
   Situation and Human Existence:
   Freedom, Security and Society.
   London: Hutchinson, 1988; Unwin Hyman, 1990
Lawall, Sarah
   Critics of Consciousness: The Existential Structures of Literature.
   Cambridge: Harvard Univ. Press, 1968
Nahas, Hélène
   La femme dans la littérature existentielle.
   Paris, 1957
Pisan (Pizan), Christine de
   Mutacion de fortune. 1404
   La Vision. 1405
Sanborn, Patricia F.
   Existentialism. New York: Pegasus, 1968
Shikibu, Murasaki
   Genji monogatari.
   The Tale of the Genji. Trans. Arthur Waley.
   Boston: Houghton Mifflin, 1936
Shklar, Judith N.
   Freedom and Independence.
   Cambridge: Cambridge Univ. Press, 1976
Smith, Dorothy
   The Everyday World as Problematic.
   Toronto: Univ. of Toronto Press, 1988

Warnock, Mary
    Existentialism. Oxford: Oxford Univ. Press, 1970

Yonke, Anette M., Benjamin D. Wright, and -
    Hero, Villain, Saint. An Adventure in the Experience of
    Individuality.
    New York, etc.: Peter Lang Publishing, 1989

AII.6   **Law, Philosophy of** *see also* Empirical Sciences: Criminology

AII.6a   **General Philosophy of Law**

Bos, Alida Maria
    Over methoden van begripsvorming in het recht.
    Een studie gebaseerd op Jeremy Benthams expositieleer.
    Deventer: Kluwer, 1967

DeCrow, Karen
    Sexist Justice.
    New York: Random House, 1974

Delhomme, Jeanne
    L'impossible interrogation. Paris: Desclée, 1971

Fawcett, Millicent
    On the Amendments Required in the Criminal Law.
    Amendment Act 1885. London: Women's Printing Society

Feldman, Martha S., W. Lance Bennett, and -
    Reconstructing Reality in the Courtroom.
    New Brunswick: Rutgers Univ. Press, 1981

Hampton, Jean, Jeffrie Murphy, and -
    Forgiveness and Mercy. Cambridge: Cambridge Univ. Press, 1988

Heller, Agnes
    Beyond Justice. Oxford: Blackwell, 1987

MacKinnon, Catharine A.
    Sexual Harassment of Working Women: A Case of Sex
    Discrimination. New Haven, CT: Yale Univ. Press, 1979
    Feminism Unmodified: Discourses on Life and Law.
    Cambridge, MA: Harvard Univ. Press, 1987

Minow, Martha
    Making All the Difference: Inclusion, Exclusion, and
    American Law. Ithaca, NY: Cornell Univ. Press, 1990

Moore, Kathleen Dean
    Pardon: Justice, Mercy, and Public Interest.
    Oxford: Clarendon Press, 1989

O'Donovan, Katherine
    Sexual Divisions in Law. London: Weidenfeld & Nicholson, 1985

Pitch, Tamar
    La devianza. Firenze: La Nuova Italia, 1975

Radcliffe, Mary Anne
The Female Advocate. 1799
Facsimile: Hildesheim and New York: Georg Olm, 1980
Rose, Gillian
Dialectic of Nihilism: Post-Structuralism and the Law.
Oxford: Blackwell, 1984
Shklar, Judith N.
Legalism: Laws, Morals, and Political Trials.
Cambridge, MA: Harvard Univ. Press (Harvard Paperbacks), 1987
The Faces of Injustice. The Storrs Lectures on Jurisprudence.
New Haven, CT: Yale Univ. Press, 1990
Spitz, Elaine
Majority Rule. Chatham, NJ: Chatham House, 1984
Sypnowich, Christine
The Concept of Socialist Law. Oxford: Clarendon Press, 1990
Tong, Rosemarie
Women, Sex, and the Law. Totowa, NJ: Rowman & Allanheld, 1984
Wichmann, Clara Meijer
Beschouwingen over de historische grondslagen der
tegenwoordige omvorming van het strafbegrip.
Leiden: E.J. Brill, 1912
Misdaad, straf en maatschappij. Utrecht: Erven J. Bijleveld, 1931
Young, Iris Marion
Justice and the Politics of Difference.
Princeton, NJ: Princeton Univ. Press, 1990

collections:

Attwood, Elspeth (ed.)
Perspectives in Jurisprudence.
Glasgow: Univ. of Glasgow Press, 1977
Ezorsky, Gertrude (ed.)
Philosophical Perspectives on Punishment.
Albany: State Univ. of New York Press, 1972
Faralli, Carla, and Enrico Pattaro (eds.)
Legal Philosophical Library: Finland
Milan: Giuffré, 1985
Legal Philosophical Library: Norberto Bobbio.
Milan: Giuffré, 1985
Lefcourt, Carol H. (ed.)
Women and the Law. New York: Clark Boardman, 1984

AII.6b   Rights
Bayefsky, Anne, and Mary Eberts (eds.)
Equality Rights and the Canadian Charter of Rights and Freedoms.
Toronto: Carswell, 1985

Dohm, Hedwig
Der Frauen Natur und Recht.
Berlin: Wedekind und Schweiger, 1876
Gibson, Mary
Worker's Rights. Totowa, NJ: Rowman and Allanheld, 1983
Totowa, NJ: Rowman & Littlefield, 1987
Gouges, Olympe des (Marie Gouze)
Les Droits de la Femme. Paris, n.d. (1791)
Déclarations des droits de la femme et de la citoyenne.
Paris: 1791
In: Susan Groag Bell and Karen Offen (eds.)
Woman: The Family and Freedom.
Stanford, CA: Stanford Univ. Press, 1983
Verklaring van de rechten van de vrouw en burgeres
(trans. Anjà Hélene). Ed. H. Schröder.
Kampen: Kok Agora, 1989
Olympe de Gouges: Oeuvres. Ed. Benoite Groult.
Paris: Mercure de France, 1986
Goyard-Fabre, Simone
Essai de critique phénoménologie du droit.
Paris: Libraire Klincksieck, 1972
Maus, Ingeborg
Bürgerliche Rechtstheorie und Faschismus.
München: Fink, 1976
Meyers, Diana T.
Inalienable Rights: A Defense.
New York: Columbia Univ. Press, 1985
Moberly, Elizabeth R.
Suffering, Innocent and Guilty. London: SPCK, 1978
Rhode, Deborah L.
Justice and Gender. Cambridge, MA: Harvard Univ. Press, 1989
Sameli, Katharina
Freiheit und Sicherheit im Recht.
Zürich: Schulteiss, 1969
Schröder, Hannelore
Die Rechtlosigkeit der Frau im Rechtsstaat.
Frankfurt: Campus, 1975
Twee honderd jaar rechten van de vrouw en burgeres
(the Clara Meijer-Wichman Lecture 1990).
Amsterdam: Liga voor de Rechten van de Mens, 1990
Thomson, Judith Jarvis
Self-Defense and Rights.
New York: Univ. of Kansas Philosophy Department, 1977
The Realm of Rights.
Cambridge, MA: Harvard Univ. Press, 1990

Westernhagen, Dorte Willrodt-von
    Recht und soziale Frage:
    Die Rechts- und Sozialphilosophie Anton Mengers.
    Hamburg: Fundament Sasse, 1975

AII.6c   Special Issues
Allen, Anita A.
    Women and Privacy. Totowa, NJ: Rowman & Littlefield 1988
    Uneasy Access: Privacy for Women in a Free Society.
    Totowa, NJ: Rowman & Littlefield 1988
Edwards, Susan
    Female Sexuality and the Law. Oxford: Robertson, 1981
Estrich, Susan
    Real Rape. Cambridge, MA: Harvard Univ. Press, 1987
Faulder, Carolyn
    Whose Body is It - The Troubling Issue of Informed Consent.
    London: Virago, 1985
Glendon, Mary Ann
    Abortion and Divorce in the Western Law.
    Cambridge, MA: Harvard Univ. Press, 1989
Hamilton, Cicely
    Marriage as a Trade. London: Chapman & Hall, 1909
Holder, Angela Roddey
    Legal Issues in Pediatrics and Adolescent Medicine.
    New Haven, CT: Yale Univ. Press, 1986
O'Neill, Onora
    Faces of Hunger - An Essay on Poverty, Justice and Development.
    London: Allen & Unwin (n.d.)

collections:
Bell, Nora (ed.)
    Who Decides: Conflicts of Rights in Health Care.
    Clifton, NJ: Humana Press, 1982
Fineman, Martha Albertson, and Nancy Sweet Thomadsen (eds.)
    At the Boundaries of Law. Feminism and Legal Theory.
    London: Routledge, 1990

AII.7   Political Philosophy
    see also History of; Foundation Empirical Science: Political
    Science; Philosophy of Language; Philosophy of Culture; Logic

AII.7a   General Political Philosophy
Adams, Carol J.
    The Sexual Politics of Meat. A Feminist-Vegetarian
    Critical Theory. Cambridge: Polity Press, 1990

Arendt, Hannah
    The Origins of Totalitarism. New York: Harcourt, 1951
    Fragwürdige Traditionsbestände in politischen Denken
    der Gegenwart. Trans. from the English by Ch. Beradt.
    Frankfurt am Main: Europ. Verl. Anst., 1957
    Elemente und Ursprünge totaler Herrschaft.
    Frankfurt am Main: Europ. Verl. Anst., 1958
    The Human Condition. Chicago: Univ. of Chicago Press, 1958
    Eichmann in Jerusalem: A Report on the Banality of Evil.
    New York: Penguin Books, 1963, 1964
    Crisis of the Republic.
    New York, etc.: Harcourt Brace Jovanovich, 1972
    Between Past and Future: eight exercises in political
    Thought. Harmondsworth: Penguin, 1977
    A Radical Philosophy. Oxford: Blackwell, 1984, 1986
Baeyer-Katte, Wanda von
    Das Zerstörende in der Politik.
    Heidelberg: Quelle u. Meyer, 1958
Bartky, Sandra Lee
    Femininity and Domination - Studies in the Phenomenology
    of Oppression. London: Routledge, 1990
Beecher, Catharine
    Letter to Persons Who Are Engaged in Domestic Service.
    New York: Leavitt & Trow, 1842
Coignet, Clarisse
    De l'affranchissement des femmes en Angleterre.
    Paris, 1874
Corradi Fiumara, Gemma
    Philosophy and Coexistence. (Preface by Paolo Filiafi Carcano.)
    (European Aspects Series A: Culture, No. 9)
    Leiden: Sijthoff, 1966
Cypser, Cora E.
    Covenant and Consensus. Katonah, NY: Kim Pathways, 1990
Douglas, Mary
    How Institutions Think.
    London: Routledge & Kegan Paul, 1987;
    Syracuse Univ. Press, 1988
Ehrenreich, Barbara, and Deirdre English
    For Her Own Good: 150 Years of Experts' Advice to Women.
    New York: Doubleday, 1978
    London: Pluto Press, 1988 [1979].
    Dutch trans.: Voor haar eigen bestwil.
    Amsterdam: Bert Bakker, 1979
Evans, Sara
    Personal Politics. New York: Knopf, 1979

Fenichel Pitkin, Hanna
    Fortune is a Woman.
    Berkeley: Univ. of California Press, 1984
Gerstenmaier, Cornelia
    Die Stimme der Stummen. Stuttgart: Seewald, 1971
Goyard-Fabre, Simone
    L'Interminable querelle du contrat social.
    Ottawa: Univ. d'Ottawa, 1983
Heller, Agnes
    A Radical Philosophy. Oxford: Blackwell, 1984, 1986
    The Power of Shame. A Rational Perspective.
    London: Routledge & Kegan Paul 1985
Henry, Maureen
    The Intoxication of Power. Dordrecht: Reidel, 1979
Kelly, Petra
    Fighting for Hope (English trans. M. Howarth).
    London: Chatto & Windus, 1984
Keuls, Eva C.
    The Reign of the Phallus - Sexual Politics in Ancient Athens.
    New York: Harper & Row, 1985
Kresic, Andrija
    Political Society and Political Mythology.
    Beograd, 1968
Mernissi, Fatima
    L'harem politique: Le prophète et les femmes.
    Paris: Albin Michel, 1987
Quillet, Jeannine
    La philosophie politique du songe du Vergier. Paris: Vrin, 1977
Romein-Verschoor, Annie
    Vrouwenwijsheid. (Texts 1923-1978 not published in
    earlier collections. Collected and annotated by Claire Rappange.
    Introduction by Emma Brunt.)
    Amsterdam: Arbeiderspers, 1980
Sayers, Janet
    Biological Politics. London: Tavistock, 1982
Soper, Kate
    Troubled Pleasures: Writings on Politics, Gender and Hedonism.
    New York: Verso, 1990
Steuernagel, Gertrude A.
    Political Philosophy as Therapy.
    Westport, CT: Greenwood Press, 1979
Takamure Itsue (ed.) Fijin sensenn (feminist journal)
Zeldin, Mary-Barbara
    Freedom and the Critical Understanding.
    Ann Arbor, MI: University Microfilms International, 1980

collections:

Albrecht, Lisa, and Rose M. Brewer (eds.)
    Bridges of Power: Women's Multicultural Alliances.
    Philadelphia: New Society Publishers, 1990
Elshtain, Jean Bethke (ed.)
    The Family in Political Thought. Brighton: Harvester, 1982
Genova, Judith (ed.)
    Power, Gender, Values.
    Edmonton: Academic Printing and Publishing, 1987
Stiehm, Judith Hicks (ed.)
    Women's Views of the Political World of Men.
    Dobbs Ferry, NY: Transnational, 1984

AII.7b   Class and Labour

Outram, Dorinda
    The Body and the French Revolution:
    Sex, Class and Political Structure. London: Yale Univ. Press, 1989
Schreiner, Olive
    Woman and Labour.
    London: Virago, 1978 [1911]. Preface by Jane Graves.
Weil, Simone, posthumous editions
    La condition ouvrière, Paris, 1951
    Oppression and Liberty. (Trans. A. Wills and J. Petrie)
    Amherst: Univ. of Massachussetts Press, 1973
    Unterdrückung und Freiheit: Politische Schriften.
    München: Rogner & Bernhard, 1975

AII.7c   Ideologies and Theories

AII.7ca   -Capitalism

Fraser, Nancy
    Power, Discourse, and Gender - Studies in Late-Capitalist
    Political Philosophy. Oxford: Blackwells's/Polity Press, 1987

AII.7cb   -Communism/Marxism *see also* History: European Traditions

Bacinetti-Florenzi Waddington, Marianna
    Alcune riflessioni sopra il socialismo e il communismo.
    Florence, 1860
Barrett, Michèle
    Women's Oppression Today: Problems in Marxist Feminist
    Analysis. London: NLB/New York: Schocken, 1980.
    Das unterstellte Geschlecht:
    Umrisse eines marxistischen Feminismus (trans.).
    Hamburg: Argument-Verlag, 1983
    Links en de vrouwenbeweging.
    Weesp: Het Wereldvenster, 1984

Dalla Costa, Mariarosa
    Selma James: Die Macht der Frauen und der Umsturz der
    Gesellschaft. Berlin: Herve, 1973
Dunayevskaya, Raya
    Philosophy and Revolution: From Hegel to Sartre, and
    from Marx to Mao.
    New York: Dell, 1973/Columbia Univ. Press
    Expanded ed., New York: \Columbia Univ. Press, 1989
Heller, Agnes, Ferenc Fehér, and -
    Diktatur über die Bedürfnisse: sozialistische
    Kritik osteuropäischer Gesellschaftsformationen.
    Hamburg: VSA-Verlag, 1979
Luxemburg, Rosa
    Gesammelte Werke. Ed. G. Adler.
    Berlin: Dietz, 1970
Vogel, Lise
    Marxism and the Oppression of Women.
    New Brunswick, NJ: Rutgers Univ. Press, 1983

collections:

Sargent, Lydia (ed.)
    Women and Revolution: A Discussion of the Unhappy
    Marriage of Marxism and Feminism. London: Virago, 1987

AII.7cc   -Democracy

Carter, April
    Direct Action and Liberal Democracy.
    New York: Harper & Row, 1973
Fraisse, Geneviève
    Muse de la Raison. La democratie exclusive et la
    différence des sexes. Aix-en-Provence: Alinea, 1989
Gould, Carol C.
    Rethinking Democracy - Freedom of Social Co-operation
    in Politics, Economy and Society.
    Cambridge/New York: Cambridge Univ. Press, 1988
Mansbridge, Jane J.
    Beyond Adversary Democracy.
    New York: Basic Books, 1980
Pateman, Carole
    The Disorder of Women: Democracy, Feminism and
    Political Theory. Cambridge: Polity Press, 1989
Pickles, Dorothy
    Democracy. London: Methuen, 1971
Smith, Maria Parris
    What Constitutes a Liberal Democracy?
    Philadelphia, 1925

AII.7cd -Fascism

Lewerenz, Elfriede
> Die Analyse des Faschismus durch die Kommunistische
> International. Berlin: Dietz, 1975

Macciocchi, Maria
> Vrouwen en fascisme. Amsterdam: Sara, 1978

AII.7ce -Feminism *see also* other ideologies; *also* Philosophy of Culture: Patriarchy; History: The Feminist Tradition, Modern and Contemporary Philosophy

AII.7ce1 -Introductions

Tong, Rosemarie
> Feminist Thought. A Comprehensive Introduction.
> London: Unwin & Hyman, 1989

AII.7ce2 -Other works

Banks, Olive
> Faces of Feminism. Oxford: Robertson, 1981

Eisenstein, Hester
> Contemporary Feminist Thought.
> London: Counterpoint, 1984

Eisenstein, Zillah
> The Radical Future of Liberal Feminism.
> New York: Longmans, 1981; Boston, 1986

Elshtain, Jean Bethke
> Power Trips and Other Journeys: Essays in Feminism as
> Civic Discourse. Madison: Univ. of Wisconsin Press, 1990

Freeman, Jo
> The Politics of Women's Liberation.
> New York: David McKay, 1975

Frye, Marilyn
> The Politics of Reality: Essays in Feminist Theory.
> Trumansburg, NY: Crossing Press, 1983

Fuller, (Sarah) Margaret
> Woman in the Nineteenth Century, 1845
> The Writings of Margaret Fuller (ed. Mason Wade), 1941

Fuss, Diana
> Essentially Speaking - Feminism, Nature and Difference.
> London: Routledge, 1989,
> New York: Routledge, 1990

Humm, Maggie
> The Dictionary of Feminist Thought.
> Hemel Hempstead, UK: Harvester Wheatsheaf
> Columbus: Ohio State Univ. Press, 1990

Irigaray, Luce
    Le temps de la différence: pour une révolution pacifique.
    Paris: LGF, 1989
Jaggar, Alison M.
    Feminist Politics and Human Nature.
    Totowa, NJ: Rowman and Allanheld, 1983;
    Brighton: Harvester, 1983
Kramarae, Cheris, and Paula A. Treichler
    A Feminist Dictionary. London: Pandora, 1985
MacKinnon, Catharine A.
    Toward a Feminist Theory of the State.
    Cambridge, MA: Harvard Univ. Press, 1989
Midgley, Mary, and Judith Hughes
    Women's Choices: Philosophical Problems Facing Feminism.
    London: Weidenfeld and Nicholson, 1983
Mitchell, Juliet, and Ann Oakley (eds.)
    What is Feminism: A Re-examination by Nancy Cott,
    Linda Gordon, Judith Stacey, Juliet Mitchell, Ann
    Oakley and six other major feminist thinkers.
    New York: Pantheon, 1986
Morgan, Robin
    The Anatomy of Freedom: Feminism, Physics and Global Politics.
    Garden City, NY: Anchor/Doubleday, 1982
O'Brien, Mary
    The Politics of Reproduction.
    London/New York: Routledge & Kegan Paul, 1981
Phelan, Shane
    Identity Politics: Lesbian Feminism and the Limits of
    Community. Philadelphia: Temple Univ. Press, 1989
Rosenberg, Rosalind
    Beyond Separate Spheres: The Intellectual Roots of
    Modern Feminism.
    New Haven, etc.: Yale Univ. Press, 1982
Rowbotham, Sheila, Lynne Segal, and Hilary Wainwright
    Beyond the Fragments: Feminism and the Making of Socialism.
    London: Merlin Press, 1979
Ruth, Sheila
    Issues in Feminism: A First Course in Women's Studies.
    Boston: Houghton Mifflin, 1980
Segal, Lynne
    Is the Future Female? Troubled Thoughts on Contemporary
    Feminism. London: Virago, 1987
Thürmer-Rohr, Christina
    Vagabundinnen. Feministische Essays.
    Berlin: Orlanda Frauenverlag, 1987

collections:

Adams, Parveen, and Elizabeth Cowie (eds.)
  The Woman in Question M/F.
  Cambridge, MA: The MIT Press, 1990

Griffiths, Morwenna, and Margaret Whitford (eds.)
  Feminist Perspectives in Philosophy.
  Basingstoke, etc.: Macmillan, 1988

al-Hibri, Azizah, and Margaret A. Simmons
  Hypatia Reborn - Essays in Feminist Philosophy.
  Bloomington: Indiana Univ. Press, 1990

Jaggar, Alison M., and Paula S. Rothenberg (eds.)
  Feminist Frameworks.
  New York: McGraw Hills, 1984

Kauffman, Linda (ed.)
  Feminism and Institutions.
  Oxford, U.K./Cambridge, MA: Basil Blackwell, 1989

Kuhn, Annette, and Ann Marie Wolpe (eds.)
  Feminism and Materialism. Women and Modes of Production.
  London: Routledge & Kegan Paul, 1978

Lauretis, Teresa de (cd.)
  Feminist Studies/Critical Studies.
  Bloomington: Indiana Univ. Press, 1986

Leidholt, Dorchen, and Janice G. Raymond (eds.)
  The Sexual Liberals and the Attacks on Feminism.
  New York, etc.: Pergamon Press, 1990

Nagl-Docekal, Herta (ed.)
  Feministische Philosophie
  (Wiener Reihe: Themen der Philosophie, Vol. 4).
  Vienna, etc.: Oldenbourg, 1990

Nicholson, Linda J. (ed.)
  Feminism/Postmodernism. New York, etc.: Routledge, 1990

Pateman, Carole, and Elizabeth Grosz (eds.)
  Feminist Challenges: Social and Political Theories
  (The Northeastern series in feminist theory.).
  Boston: Northeastern Univ. Press, 1986
  Sydney/London/Boston: Allen & Unwin

Phillips, Anne (ed.)
  Divided Loyalties. Dilemmas of Sex and Class.
  London, 1987

Phillips, Anne (ed.)
  Feminism and Equality.
  Oxford: Blackwell, 1987

Weed, Elizabeth (ed.)
  Coming to Terms: Feminism, Theory, Politics.
  New York: Routledge, 1989

AII.7cf   -Humanism
Soper, Kate
>Humanism and Antihumanism.
>London: Hutchinson, 1986

AII.7cg   -Liberalism
Mendus, Susan
>Toleration and the Limits of Liberalism.
>London (Basingstoke): Macmillan, 1989

Pateman, Carole
>The Problem of Political Obligation: A Critical
>Analysis of Liberal Theory.
>Chichester/New York: John Wiley, 1979

Wood, Ellen Meiksins
>Mind and Politics: An Approach to the Meaning of
>Liberal and Socialist Individualism.
>Berkeley: Univ. of California Press, 1972

collections:

Mendus, Susan, and David Edwards (eds.)
>On Toleration.
>Oxford: At the Clarendon Press, 1988

AII.7ch   -New Right
Seidel, Gill
>The Ideology of the New Right.
>Cambridge: Polity Press, 1986

collections: see "Language in general"

AII.7ci   -Patriarchy, Political
Bonnevie, Margarete
>Patriarkatets siste skanse. Oslo: Aschehoug, 1948
>Fra mannssamfunn til menneskesamfunn.
>Oslo: Cappelen, 1968 [1955]
>Fra likestilling til undertrykkelse.
>Oslo: Dreyer, 1964

Coward, Rosalind
>Patriarchal Precedents: Sexuality and Social Relations.
>London, etc.: Routledge & Kegan Paul, 1983

Figes, Eva
>Patriarchal Attitudes. Women in Society.
>London: Faber and Faber Ltd., 1970

Lerner, Gerda
>The Creation of Patriarchy.
>Oxford: Oxford Univ. Press, 1986

collections:

Holter, Harriet (ed.)
Patriarchy in a Welfare Society.
Oslo: Universitetsforlaget, 1984

Moi, Toril (ed.)
French Feminist Thought: Politics, Patriarchy and
Sexual Difference. Oxford: Blackwell, 1987

AII.7cj   -Racism *see also* Individual Philosophers: Weininger

Guillaumin, Colette
L'idéologie raciste. Paris/The Hague: Mouton, 1972

-Sexism *see* Anthropology; "Language in general";
Patriarchy; General Philosophy of Religion; Political
Philosophy, History of

AII.7ck   -Socialism

Eisenstein, Zillah (ed.)
Capitalist Patriarchy and the Case for Socialist
Feminism. New York: Monthly Review Press, 1979

Fiedler, Helene
Gemeinsam zum Sozialismus.
Berlin: Dietz, 1969

Roland Holst-van der Schalk, Henriëtte
De revolutionaire massa-aktie: een studie.
Rotterdam: W.L. & J. Brusse, 1918
De strijdmiddelen der sociale revolutie.
Amsterdam: Bos, 1918
De geestelijke ommekeer en de nieuwe taak van het
socialisme. Arnhem: Van Loghum Slaterus, 1931

Scott, Hilda
Does Socialism Liberate Women: Experiences From Eastern
Europe. Boston: Beacon Press, 1974

Weinbaum, Batya
The Curious Courtship of Women's Liberation and Socialism.
Boston: South End Press, 1978

Wood, Ellen Meiksins
The Retreat From Class: A New 'True' Socialism.
London: Verso, 1986

AII.7cl   -Utopianism

Benhabib, Seyla
Critique, Norm, And Utopia -
A Study of the Foundations of Critical Theory.
New York: Columbia Univ. Press, 1986

Goodwin, Barbara, and Keith Taylor
The Politics of Utopia: A Study in Theory and Practice.
New York: St. Martin's Press, 1982

Hansot, Elisabeth
Perfection and Progress: Two Modes of Utopian Thought.
Cambridge, MA: MIT Press, 1974

Heller, Agnes and Ferdinando Adornato
Das Leben ändern: radikale Bedürfnisse, Frauen
und Utopie: Gespräche mit Ferdinando Adornato
(from Italian). Hamburg: VSA, 1981

Motroschilova, N.V. (Nelli, Vasilevna)
Marcuses Utopie der Antigesellschaft.
Berlin: Akademie-Verlag, 1971

Serra, Teresa
L'utopia controrivoluzionario. Napels: Guida, 1977

AII.7d   Sexual/gender Oppression and Politics *see also*: Aesthetics:
Visual Arts; Culture: Academy; Law; Rights

Astell, Mary
An Essay in Defence of the Female Sex. Pamphlet
Attributed to Mary Astell. London, 1696

Bartky, Sandra Lee
Femininity and Domination. Studies in the Phenomenology
of Oppression. New York: Routledge, 1990

Beecher, Catharine
An Essay on Slavery and Abolitionism with Reference to
the Duty of American Females.
Philadelphia: Henry Perkins, 1837

Bernard, Jessie
Women and the Public Interest - An Essay on Policy and
Protest. Chicago/New York: Aldine Altherton, 1971

Beauvoir, Simone de
Le deuxième sexe I-II.
I. Les faits et les mythes, II. L'expérience vécue.
Paris: Gallimard, 1949, 51982
The Second Sex (trans. and ed. by H.M. Parshley).
New York: Random House, Vintage Books, 1953
Dutch trans. Utrecht, 1976
Wij vrouwen, eds. Claude Francis and Fernande Gauthier,
introduction Jeanne Holierhoek; Hilversum, 1981

Brownmiller, Susan
Against Our Will: Men, Women and Rape.
New York: Simon & Schuster, 1975

Carter, Angela
The Sadeian Woman and the Ideology of Pornography.
New York: Pantheon Books, paperback 1988

Dworkin, Andrea
    Womanhating: A Radical Look at Sexuality.
    New York: Dutton, 1974
    Pornography: Men Possessing Women.
    London: The Women's Press, 1981
    New York: G.P. Putnam's Sons, Perigree Books, 1981
    Our Blood.
    London: The Women's Press, 1982
    Right-Wing Women: the Politics of Domesticated Females.
    London: The Women's Press/New York: Putnam Publishers, 1983
    Letters from a War Zone. Writings 1976-1987.
    London: Secker & Warburg, 1987; New York: Dutton, 1989
    Intercourse. 1987. London: Arrow Books, 1988
    Paren (Dutch trans. of Intercourse).
    Baarn: Anthos/Bosch & Keuning, 1989

Ethelmer, Ellis (Elizabeth Wollstenholme Elmy)
    Woman Free. Congleton: Women's Emancipation Union, 1893

Ferguson, Ann
    Sexual Democracy: Women, Oppression, and Revolution.
    Boulder, CO: Westview Press, 1989

Fox, Margaret Fell
    Woman's Speaking Justified. 1677

Friedan, Betty
    The Feminine Mystique. Gollancz, 1963
    De mystieke vrouw (trans. of (1963)).
    Amsterdam: Rainbow, 1985

Gage, Mathilda Joslyn
    Woman, Church and State. c. 1893.
    Reprinted Watertown, MA: Persephone Press, 1980

Johnsen, Kari Mundal
    Hva er kvinnesak? Et forsök på klargjöring, og et
    oppgjör med noen herskende tendenser i kvinnedebatten.
    Oslo: Gyldendal, 1979

Klein, Ethel
    Gender Politics: From Consciousness to Mass Politics.
    Cambridge, MA: Harvard Univ. Press, 1984

Landes, Joan B.
    Women and the Public Sphere.
    Ithaca, NY: Cornell Univ. Press, 1988

LeMoncheck, Linda
    Dehumanizing Women: Treating Persons as Sex Objects.
    Totowa, NJ: Rowman & Allanheld, 1985

Luker, Kristin
    Abortion and the Politics of Motherhood.
    Berkeley: Univ. of Calfornia Press, 1984

Masham, Damaris Cudworth
  Occasional Thoughts in Reference to a Virtuous or Christian Life.
  London: A. and J. Churchil, 1705
Millett, Kate
  Sexual Politics.
  Garden City, NY: Doubleday, 1970/Ballentine Books, 1978
  Sexe en macht. Amsterdam: Meulenhoff, 1975
  Sexus und Herrschaft. Die Tyrannei des Mannes in
  unserer Gesellschaft. Reinbeck: Rowohlt, 1985
Mitchell, Juliet, and Ann Oakley (eds.)
  The Rights and Wrongs of Women.
  Harmondsworth: Penguin, 1976
  Women: The Longest Revolution. London: Virago, 1984
Moi, Toril
  Sexual/Textual Politics. London: Methuen, 1985
Pankhurst, Christabel
  Plain Facts About a Great Evil.
  (The Great Scourge and How to End It.)
  London: Women's Social and Political Union, 1913
Pateman, Carole
  The Sexual Contract. Cambridge: Polity Press, 1988
  Stanford, CA: Stanford Univ. Press, 1988
Petchesky, Rosalind P.
  Abortion and Woman's Choice. New York: Longman, 1984
Pisan (Pizan), Christine de
  Épitre au dieu d'amour. 1399; Dit de la rose. 1402
Randall, Vicky R.
  Women and Politics: An International Perspective.
  Chicago: Univ. of Chicago Press, 1988
Raymond, Janice G.
  The Transsexual Empire: The Making of the She-Male.
  Boston: Beacon Press, 1979
Roberts, Jane
  Psychic Politics.
  Englewood Cliffs, NJ: Prentice-Hall, 1976
Schuurman (or Schurman), Anna Maria van
  Dissertatio de ingenii muliebris ad doctrinam et
  meliores litteras aptitudine. Leiden, 1641. Trans. as:
  Question celebre. S'il est necessaire, ou non, que les
  filles soient scavantes. Agitée de part et d'autre, par
  Mademoiselle Anna Marie de Schurman Holandoise, et le
  Sr. André Rivet Poitevin. Trans. from Lat. by G.C.
  Colletet. Paris, 1646
  The Learned maid, or Whether a maid may be a scholar?
  London: John Redmayne, 1659

Sophia, a person of Quality [pseudonym]
    Woman Not Inferior to Man or, A Short and Modest Vindication
    of the Natural Right of the Fair Sex to a Perfect Equality of
    Power, Dignity, and Esteem, with the Men.
    London, 1739
Starhawk
    Dreaming the Dark: Magic, Sex and Politics.
    Boston: Beacon Press, 1982
Sullerot, Evelyne
    Demain les femmes.
    Paris: Laffront, 1965
Taylor, Harriet
    German trans. by Sigmund Freud:
    Über Frauenemanzipation, in:
    Schröder (ed.) 1976 sub Individual philosophers: Mill
Wheeler, Anna Doyle, William Thompson, and -
    An Appeal of One-Half of the Human Race, Women, Against
    the Pretensions of the Other Half, Men, To Retain Them in
    Political and Thence in Civil and Domestic Slavery
    London, 1825. London: Virago, 1983
Wolgast, Elizabeth Hankins
    Equality and the Rights of Women.
    New York: Cornell Univ. Press, 1980
Wollstonecraft, Mary
    Female Reader. London: Johnson, 1789
    The Female Reader: A Facsimile Reproduction.
    Delmar, NY: Scholars' Facsimiles & Reprints, 1980
    A Vindication of the Rights of Woman. 1792
    Harmondsworth: Penguin, 1978
    The Rights of Woman (together with John Stuart Mill's
    The Subjection of Women; with introduction by Pamela Frankau).
    London: Dent/New York: Dutton, 1954 or 1955
    Collected Letters of Mary Wollstonecraft (ed. Ralph M. Wardle.)
    Ithaca, NY and London: Cornell Univ. Press, 1979
Wollstonecraft, Mary, and William Godwin
    A Short Residence in Sweden, Norway and Denmark, and
    Memoirs of the Author of the Rights of Woman.
    New York: Viking Penguin, 1988
Woolf, Virginia
    A Room of Ones Own. London: The Hogarth Press, 1928
    London: Grafton Books, 1988
    Three Guineas. London, 1938
    Women and Writing. (Introduction by M. Barrett.)
    London: The Women's Press, 1975
    The Essays of Virginia Woolf. Vols. I-II
    (ed. A. McNeillie). London: The Hogarth Press, 1986

collections:

Conway, Jill, Susan C. Bourque, and Joan Wallach Scott (eds.)
Learning About Women: Gender, Politics, and Power.
Ann Arbor: Univ. of Michigan Press, 1989

Deuber-Mankowsky, Astrid, Ulrike Ramming, and
Elfriede Walesca Tielsch (eds.)
1789/1989 - Die Revolution hat nicht stattgefunden.
Dokumentation des V. Symposions der Internationalen
Assoziation von Philosophinnen.
Tübingen: Edition Discord, 1989

Dreifus, Claudia (ed.)
Seizing Our Bodies: The Politics of Women's Health.
New York: Random, 1977

Ferguson, Frances, R. Howard Bloch, and - (eds.)
Misogyny, Misandry, and Misanthropy -
Rethinking Gender and Symbolic Violence.
Special issue of Representations, Autumn 1987, No. 20.

Gould, Carol C. (ed.)
Beyond Domination: New Perspectives on Women and
Philosophy.
Totowa, NJ: Rowman & Allanheld, 1984

Morgan, Robin (ed.)
Sisterhood is Powerful.
New York: Random House, 1970

AII.7e   War and Peace

Astell, Mary
Moderation Truly Stated: or a Review of a Late Pamphlet entitled
Moderation a Vertue with a Prefactory Discourse to
Dr. D'Aveanant concerning His late Essays on Peace and War.
London, 1704
A Fair Way with the Dissenters and their Patrons.
London, 1704

Bok, Sissela
A Strategy for Peace.
New York: Pantheon Books, 1989

Elshtain, Jean Bethke
Women and War.
New York: Basic Books, 1987

Harris, Adrienne E., and Ynestra King
Rocking the Ship of State: Toward a Feminist Peace Politics.
Boulder, CO: Westview Press, 1989

Oldfield, Sybil
Women Against the Iron Fist:
Alternatives to Militarism 1900-1989.
Oxford: Blackwell, 1989

Pisan (Pizan), Christine de
    Lamentation. 1410
    Livre de la paix. 1412-13
    The "Livre de la Paix" of Christine de Pisan.
    A critical edition with Introduction and Notes.
    Ed. Charity Cannon Willard. The Hague: Mouton, 1958
    The Book of Fayettes of Armes and of Chyualrie (c. 1410)
    Trans. William Caxton, ed. A.T.P. Byles, 1932.
    Reprinted London: Humphrey Milford/Oxford: Univ. Press, 1973
Ruddick, Sara
    Maternal Thinking: Towards a Politics of Peace.
    Boston: Beacon, 1989
Teichman, Jenny
    Pacifism and the Just War. A Study in Applied Philosophy.
    Oxford: Blackwell, 1986

collections:

Cooper, Helen M., Adrienne Auslander Munich, and Susan Merrill
    Squier (eds.)
    Arms and the Woman: War, Gender, and Literary Representation.
    Chapel Hill: Univ. of North Carolina Press, 1989

AII.8   **Social Philosophy** *see also* Culture: Academy; Political
         Philosophy; Fichte; Philosophy Traditions: Feminist Traditions

AII.8a   **General Social Philosophy** *see also* Action; Existence;
         Ideologies and Theories: Feminism
Asperen, G.M. van
    De goede maatschappij - Inleiding in de sociale filosofie.
    Assen: Van Gorcum (*series Terreinverkenningen in de filosofie*), 1978
    Tussen coöperatie en conflict: Inleiding in de sociale filosofie.
    Assen, etc.: Van Gorcum, 1986
Assiter, Alison
    Pornography, Feminism and the Individual.
    London: Pluto Press, 1989
Bäumer, Gertrud
    Die soziale Idee in der Weltanschauungen des 19.
    Jahrhunderts. Grundzüge der modernen Sozialphilosophie.
    Heilbron, 1910
Beecher, Catharine
    The Evils Suffered by American Women and American
    Children: The Causes and the Remedy.
    New York: Harper & Bros., 1846
Bernard, Jessie
    The Female World. New York: Macmillan, 1981
    The Sex Game. New York: Atheneum, 1973

Blackwell, Antoinette Brown
  Shadows of our Social System. 1855
  The Social Side of Mind and Action.
  The Neale Publishing Co., 1915
Blanchette, Olivia
  For a Fundamental Social Ethic: A Philosophy of Social Change.
  New York: Philosophical Library, 1973
Coote, Anna, and Beatrix Campbell
  Sweet Freedom. Oxford: Blackwell, 1982
Doane, J., D. Hodges
  Nostalgia and Sexual Difference:
  The Resistance to Contemporary Feminism.
  New York: Methuen, 1987
Easton, Susan M.
  Humanist Marxism and Wittgensteinian Social Philosophy.
  Manchester: Manchester Univ. Press, 1983
Ethelmer, Ellis (Elizabeth Wollstenholme Elmy)
  The Human Flower. Congleton: Mrs. W. Elmy, 1882
  Phases of Love. Congleton: Mrs. W. Elmy, 1897
Firestone, Shulamith
  The Dialectic of Sex. London: Cape, 1970
Fraser, Nancy
  Unruly Practices:
  Power and Gender in Contemporary Social Theory.
  Minneapolis: Univ. of Minnesota Press, 1989
Gilman, Charlotte (Perkins)
  The Man Made World: Or Our Androcentric Culture, 1911.
  Reprinted, New York: Science Book Press, 1970
Hartsock, Nancy C.M.
  Money, Sex and Power: Toward a Feminist Historical Materialism.
  New York: Longman, 1983
James, Susan
  The Content of Social Explanation.
  Cambridge: Cambridge Univ. Press, 1984
Lilja, Elisabeth
  Välfärdsskapandets dilemma: Om människan och hennes
  behov i kommunal socialvårdspraktik.
  Stockholm: Nordiska Inst. för samhällsplanering, Avh. nr. 7, 1989
Lister, Ruth
  The Exclusive Society: Citizenship and the Poor London Child.
  Pov. Action, 1990
Lonzi, Carla
  Sputiami su Hegel, e altri scritti.
  Milan: Scritti di Rivolta Femminile, 1974

Luigi, Rosa
La società dell'uomo.
Milan: Giuffré, 1982

Motroschilova, N.V. (Nelli, Vasilevna)
Posnanije i Obstschestwo.
Moscow: Isdatelstevo Mysl, 1969

Rose, Gillian
Hegel Contra Sociology.
Atlantic Highlands, NJ: Humanities Press, 1981

Royer, Clémence Augustine
L'origine de l'homme et des sociétés. c. 1870

Sabrosky, Judith A.
From Rationality to Liberation.
Westport, CT: Greenwood Press, 1979

Shelley, Mary
The Last Man. 1826

Spelman, Elizabeth V.
Inessential Woman: Problems of Exclusion in Feminist Thought.
Boston: Beacon, 1989

Staël-Holstein, Anne-Louise Germaine Necker de
De la Littérature considérée dans ses rapports avec
les institutions sociales, 1800

Wichmann, Clara Meijer
Mens en maatschappij.
Arnhem: Van Loghum & Slaterus, 1923
Bevrijding. Arnhem: Van Loghum & Slaterus, 1924
Inleiding tot de philosophie der samenleving.
Haarlem: Erven F. Bohn, 1925
Vrouw en maatschappij. Utrecht: Erven J. Bijleveld, 1936

Wilke, Ursula
Risiko und soziale Persönlichkeit.
Berlin: Deutscher Verlag der Wissenschaften, 1977

Young, Iris Marion
Throwing Like a Girl and Other Essays in Feminist
Philosophy and Social Theory.
Bloomington: Indiana Univ. Press, 1990

collections:

Abbott, Pamela, and Roger Sapsford (eds.)
Women and Social Class.
London: Tavistock, 1987

Beer, Ursula (ed.)
Klasse Geschlecht. Feministische Gesellschaftstheorie
und Wissenschaftskritik.
Bielefeld: AJZ-Verlag, 1987

Benhabib, Seyla, and Drucilla Cornell (eds.)
Feminism as Critique: Essays on the Politics of Gender
in Late Capitalist Society.
Cambridge: Polity Press, 1987

Diaz-Diocaretz, Myriam, and Iris M. Zavala (eds.)
Women, Feminist Identity and Society in the 1980's -
Selected Papers (Series Critical Theory).
Amsterdam: John Benjamins, 1985

Heller, Agnes (ed.)
Individuum und Praxis.
Frankfurt am Main: Suhrkamp, 1975

Kauffman, Linda (ed.)
Feminism and Institutions. Dialogues of Feminist Theory.
Oxford: Basil Blackwell, 1989

Kulke, Christine (ed.)
Rationalität und sinnliche Vernunft:
Frauen in der patriarchalen Realität.
Pfaffenweiler: Centaurus-Verlagsges., 1985, 1988

Newton, Judith, and Deborah Rosenfelt (eds.)
Feminist Criticism and Social Change.
New York: Methuen, 1986

AII.8b   Gender and Role

Blom, Ida et al.
Kjönnsroller og likestilling
Oslo: Universitetsforlaget, 1983

Cixous, Hélène, and Catherine Clément
La jeune née. Paris: Union générale d'éditions, c. 1975
The Newly Born Woman (trans. Betsy Wing).
Minneapolis: Univ. of Minnesota Press, 1986

Epstein, Cynthia Fuchs
Deceptive Distinctions - Sex, Gender, and the Social Order.
New Haven, CT: Yale Univ. Press, 1989
Ithaca, NY: Russel Sage Foundation, 1989

Ferguson, Kathy E.
Self, Society and Womankind: The Dialectic of
Liberation. Westport, CT: Greenwood Press, 1980

Hijab, Nadia
Womanpower - The Arab Debate on Women at Work.
Cambridge: Cambridge Univ. Press, 1988

Janeway, Elizabeth
Man's World, Woman's Place: A Study in Social Mythology.
New York: Morrow, 1971
Powers of the Weak.
New York: Alfred A. Knopf, 1980

Lemoine-Luccioni, Eugenie
Partage des femmes. Paris: Seuil, 1976
Myrdal, Alva, and Viola Klein
Women's Two Roles: Home and Work.
London: Routledge & Kegan Paul, 1956 (1970)
Pisan (Pizan), Christine de
La cité des dames. 1407
Trans. and ed. by Earl Jeffrey Richards as:
Christine de Pizan. The Book of the City of Ladies.
New York: Persea, 1982
Le Livre des trois vertus, or Le Trésor de la cité des dames. 1407.
The Treasure of the City of the Ladies. Trans. Sarah Lawson.
Harmondsworth. UK: Penguin Books, 1974
Smit, Joke Kool, E. Engelsman, H. Misset, and H. D'Ancona
Rok en Rol. Amsterdam: De Arbeiderspers, 1969
Young, Iris Marion
Throwing Like a Girl and Other Essays in Feminist
Philosophy and Social Theory.
Bloomington: Indiana Univ. Press, 1990

collections:
Gornick, Vivian, and Barbara K. Moran (eds.)
Woman in Sexist Society. New York: Basic Books, 1971

AII.8c **Home, Family, Work** *see also* **Culture; Political Philosophy**
Allen, Polly Wynn
Building Domestic Liberty -
Charlotte Perkins Gilman's Architectural Feminism.
Amherst: Univ. of Massachusetts Press, 1988
Bernard, Jessie
Women, Wives, Mothers: Values and Options.
Chicago: Aldine, 1975
Bonnevie, Margarete
Ekteskap og arbeide. Oslo: Aschehoug, 1932
Äktenskap och arbete. Uppsala, 1932
Familiekrisen og botemidler til den. Oslo: Aschehoug, 1935
Foreman, Ann
Femininity as Alienation: Women and the Family in
Marxism and Psychoanalysis. London: Pluto Press, 1977
Gilman, Charlotte (Perkins)
The Home: Its Work and Influence. 1903
New ed. by William O'Neill,
Urbana: Univ. of Illinois Press, 1972
Gössmann, Elisabeth
Mann und Frau in Familie und Öffentlichkeit.
Munich: Hueber, 1964

Nicholson, Linda J.
    Gender and History -
    Limits of Social Theory in the Age of the Family.
    New York: Columbia Univ. Press, 1986

Wilkes, Ruth
    Social Work With Undervalued Groups.
    London: Tavistock (n.d.)

collections:

Bell, Susan Groag, and Karen Offen (eds.)
    Woman: The Family and Freedom.
    Stanford: Stanford Univ. Press, 1983

B.   Historical Disciplines

B1   Archives, Surveys and Reference Guides

Canto, Monique
    L'intrigue philosophique:
    Collections de commentaires d'auteurs anciens.
    Paris: "Les Belles Lettres," 1987

Collinson, Diané
    Fifty Major Philosophers -
    A Reference Guide.
    London: Routledge, 1988

Gössmann, Elisabeth (ed.)
    Archiv für philosophie- und theologiegeschichtliche
    Frauenforschung.
    (planned to comprise 10 vols.)
    Vol. 1: Das wohlgelahrte Frauenzimmer.
    Munich: Iudicium, 1984
    Vol. 2: Eva - Gottes Meisterwerk.
    Munich: Iudicium, 1985
    Vol. 3: Johann Caspar Eberti: Eröffnetes Cabinet des
    Gelehrten Frauen-Zimmers (1706).
    Munich: Iudicium, 1986
    Vol. 4: Ob die Weiber Menschen seyn, oder nicht?
    Munich: Iudicium, 1988

Waithe, Mary Ellen (ed.)
    A History of Women Philosophers.
    (4 vols. planned)
    Vol. I: Ancient Women Philosophers: 600 B.C.-500 A.D.
    Dordrecht/Boston/Lancaster: Nijhoff/Kluwer, 1987
    Vol. II: Medieval, Renaissance and Enlightenment Women
    Philosophers: 500-1600.
    Dordrecht, Boston, London: Kluwer Academic Publishers, 1989

B2 **General History of Philosophy** *see also* **General Philosophy; Individual Philosophers**

B2.a **Classical Philosophy** *see also* **Political Philosophy**

Ballew, Lynne
> Straight and Circular: A Study of Imagery in Greek Philosophy.
> Assen: Van Gorcum, 1979.

Bordes, Jacqueline
> Politeia dans la pensée grecque jusq'á Aristote.
> Paris: Les Belles Lettres, 1982

Boyce, Mary
> A Persian Stronghold of Zoroastrianism.
> New York: Oxford Univ. Press, 1977

Colish, Marcia L.
> The Stoic Tradition From Antiquity to the Early Middle Ages I-II.
> I: Stoicism in Classical Latin Literature.
> II: Stoicism in Christian Latin Thought Through
> the Sixth Century.
> Leiden, etc.: E.J. Brill, 1985

Freeman, Kathleen
> Ancilla to the Pre-Socratic Philosophers.
> Oxford: Blackwell, 1948
> God, Man and State: Greek Concepts.
> London: Macdonald, 1975

Hadot, Ilsetraut
> Le problème du néoPlatonisme Alexandrin: Hiérocles
> et Simplicius. Paris: Etudes Augustiniennes, 1978
> Arts libéraux et philosophie dans la pensée antique.
> Paris: Augustiniennes, 1984

Hall, Edith
> Inventing the Barbarian:
> Greek Self-Definition Through Tragedy.
> Oxford, 1989

Hamilton, Edith
> The Greek Way. London: J.M. Dent & Sons, 1930
> The Great Age of Greek Literature (enlarged ed. of (1930).
> New York: Norton, c. 1942
> The Greek Way to Western Civilization.
> New York: American Library, 1942
> The Roman Way. New York: Norton, 1932

Isnardi Parente, Margherita
> Sofistica e democrazia antica.
> [Sansoni Scuola aperta; 83]. Firenze: Sansoni, 1977

Keuls, Eva C.
> The Reign of the Phallus - Sexual Politics in Ancient Athens.
> New York: Harper & Row, 1985

Lanata, Giuliana
  Poetica pre-platonica: Testimonianze e frammenti.
  Florence: Italia, 1963
Osborne, Catherine
  Rethinking Early Greek Philosophy:
  Hippolytus of Rome and the Presocratics.
  London: Duckworth, 1987
Richlin, Amy
  The Garden of Priapus - Sexuality and Aggression in
  Roman Humor.
  New Haven, CT, and London: Yale Univ. Press, 1983
Romilly, Jacqueline de
  La loi dans la pensée Grècque.
  Paris: Belles Lettres, 1971
  Time in Greek Tragedy. Ithaca, NY: Cornell Univ. Press, 1968
  Le temps dans la tragédie Grècque. Paris: Vrin, 1971
  Magic and Rhetoric in Ancient Greece.
  Cambridge, MA: Harvard Univ. Press, 1975
Rosengarten, Yvonne
  Sumer et le sacré: Le jeu des préscriptions.
  Paris: Boccard, 1977
Scholten, Jenny
  Retoren en Democratie. Functies en disfuncties van de
  retorika in klassiek Athene.
  Groningen: Groningen Univ., 1990
Swift-Riginos, Alice
  Platonica. Leiden: Brill, 1976
Valimigli, Manara
  Poeti e filosofi di Grecia.
  Bari: G. Laterza e figli, 1941, 1951
  (Biblioteca di cultura moderna)
Vogel, C.J. de
  Greek Philosophy. A Collection of Texts Supplied With
  Some Notes and Explanations I-III.
  Leiden: Brill, 1950-1959
  Vol. I: Thales to Plato, 1969
  Vol. II: Aristotle, the Early Peripatetic School and
  the Early Academy, 1967
  Vol. III: The Hellenistic-Roman Period, 1973
  Theoria. Studies over de Griekse wijsbegeerte.
  Assen: Van Gorcum, 1967
  Girishiya tetsu gaku to shukyo/[Koruneriga J. do
  Fuogeru], Fejisawa Reifu, Inagaki Rioten,
  Kato Noboro ta yaku. Tokyo: Chikuma, 1969
  Philosophia. Assen: Van Gorcum, 1970
  Rethinking Plato and Platonism. Leiden: Brill, 1986

Weil, Simone
    Intimations of Christianity among the Ancient Greeks.
    New York: Methuen (Ark Paperbacks), 1987
Wurz, Maria
    Die Seelenlehre der alten Stoa. Dargestellt nach der
    von H. von Annim gesammelte Fragmenten der alten
    Stoiker. Vienna: diss., 1933

collections:

Annas, Julia (ed.; founding editor)
    Oxford Studies in Ancient Philosophy, Vol. I.
    Oxford: Oxford Univ. Press, 1983
    Oxford Studies in Ancient Philosophy, Vol. VI.
    Oxford: Clarendon Press, 1984
    Supplementary Volume 1988.
    Oxford: Clarendon Press, 1988
    Oxford Studies in Ancient Philosophy, Vol. VII.
    Oxford: Clarendon Press, 1989
    Oxford Studies in Ancient Philosophy, Vol. VIII.
    Oxford: Clarendon Press, 1990
Huby, Pamela, and Gordon Neal (eds.)
    The Criterion of Truth.
    Liverpool: Liverpool Univ. Press, 1989
Nussbaum, Martha, and Malcolm Schofield (eds.)
    Language and Logos. Studies in Ancient Greek Philosophy.
    Cambridge: Cambridge Univ. Press, 1982
Taran, Sonya Lida (ed., with an introduction)
    The Greek Anthology I-II.
    New York: Garland, 1987

B2.b   Rome

Gardner, Jane F.
    Women in Roman Law and Society.
    Bloomington: Indiana Univ. Press, 1986
Rawson, Elizabeth
    Intellectual Life in the Late Roman Republic.
    Baltimore: Johns Hopkins Univ. Press, 1985

B2.c   Medieval Philosophy

Arcari, Paola Maria
    Idee e sentimenti politici dell'alto medio evo.
    Milan: Giuffre, 1968
Carruthers, Mary
    The Book of Memory: A Study of Memory in Medieval Culture.
    Cambridge: Cambridge Univ. Press, 1990

Gössmann, Elisabeth
  Glaube und Gotteserkenntnis im Mittelalter.
  Freiburg, etc.: Herder, 1971
Gössmann, Elisabeth
  Antiqui und Moderni im Mittelalter: eine geschichtliche
  Standortbestimmung Veröffentl. des Grabmann-Inst.
  zur Erforschung der mittelalterl. Theol. u. Philosophie. N.F. 23.
  Munich, etc.: Schöningh Packerborn, 1974
Handlin, Joanna F.
  Action in Late Ming Thought.
  Berkeley: Univ. of California Press, 1983
Harvey, E. Ruth
  The Inward Wits: Psychological Theory in the Middle
  Ages and the Renaissance.
  London: Warburg Institute, 1975
Lynch, Kathryn L.
  The High Medieval Dream Vision -
  Poetry, Philosophy, and Literary Form.
  Stanford, CA: Stanford Univ. Press, 1988
Riet, S. van
  Avicenna Latinus. The Hague: Leiden, 1983
Sirat, Colette
  A History of Jewish Philosophy in the Middle Ages.
  Cambridge: Cambridge Univ. Press, 1985

collections and translations:
Lewin, Carol, and Jeanie Watson (eds.)
  Ambiguous Realities: Women in the Middle Ages and the
  Renaissance. Detroit: Wayne State Univ. Press, 1988
Link-Salinger, Ruth (ed.)
  A Straight Path: Studies in Medieval Philosophy and Culture.
  Washington, DC: Catholic Univ. of America Press, 1988
Wilson, Katherina M. (ed.)
  Medieval Women Writers.
  Athens: Univ. of Georgia Press, 1984
Wood, Rega
  Adam de Wodeham: Tractatus de indivisibilius.
  Dordrecht: Kluwer Academic Publishers, 1988

B2.d   Renaissance *see also* **Medieval Philosophy**
Heller, Agnes
  Renaissance man (trans. from Hungarian by Richard E. Allen).
  London, etc.: Routledge and Kegan Paul, 1978
  German trans. by Hans-Henning Paetzke,
  Frankfurt am Main: Suhrkamp, 1988

Johnson, Paula
  Form and Transformation in Music and Poetry of the
  English Renaissance. New Haven, CT: Yale Univ. Press, 1972

Kahn, Victoria
  Rhetoric, Prudence and Skepticism in the Renaissance.
  Ithaca, NY: Cornell Univ. Press, 1985

Koenigsberger, Dorothy
  Renaissance Man and Creative Thinking.
  Atlantic Highlands, NJ: Humanities Press, 1979

Struever, Nancy S.
  The Language of History in the Renaissance.
  Princeton, NJ: Princeton Univ. Press, 1970

Vedrine, Hélène
  Les philosophies de la Renaissance.
  Paris: P.U.F., 1971

Yates, Frances A.
  Collected Essays I-III.
  London, etc.: Routledge & Kegan Paul, 1982-1984
  Vol. I: Lull and Bruno, 1982.
  Vol. II: Renaissance and Reform: The Italian Contribution, 1983.
  Vol. III: Ideas and Ideals in the North European
  Renaissance, 1984.
  The Art of Memory. London: Routledge & Kegan Paul, 1966;
  Chicago: Univ. Press, 1974; Harmondsworth, 1978
  L'Illuminismo dei Rosa-Croce. Turin: Einaudi, 1976
  The Rosicrucian Enlightenment.
  London: Routledge & Kegan Paul, 1986
  The Occult Philosophy In the Elizabethan Age.
  London: Routledge & Kegan Paul, 1979. Ark Paperback, 1983

collections:

Ferguson, Margaret W., Maureen Quilligan, and Nancy J. Vickers (eds.)
  Rewriting the Renaissance: The Discourses of Sexual
  Difference in Early Modern Europe.
  Chicago: Univ. of Chicago Press, 1986

B2.e **Modern and contemporary philosophy** *see also*
  Social Philosophy; Philosophy of Language, History of;
  Individual Philosophers; Philosophical Traditions

Braidotti, Rosi
  Féminisme et philosophie. La philosophie contemporaine
  comme critique du pouvoir par rapport à la pensée
  féministe. Paris: Univ. of Paris, diss., 1981

Brookner, Anita
  Greuze: The Rise and Fall of an Eighteenth-Century
  Phenomenon. London: Elek, 1972

Bulciolu, Maria Teresa
    L'école Saint-Simonienne et la femme.
    Pisa: Goliardica, 1980
Butler, Judith P.
    Subjects of Desire: Hegelian Reflections in Twentieth-
    Century France.
    Oxford: Blackwell/Columbia Press, 1987
Coignet, Clarisse
    De Kant à Bergson: réconciliation de la religion et de
    la science dans un spiritualisme nouveau.
    Paris: Alcan, 1911
Conry, Yvette
    L'Introduction du Darwinisme en France au XIXe siècle.
    Paris: Vrin, 1974
Fuller, (Sarah) Margaret
    Woman in the Ninteenth Century - 1845.
    New York: Norton, 1971
Furst, Lilian R.
    The Contours of European Romanticism.
    London: Macmillan, 1979
Goyard-Fabre, Simone
    La philosophie des Lumières and France.
    Paris: Klincksieck, 1972
Haight, Jeanne
    The Concept of Reason in French Classical Literature 1635-1690.
    Toronto: Univ. of Toronto Press, 1982
Harth, Erica
    Ideology and Culture in Seventeenth-Century France.
    Ithaca, NY: Cornell Univ. Press, 1983
Jacob, Margaret C.
    The Newtonians and the English Revolution 1689-1720.
    Ithaca, NY: Cornell Univ. Press, 1976
    The Radical Enlightenment. London: Allen & Unwin, 1981
Jones, Greta
    Social Darwinism and English Thought.
    Atlantic Highlands, NJ: Humanities Press, 1980
Kabitoglou, Douka E.
    Plato and the English Romantics.
    London, etc.: Routledge, 1990
Kuhn, Anna K.
    Christa Wolf's Utopian Vision - From Marxism to Feminism.
    Cambridge: Cambridge Univ. Press, 1988
Pepperle, Ingrid
    Junghegelianische Geschichtsphilosophie und Kunsttheorie.
    Berlin: Akademie, 1978

Pompeo Faracovi, Ornella
Il marxismo francese contemporaneo fra dialettica e
struttura (1945-1978). Milan: Feltrinelli, 1972

Rovighi, Sofia Vanni
Storia della filosofia moderna - Dalla rivoluzione
scientifica a Hegel. Brescia: La Scuola, 1976

Scherrer, Jutta
Die Petersburger religiös-philosophischen
Vereinigungen. Berlin: Freie Univ., 1973

Stich, Herta
Von Herders "Ideen zur Philosophie der Geschichte der
Menschheit" über Kant, Fichte, Schelling, bis zu
Hegel's "Vorlesungen Über die Philosophie der
Geschichte." Vienna: diss., 1936

Thijssen-Schoute, C. Louise
Over Nicolaas J. Wieringa.
Groningen: Groningen Univ., 1939

Valimigli, Manara, and Benedetto Croce
Carteggio a cura di Marcello Gigante. Napels: Bibliopolis, 1976

Weedon, Chris
Feminist Practice and Poststructuralist Theory.
Oxford, etc.: Blackwell, 1987

collections:

Chatterjee, Margaret (ed.)
Contemporary Indian Philosophy, Series I, II.
New York: Humanities Press;
London: Allen & Unwin; 1974

B3   History of Specific Philosophical Disciplines

B3.1   Anthropology, History of Philosophical
see also Science, Philosophy of; Science, History of;
Renaissance; American Traditions; The Feminist Tradition

B3.1a   Images of "Man"

B3.1aa   -Surveys and Non-periodized Topics

Agonito, Rosemary
History of Ideas on Women - A Source Book.
New York: G. P. Putnam's Sons, 1977

Murray, Penelope (ed.)
Genius: The History of an Idea.
Oxford/Cambridge, MA: Blackwell, 1989

North, Helen F.
  From Myth to Icon.
  New York: Cornell Univ. Press, 1979
O'Faolain, Julia, and Lauro Martinez (eds.)
  Not in God's Image.
  London: Temple Smith, 1973
Rogers, Katharine M.
  The Troublesome Helpmate - A History of Misogyny in Literature.
  Seattle: Univ. of Washington Press, 1966
Springborg, Patricia
  Patriarchal Monarchy and the Feminine Principle.
  London: Unwin & Hyman, 1990
Waal Malefijt, Annemarie de
  Images of Man. A History of Anthropological Thought.
  New York: Alfred A. Knopf, 1976

B3.1ab   -Ancient Philosophy
Allen, Prudence
  The Concept of Woman: The Aristotelian Revolution
  750 BC - AD 1250.
  Montreal and London: Eden Press, 1985
Cantarella, Eva
  Pandora's Daughters. The Role and the Status of Women
  in Greek and Roman Antiquity.
  Baltimore: Johns Hopkins Univ. Press, 1987
Cavarero, Adriana
  Nonostante Platone. Figure femminili nella
  filosofia antica. Roma: Editori Riuniti, 1990
Lefkovitz, Mary R.
  Women in Greek Myth.
  Baltimore: Johns Hopkins Univ. Press, 1987
Reesor, Margaret E.
  The Nature of Man in Early Stoic Philosophy.
  London: Duckworth, 1989

B3.1ac   -Gnosticism
King, K.L.
  Images of the Feminine in Gnosticism
  (Studies in Antiquity and Christianity, 4).
  Philadelphia: Fortress Press, 1988
Sfameni Gasparro, Giulia
  Enkretia e antropologia. Le motivazioni protologiche
  della continenza e della verginità nel cristianesimo
  dei primi secoli e nello gnosticismo.
  Rome: Institutum Patristicum "Augustinianum," 1984

B3.1ad   -Medieval Philosophy

Börresen, Kari Elisabeth
  Subordination et équivalence. Nature et rôle de la
  femme d'après Augustin et Thomas d'Aquin.
  Oslo: Universitetsforlaget/Paris: Maison Mame, 1968
  Natura e ruolo della donna in Agostino e Tommaso
  d'Aquino (updated trans. of (1968)).
  Assisi: Cittadella editrice, 1979
  Subordination and Equivalence. The Nature and Role of Woman
  in Augustine and Thomas Aquinas (updated trans. of (1968)).
  Washington, DC: Univ. Press of America, 1981
  Anthropologie médiévale et théologie mariale.
  Oslo: Universitetsforlaget, 1971

Bynum, Caroline Walker
  Fragmentation and Redemption. Essays on Gender and the
  Human Body in Medieval Religion.
  Cambridge, MA: MIT Press, 1990
  New York: Zone Books, 1991

B3.1ae   -Modern and Contemporary Philosophy

Ingrisch, Doris
  Das Rollenbild der Frau bei den Frühsozialisten.
  Linz: Trauner, 1985

Karlsen, Carol F.
  The Devil in the Shape of a Woman - Witchcraft in
  Colonial New England.
  New York: Norton, 1988

Korotin, Ilse
  Philosophische Dispositionen zum Frauenbild im
  Nationalsozialismus. Vienna: diss., 1990

Larner, Christina
  Witchcraft and Religion: The Politics of Popular Belief
  (ed. and introduced by Alan Macfarlane).
  Oxford: Blackwell, 1986

Linden, Mareta
  Untersuchungen zum Anthropologiebegriff des 18.
  Jahrhunderts. Bern: Lang, 1976

Matthews, Jill Julius
  Good and Mad Women: The Historical Construction of
  Femininity in Twentieth-Century Australia.
  Sydney: Allen & Unwin, 1984

Nead, Lynda
  Myths of Sexuality: Representations of Women in
  Victorian Britain.
  Oxford: Blackwell, 1988

Osmond, Rosalie
Mutual Accusation. Seventeenth-Century Body and Soul
Dialogues in Their Literary and Theological Context.
Cheektowaga, NY: Univ. of Toronto Press, 1990
Salvaggio, Ruth
Enlightened Absence: Neoclassical Configurations of
the Feminine. Urbana: Univ. of Illinois Press, 1988
Steinbrügge, Liselotte
Das moralische Geschlecht:
Theorien und literarische Entwürfe über die Natur der
Frau in der französischen Aufklärung.
Weinheim: Beltz, 1987
Viestad, Else
Kjönn og ideologi: en studie av kvinnesynet hos Locke, Hume,
Rousseau og Kant. Oslo: Solum forlag, 1989
Walousek, Ella
Die Überwinduns der Physiognomie im 18.
Jahrhandert: Ansdrucks theorie von Descartes bis Ensel.
Vienna: diss., 1934

collections:

Börresen, Kari Elisabeth (ed.)
Image of God and Gender Models in Judaeo-Christian Tradition.
Oslo: Solum Forlag, 1990
Mahowald, Mary Briody (ed.)
Philosophy of Woman - An Anthology of Classic &
Current Concepts. Indianapolis, IN: Hackett, 1983
Mendus, Susan, and Jane Rendall (eds.)
Sexuality and Subordination - Interdisciplinary Studies
of Gender in the Nineteenth Century. London: Routledge, 1988
Stopczyk, Annegret (ed.)
Was Philosophen über Frauen Denken.
Munich: Matthes & Seitz Verlag, 1980

B3.1b   Motherhood
Badinter, Elisabeth
L'amour en plus: histoire de l'amour maternel (XVIIe-XXe siècle).
Paris: Flammarion, 1980
Det naturligste av verden? Om morskjærlighetens
historie (Norwegian trans. of (1980) by Marit Notaker,
preface by Sölvi Sogner). Oslo: Universitetsforlaget, 1981
De mythe van de moederliefde
(trans. of (1980) by V. Huijbregts and M. Lyon).
Utrecht: Erven J. Bijleveld, 1983;
Amsterdam: Maarten Muntinga, 1989 (Rainbow Pocketboek)

B3.2 **Epistemology, History of** *see also* History of Science;
Individual Philosophers: a.o. C.I. Lewis

Alanen, Lilli
Studies in Cartesian Epistemology and Philosophy of Mind.
Helsinki: Acta Philosophica Fennica 33, 1978, 1982

Arens, Katherine
Structures of Knowing. Psychologies of the Nineteenth Century.
Dordrecht: Kluwer Academic Publishers, 1988

Colish, Marcia L.
The Mirror of Language: A Study in the Medieval Theory
of Knowledge.
New Haven, CT: Yale Univ. Press, 1968

Ende, Helga
Der Konstruktionsbegriff im Umkreis des deutschen Idealismus.
Weisenheim am Glan: Studien zur
Wissenschaftstheorie 7, 1973

Giordano, Maria
Cartesio epistemologo.
Bari: Ecumenica, 1981

Küster, Margarete
Der Begriff der Intution in de nachkantischen deutschen
Philosophie (unter Berücksichtigung Bergsons).
Vienna: diss., 1932

Morantz-Sanchez, Regina Markell
Sympathy and Science -
Women Physicians in American Medicine.
New York: Oxford Univ. Press, 1985

Stough, Charlotte L.
Greek Skepticism: A Study of Epistemology.
Berkeley: Univ. of California Press, 1969

Tachau, Katherine H.
Vision and Certitude in the Age of Ockham. Optics,
Epistemology and the Foundations of Semantics 1250-1345.
Leiden, etc.: E.J. Brill, 1988 (series Studien und
Texte zur Geistesgeschichte des Mittelalters, ed.
Albert Zimmermann)

Tielsch, Elfriede Walesca
Der kritische Empirismus der Antike in seiner
Bedeutung für die Naturwissenschaft.
Königstein (Ts): Forum Academicum, 1981

collections and translations:

Limbrick, Elaine, and Douglas F.S. Thomson
Franciscus Sanchez: That Nothing is Known.
Cambridge: Cambridge Univ. Press, 1988 (Dec.)

B3.3   **Ethics and Morality, History of** *see also* Montaigne

Braun, Hedwig
     Einfluss des Darwinismus auf die Ethik.
     Vienna: diss., 1915

Favre, Julie Velten
     La Morale de Socrate. Paris: Alcan, 1888
     La Morale des Stoïciens. Paris: Alcan, 1888
     La morale d'Aristote. Paris: Alcan, 1889
     La morale de Ciceron. Paris: Fischbacher, 1891
     La morale de Plutarche (Préceptes et examples) avec les
     discours de MM. Chantavoine, Lemonnier et Joseph Fabre
     prononcés aux obsèques de Mme. Jules Favre et Une
     notice sur Mme. Jules Favre par Mademoiselle L.
     Belugou, Directrice de l'École Normale Supérieure de
     Sèvres. Paris: Paulin et Cie., 1909

Huby, Pamela
     Greek Ethics.
     London, etc.: Macmillan (series New Studies in Ethics), 1967
     New York: St. Martin's Press (idem), 1967

Nussbaum, Martha
     The Fragility of Goodness:
     Luck and Ethics in Greek Tragedy and Philosophy.
     Cambridge: Cambridge Univ. Press, 1986

Warnock, Mary
     Ethics since 1900. London: Oxford Univ. Press, 1963/1978 [1960]
     Existentialist Ethics.
     London, etc.: McMillan (series New Studies in Ethics)
     New York: St. Martin's Press (idem), 1967

Wyschogrod, Edith
     Spirit in Ashes - Hegel, Heidegger and Man-made Mass Death.
     New Haven, CT: Yale Univ. Press, 1985

B3.4   **Logic, History of**
     see also Philosophical Logic; Individual Philosophers

B3.4a   **General Themes**

Nye, Andrea
     Words of Power. A Feminist Reading of the History of Logic.
     New York: Routledge, 1990

Pape, Ingetrud
     Tradition und Transformation der Modalität.
     Hamburg: Meiner, 1968

Proust, Joëlle
     Question de forme. (Before 1989)
     Questions of Form: Logic and the Analytic Proposition
     from Kant to Carnap. Trans. by A. Brenner Anastasios.
     Minneapolis: Univ. of Minnesota Press, 1989

B3.4b   Ancient Logic

Beil, Joanne Mary
    From Poetry to Philosophy: the Beginnings of Logic in Early
    Greek Thought.
    Los Angeles: Univ. of Southern California, diss., 1981

Buck-Morse, Susan
    Origen de la dialectica negativa.
    Mexico: Siglo XXI, 1981

Grimm, Laura
    Definition in Plato's Meno -
    An Inquiry in the Light of Logic and Semantics into the Kind of
    Definition Intended by Socrates When He Asks "What is virtue?"
    Oslo: Det Norske Videnskaps-Akademi i Oslo,
    II. Hist.-filos. klasse: Skrifter N.s. No. 2, 1962

Kneale, Martha, William Kneale, and -
    The Development of Logic.
    Oxford: Clarendon Press, 1984 [1962]

Mansion, Suzanne
    Jugement d'existence chez Aristote.
    Louvain: Ed. de l'Institut Supérieur de Philos., 1946

Repici, Luciana
    La logica di Teofrasto -
    Studio critico e raccolta dei frammenti e delle
    testimonianze. Bologna: Mulina, 1977

Rose, Lynn E.
    Aristotle's Syllogistic.
    Springfield, IL: Chas. C. Thomas, 1968

Virieux-Reymond, Antoinette
    La logique et l'épistemologie des stoïciens.
    Lausanne: 1950

Waterlow, Sarah
    Passage and Possibility: A Study of Aristotle's Modal Concepts.
    Oxford: Clarendon Press, 1982

B3.4c   Medieval Logic

Ashworth, E. J.
    The Tradition of Medieval Logic and Speculative Grammar.
    Toronto: Pontifical Institute of Medieval Studies, 1978

Bartolomei, Maria Christina
    Tomismo e principio di non-contraddizione.
    Padua: Cedam, 1973

Corrigan, Mary
    A Study of the Aristotelian Sources of the "summa
    totius logicae Aristotelis."
    Bronx, NY: Fordham Univ., diss., 1934

Desjardins, Rosemary
   The Rational Enterprise: "Logos" in Plato's "Thaetetus."
   Philadelphia: Univ. of Pennsylvania, diss., 1975
Fumagalli, Maria Teresa Beonio-Brocchieri
   The Logic of Abelard.
   Dordrecht: Reidel, 1969
Karger, Elizabeth Christiane
   A Study in William of Ockham's Modal Logic.
   Berkeley: Univ. of California, diss., 1976
Mc Dermott, Agnes Charlene Senape
   The Assertion and Modal Propositional Logic of the Pseduo-Scotus.
   Philadelphia: Univ. of Pennsylvania, diss., 1964
Roberts, Helen Louise Nisbet
   An Introduction to the Terminist Logic of John Buridan.
   New York: Columbia Univ., diss., 1952
Spruyt, Joke
   Peter of Spain on Composition and Negation.
   Nijmegen: Ingenium Publishers, 1989
Stump, Eleonore
   Dialectic and its Place in the Development of Medieval Logic.
   Ithaca, NY: Cornell Univ. Press, 1983, 1989

   collections and translations:
Ashworth, E.J.
   Paul of Venice: Logica Magna -
   Part II Fascicule 8, Tractatus Obligationibus.
   Oxford: Claredon Press, 1988
Clarke, Patricia (trans.)
   Paul of Venice: Logica Magna.
   New York: Oxford Univ. Press, 1981
Stump, Eleonore, Norman Kretzmann and -
   The Cambridge Translations of Medieval Philosophical
   Texts. Vol. 1: Logic and the Philosophy of Language.
   Cambridge and New York: Cambridge Univ. Press, 1988

B3.4d   Renaissance Logic
Ashworth, E. J.
   The "Logica Hamburgensis" of Joachim Jungius.
   Bryn Mawr, PA: Bryn Mawr College, diss., 1965
   Language and Logic in the Post-Medieval Period.
   Dordrecht and Boston: Reidel, 1974
Del Torre, Maria Assunta
   Studi su Cesare Cremonini -
   Cosmologia e logica nel tardo aristotelismo padovano.
   Padua: Univ. di Padova, 1968

Jardine, Lisa
    Francis Bacon: Discovery and the Art of Discourse.
    Cambridge: Cambridge Univ. Press, 1974

Lusignan, Francine
    L'Artis Logicae plenior institutio de John Milton:
    êtat de la question et position.
    Montreal: Univ. de Montreal, diss., 1974

collections:

James, Patricia, James Dickoff, and - (trans.)
    Art of Thinking: Port-Royal Logic.
    New York: Macmillan, 1964

B3.4e   German Logic in the Interregnum

B3.4ea   -Leibniz

Ishiguro, Hidé
    Leibniz' Philosophy of Logic and Language.
    London: Duckworth, 1972
    Revised ed. Cambridge: Cambridge Univ. Press, 1990

Kauppi, Railli
    Über die Leibnizsche Logik, mit besondere
    Berücksichtigung der Intension und Extension.
    Helsinki: Acta Philosophica Fennica, 1969
    New York: Garland Publishers, 1985

B3.4eb   -German Idealism

Aebi, Magdalena
    Kants Begründung der 'Deutschen Philosophie'-
    Kants transzendentale Logik: Kritik ihrer Begründung.
    Basel, 1947

Bachstütz, Laura
    Die analytischen und synthetischen Urteile bei Kant und
    die Logikern nach Kant. Vienna: diss., 1916

Hackenesch, Christa
    Die Logik der Andersheit. Eine Untersuchung zu Hegels
    Begriff der Reflexion. Frankfurt a.M.: Athenäum, 1987

Jarczyk, Gwendoline
    Système et liberté dans la logique de Hegel.
    Paris: Aubier-Montagne, 1980

Maier, Anneliese
    Kants Qualitätskategorien. Berlin: Metzner, 1930

Souche-Dagues, Denise
    Logique et politique Hégeliennes.
    Paris: Vrin, 1983

B3.4ec   -Husserl

Bachelard, Suzanne
    A Study of Husserl's Formal and Transcendental Logic
    (trans. L. Embrée.). Evanston, IL: Northwestern Univ. Press, 1968
Tito, Johanna
    Logic in the Husserlian Context.
    Evanston, IL: Northwestern Univ. Press, 1990

B3.4f   Modern Logic see also Frege, Peirce, Quine, Russell

Bowne, Gwendolyn Duell
    The Development of the Philosophy of Logic 1800-1908.
    Columbus: Ohio State Univ., diss., 1963
Leo, Rosella Fabbrichesi
    I grafi esistenziali di Charles Peirce.
    Milano: Annali della Facolta, 1983
    La polemica sull'iconomismo.
    Naples: Scientifiche Italiane, 1983.
Michael, Emily Poe
    The Early Logic of Charles S. Peirce.
    Philadelphia: Univ. of Pennsylvania, diss., 1973
Olds, Marianne E.
    The Nature and Function of the Logical Constructions of
    Bertrand Russell. Radcliffe College, diss., 1952
Simili, Rafaella
    Logica metodo e scienze in Gran Bretagna 1860-1930.
    Torino: Loescher, 1986

B3.5   Mysticism and Spirituality, History of see also Language:
    Special Language Forms; Individual Philosophers

Bynum, Caroline Walker
    Jesus as Mother:
    Studies in the Spirituality of the High Middle Ages.
    Berkeley/Los Angeles: Univ. of California Press, 1982, 1987
    Holy Feast and Holy Fast:
    The Religions Significance of Food to Medieval Women.
    Berkeley: Univ. of California Press, 1987
Erkenstein, Lina
    Women Under Monasticism.
    New York: Russell and Russell, 1963
Mechthild of Hackeborn
    The Book of Gostlye Grace of Mechtild of Hackeborn.
    Ed. Teresa Halligan.
    Toronto: Pontifical Institute of Medieval Studies, 1979
Menzies, Lucy
    The Saints in Italy.
    (England:) William Brendon and son, 1924

bibliographies:

Lewis, Gertrude Jaron, F. Willaert, and M.-J. Govers
Bibliographie zur deutschen mittelalterlichen
Frauenmystik. With an appendix on Beatrice of Nazareth
and Hadewych. Berlin: Erich Schmidt Verlag, 1989

editions:

Schmidt, Margot, and Dieter R. Bauer (eds.)
"Eine Höhe über die nichts geht":
Spezielle Glaubenserfahrung in der Frauenmystik?
Stuttgart-Bad Cannstatt: Fromman-Holzboog, 1986

B3.6   Philosophy of Language, History of
see also Language: Special Language Forms; Russell

Borutti, Silvana
Significato: Saggio sulla semantica filosofica del' 900.
Bologna: Zanichelli, 1983

Colish, Marcia L. *see* Epistemology, History of

Ferguson, Frances *see* William Wordsworth

Fiesel, Eva
Die Sprachphilosophie der Romantik.
Tübingen, 1927

Tachau, Katherine H. *see* Epistemology, History of

Weber, Hanna
Herders Sprachphilosophie: Eine Interpretation in
Hinblick auf die moderne Sprachphilosophie.
Berlin: Ebering, 1939

collections: see Logic, History of; Wittgenstein

B3.7   Political Philosophy, History of
see also Individual Philosophers; Philosophy of Language;
Special Language Forms

Dohm, Hedwig
Die Antifeministen. Berlin: F. Dümmer Verlag, 1902

Farrar, Cynthia
The Origins of Democratic Thinking:
The Invention of Politics in Classical Athens.
Cambridge: Cambridge Univ. Press, 1988; Paperback Library, 1989

Isnardi Parente, Margherita
Città e regime politici nel pensiero greco.
Torino: Loescher, 1979

Kleinau, Elke
Die freie Frau. Soziale Utopien des frühen 19.
Jahrhunderts. Düsseldorf: Schwann, 1987

Kobé, Eva
  Die Idee eines Dritten Reiches im deutschen Idealismus.
  Vienna: diss., 1939 (22 March)
Okin, Susan Moller
  Women in Western Political Thought.
  Princeton, NJ: Princeton Univ. Press, 1979
  London: Virago, 1980 (paper)
Saxonhouse, Arlene W.
  Women in the History of Political Thought:
  Ancient Greece to Machiavelli.
  New York: Praeger, 1985
Taylor, Barbara
  Eve and the New Jerusalem: Socialism and Feminism in
  the Nineteenth Century.
  London: Virago, 1983
Thibert, Marguerite
  Le féminisme dans le socialisme français.
  Paris: M. Giard, 1926
Wood, Ellen Meiksins, and Neal Wood
  Class Ideology and Ancient Political Theory.
  Oxford: Blackwell, 1978

  collections:
Clark, Lorenne M.G., and Lynda Lange (eds.)
  The Sexism of Social and Political Theory:
  Women and Reproduction from Plato to Nietzsche.
  Toronto: Univ. of Toronto Press, 1979
Fontana, Biancamaria (ed.)
  Constant: Political Writings.
  Cambridge: Cambridge Univ. Press, 1988
Kennedy, Ellen, and Susan Mendus (eds.)
  Women in Western Political Philosophy: Kant to Nietzsche.
  Brighton: Harvester (Wheatsheaf Books), 1987
Schröder, Hannelore (ed.)
  Die Frau ist frei geboren. Texte zur Frauenemanzipation
  I-II (with introd. and commentary).
  Munich: Beck 1979/81

B4   **Religion, Historical Philosophy of** see also Anthropology:
         Gnosticism; Mysticism and Spirituality; Individual
         Philosophers
Buckley, Jorunn Jacobsen
  Female Fault and Fulfilment in Gnosticism.
  Chapel Hill: Univ. of North Carolina Press, 1986

Pagels, Elaine H.
  The Gnostic Gospels.
  London: Weidenfeld and Nicholson, 1979
  Adam, Eve and the Serpent.
  New York: Random House, 1988
Zaleski, Carole
  Otherworlds Journeys: Accounts of Near-Death Experience
  in Medieval and Modern Times.
  Oxford: Oxford Paperbacks, 1989

B5   Science, History of

B5.1   Bibliographies/biographical Drectories
Ireland, Norma Olin
  Index to Scientists of the World from Ancient to Modern
  Times: Biographies & Portraits. Saxon, 1962
Ogilvie, Marilyn Bailey
  Women in Science: Antiquity through the Nineteenth Century
  A Biographical Dictionary with Annotated Bibliography.
  Cambridge, MA: MIT Press, 1986
Whitrow, Magda
  ISIS Cumulative Bibliography. London: Mansell, 1971

B5.2   History of Scientists, (auto)biographies
  see also Culture: Philosophy of the Academy
Alic, Margaret
  Hypatia's Heritage: A History of Women in Science from
  Antiquity through the Nineteenth Century.
  Boston: Beacon Press, 1987
Feyl, Renate
  Der lautlose Aufbruch. Frauen in der Wissenschaft.
  Berlin: Neues Leben, 1981
Goodfield, June
  An Imagined World [on Anna Brito and her work].
  Harmondsworth: Penguin, 1982
Gornick, Vivian
  Women in Science. New York: Simon & Schuster, 1983
Keller, Evelyn Fox
  A Feeling For the Organism -
  The Life and Work of Barbara McClintock.
  San Francisco: Freeman, 1983
Koblitz, Ann H.
  A Convergence of Lives. Sofia Kovalevskaia:
  Scientist, Writer, Revolutionary.
  Boston: Birkhauser, 1983

Levi-Montalcini, Rita
   In Praise of Imperfection - My Life and Work.
   New York: Basic Books, 1988
Lipinska, Melanie
   Histoire des femmes médécins. Paris: G. Jacques et cie., 1900
Rossiter, Margaret
   Women Scientists in America - Struggles and Strategies to 1940.
   Baltimore: Johns Hopkins Univ. Press, 1982
Sayre, Anne
   Rosalind Franklin and DNA: A Vivid View of What it is
   Like to be a Gifted Woman in an Especially Male Profession.
   New York: Norton, 1975
Schiebinger, Londa
   The Mind Has No Sex? Women in the Origins of Modern Science.
   Cambridge, MA: Harvard Univ. Press, 1989
Stein, Dorothy
   Ada: A Life and a Legacy.
   [Augusta Ada Byron, inventor of computer programming]
   Cambridge, MA: MIT Press, 1987

   collections:
Abir-Am, Pnina G., and Dorinda Outram (eds.)
   Women in Science, 1787-1979: Uneasy Careers and
   Intimate Lives. Preface by Margaret W. Rossiter.
   New York: University Press Books (Rutgers), 1988

B5.3   General History of Science
Germain, Sophie *see* Philosophy of Science
Kremer-Marietti, Angèle
   Les racines philosophiques de la science.
   Brussels: Pierre Margada, 1987
Phillips, Patricia
   The Scientific Lady: A Social History of Women's
   Scientific Interests 1570-1918.
   London: Weidenfeld and Nicholson, 1990
Riet, S. van
   L'essor de la philosophie et des sciences á Bagdad
   ferment de la pensée médiévale and Europe.
   Amsterdam, etc.: North-Holland, 1987
Schiebinger, Londa
   The Mind Has No Sex? Women in the Origins of Modern
   Science. Cambridge, MA: Harvard Univ. Press, 1989
Shapiro, Barbara J.
   Probability and Certainty in Seventeenth-century England.
   Princeton, NJ: Princeton Univ. Press, 1983

Shuttleworth, Sally, John Christie and -
Nature Transfigured: Literature and Science, 1700-1900.
Manchester: Manchester Univ. Press, 1989

Sinkles, Georgette
Medieval Theories of Composition and Division.
Ithaca, NY: Cornell Univ., diss., 1985

Siraisi, Nancy G.
Arts and Sciences at Padua: The Studium before 1350.
Toronto: Pontifical Institute of Medieval Studies, 1973

Ströker, Elisabeth
Wissenschaftsgeschichte als Herausforderung.
Frankfurt a.M.: Klostermann, 1976

collections:

Newman, Louise Michele (ed.)
Men's Ideas/Women's Realities - Popular Science, 1870-1915
(textbook). New York, etc.: Pergamon Press, 1985

B5.4   Biology and Medicine

Angier, Natalie
Natural Obsessions: The Search for the Oncogene.
Boston: Houghton Mifflin, 1988

Bernier, Réjane
Aux sources de la biologie.
Montreal: Presses Univ. de Quebec, 1975

Jordanova, Ludmilla
Sexual Visions: Images of Gender in Science and
Medicine Between the Eighteenth and Twentieth Centuries.
New York, London, etc.: Harvester Wheatsheaf, 1989

Lesky, Eva
Die Zeugungs- und Vererbungslehren der Antike und ihr
Nachwirken.
Mainz: Verlag dere Akademie der Wissenschaften und der
Literatur, Abh. der Geistes- und Sozialwiss. Klasse 19, 1950

Perone, Bobette, H. Henrietta Stockel, and Victoria Krueger
Medicine Women, Curanderas, and Women Doctors.
Oklahoma Univ. Press, 1989

Russett, Cynthia Eagle
Sexual Science: The Victorian Construction of Womanhood.
Cambridge, MA/London: Harvard Univ. Press, 1989

collections:

Conry, Yvette
Correspondence entre Charles Darwin et Gaston de
Saporta. Paris: P.U.F., 1972

Jacobi, Jolande (ed., with an introduction)
    Paracelsus - Selected Writings (trans. Norbert
    Guterman). Lawrenceville, NJ: Princeton Univ. Press, 1988

B5.5   Physical Sciences

Baffioni, Carmela
    Atomismo e antiatomismo nel pensiero Islamica.
    Naples, 1982

Douglas, Mary
    Natural Symbols: Explorations in Cosmology.
    London: Barrie & Rockliff, 1970

Dumée, Jeanne
    Entretiens sur l'opinion de Copernic touchant la
    mobilité de la terre. c. 1720

Hammer-Jensen, Ingeborg
    Den Ældste Atomlære. (Indtil Aristoteles.)
    Copenhagen: forlagt af Tillge's Boghandel, 1908

Jungnickel, Christa, and R. McCormach
    The Intellectual Mastery of Nature:
    Theoretical Physics From Ohm to Einstein I-II.
     I: The Torch of Mathematics, 1800-1870.
     II: The Now Mighty Theoretical Physics, 1870-1925.
    Chicago: Univ. of Chicago Press, 1986

Leavenworth, Isabel
    The Physics of Pascal. New York, 1930

Lyle, Emily
    Archaic Cosmos: Polarity, Space and Time.
    Polygon Books, 1990

Maier, Anneliese
    Die Mechanisierung des Weltbildes. Leipzig: 1938
    Das Problem der intensiven Grösse in der Scholastik.
    Leipzig: 1939.
    Die Impetustheorie der Scholastik. Vienna: 1940
    An der Grenze von Scholastik und Naturwissenschaft.
    Essen: 1943
    Die Vorläufer Galileis im 14. Jahrhundert: Studien zur
    Naturphilosophie der Spätscholastik.
    Rome: Ed. di 'storia e letteratura', 1949
    Die scholastische Wesensbestimmung der Bewegung als
    forma fluens oder fluxus formae und ihre Beziehung zu
    Albertus Magnus, Angelicum XXI (1946). Trans. as:
    On the Threshold of Exact Science (ed. Steven D. Sargent).
    Philadelphia: Univ. of Pennsylvania Press, 1982
    Scienza e filosofia nel medioevo.
    Milan: Jaca, 1984

Nersessian, Nancy
   Faraday to Einstein -
   Constructing Meaning in Scientific Theories.
   Dordrecht: Nijhoff, 1984
Ströker, Elisabeth
   Theoriewandel in der Wissenschaftsgeschichte: Chemie im 18.
   Jahrhundert Frankfurt a.M.: Klostermann, 1982
Tonnelat, Marie-Antoinette
   Histoire du principe de relativité.
   Paris: Nouvelle Bibliothèque Scientifique, 1971

B5.6   **Mathematics** *see also* Hilbert
Eisele, Carolyn
   The New Elements of Mathematics by Charles S. Peirce:
   Mathematical Philosophy. The Hague: Mouton, 1976
   Studies in the Scientific and Mathematical Philosophy
   of Charles S. Peirce: Essays by C. Eisele (ed. R.M. Martin).
   The Hague, etc.: Mouton, 1979
Krämer, Sybille
   Symbolische Machinen:
   Die Idee der Formalisierung in geschichtlichem Abriss
   Darmstadt: Wissenschaftliche Buchgesellschaft, 1988
Michalek, Margarete
   Die Philosophie der Mathematik bei Hume und Kant. Eine
   Erkenntnistheoretische Untersuchung.
   Vienna: diss., 1946
Sachs, Eva
   Die Fünf Platonische Körper:
   Zur Geschichte der mathematische und der Elementenlehre
   Platons und der Pythagoreer. 1917
   Reprinted New York: Arno Press, 1976
Sylla, Edith Dudley
   The Oxford Calculators and the Mathematics of Motion,
   1320-50. Physics and Measurements by Latitudes.
   Cambridge, MA: Harvard Univ., 1970
Wubnig, Judy, Gottfried Martin, and -
   Arithmetik and Combinatorics: Kant and his Contemporaries.
   Carbondale: Southern Illinois Univ. Press, 1985

B6   **Individual Philosophers, Studies of (works by) -**
      see also History of Epistemology; Logic

-Abbagnano, Nicola, 1901-
Dentone, Adriana
   La possibilitá in Nicola Abbagnano. Milan: Marzorati, 1971

-Abelard, Peter, 1079-1142 *see also* Logic, History of; Héloïse

Beonio-Brocchieri, M. Teresa *see also* Fumagalli
Abelardo. Bari: Laterza, 1974

Pernoud, Régine
Héloïse et Abélard. Paris: Éditions Albin Michel, 1981

editions:

Radice, Betty (ed.)
The Letters of Abelard and Heloise.
Middlesex/Baltimore/Victoria, Australia: Penguin, 1974

-Althusser, Louis, 1918- *see also* European Traditions

Assiter, Alison
Althusser and Feminism.
London, etc.: Pluto Press, 1990

Glucksmann, Miriam
Structuralist Analysis in Contemporary Social Thought:
A Comparison of the Theories of Claude Lévi-Strauss and
Louis Althusser.
London: Routledge and Kegan Paul, 1974

-Ambrose of Milan, 340(?)-397

Subrero, Margherita Oberti
L'etica sociale di Ambrogio di Milano.
Turin: Asteria, 1970

-Anselm, St., 1033-1109

Evans, Gillian R.
Anselm and Talking About God. Oxford: Clarendon, 1978
Anselm and a New Generation. Oxford: Clarendon, 1980

-Arendt, Hannah, 1906-1975

Arendt, Hannah et al.
Hannah Arendt. Brussels: Édition Ousia, 1985

Barnouw, Dagmar
Visible Spaces. Hannah Arendt anad the German-Jewish
Experience. Baltimore: John Hopkins Univ. Press, 1990

Bowen-Moore, Patricia
Hannah Arendt's Philosophy of Natality.
London: Macmillan, 1989

Bradshaw, Leah
Acting and Thinking: The Political Thought of Hannah Arendt.
Cheektowaga, NY: Univ. of Toronto Press, 1989

Canovan, Margaret
The Political Thought of Hannah Arendt.
London: Methuen, 1977

Young-Bruehl, Elizabeth
    Hannah Arendt: For Love of the World.
    New Haven, CT: Yale Univ. Press, 1982

collections:
Kaplan, Gisela T., and Clive S. Kessler (eds.)
    Hannah Arendt. Thinking, Judging, Freedom.
    London: Allen & Unwin/Sydney: Unwin and Hyman, 1989

-Aristotle, 384-322 B.C.
    see also Classical Philosophy; Ethics and Morality,
    History of -; Logic, History of -; Plato

-General
Grene, Marjorie
    A Portrait of Aristotle.
    Chicago: Univ. of Chicago Press, 1979
Hamesse, Jacqueline
    Les Auctoritates Aristotelis: Un florilège medieval.
    Louvain: Presses Universitaires, 1974
Rousseau, Mary F.
    The Apple or Aristotle's Death.
    Milwaukee: Marquette Univ. Press, 1969
Schüssler, Ingeborg
    Aristoteles: Philosophie und Wissenschaft.
    Frankfurt: Klostermann, 1982

-Ethics and Politics
Bridie, Sarah
    Ethics With Aristotle.
    Oxford and New York: Oxford Univ. Press, 1990
Heller, Agnes
    Die Ethik des Aristoteles. 1954
    Az aristotelési etika es az antik ethos. Budapest: Kiado, 1966

collections:
Nussbaum, Martha
    Politieke dieren: Aristoteles over de natuur en het
    menselijk bedrijf. (Pierre Bayle-Lecture 1990).
    Baarn: Anthos, 1990
Rorty, Amelie Oksenberg (ed.)
    Essays on Aristotle's Ethics.
    Los Angeles: Univ. of California Press, 1980
Sherman, Nancy
    The Fabric of Character: Aristotle's Theory of Virtue
    Oxford: Clarendon Press, 1989

-**Logic** *see* History of Logic

-**Metaphysics**
Annas, Julia
   Aristotle: Metaphysics, Books M and N (trans.).
   New York: Clarendon Press, 1976. Paper, 1988
Gill, Mary Louise
   Aristotle on Substance. The Paradox of Unity.
   Princeton, NJ: Princeton Univ. Press, 1989
Witt, Charlotte
   Substance and Essence in Aristotle - An Interpretation
   of Metaphysics VII-IX.
   Cornell Univ. Press, 1989

-**Causality and Nature**
Modrak, Deborah K.W.
   Aristotle: The Power of Perception.
   Chicago: Univ. of Chicago Press, 1987
Nussbaum, Martha (ed., trans.)
   Aristotle's "De motu animalium"
   (text with transl.).
   Princeton, NJ: Princeton Univ. Press, 1978
Waterlow, Sarah
   Nature, Change, and Agency in Aristotle's Physics.
   Oxford: Clarendon Press, 1982
Weiss, Helene
   Kausalität und Zufall in der Philosophie des
   Aristoteles. Basel, 1942

-**Astell, Mary, 1666-1731**
Perry, Ruth
   The Celebrated Mary Astell.
   Chicago: Univ. of Chicago Press, 1986
Smith, Florence M.
   Mary Astell.
   New York: Columbia Univ. Press, 1916

-**Augustine, St., 354-430** *see also* Anthropology, History of
   Philosophical -; Rousseau
Arendt, Hannah
   Der Liebesbegriff bei Augustin:
   Versuch einer philosophischen Interpretation.
   Berlin: Julius Springer, 1929
Bogan, Sr Mary Inez (trans.)
   Saint Augustine: The Retractations.
   Washington, DC: Catholic Univ. of America Press, 1968

Peitschach, Elisabeth
  Augustins Soliloquien, Descartes Meditationen. Ein
  Vergleichender Beitrage zur Metaphysik.
  Vienna: diss., 1944
Wolfskeel, C.W.
  De immortalitate animae - Een behandeling van één van
  de vroege geschriften van Augustinus.
  Utrecht: Utrecht Univ., 1973
  De Immortalitate animae
  (English trans. of (1973)).
  Amsterdam: Grüner, 1977.

-Bachelard, Gaston, 1884-1962

Jones, Mary McAuester
  Gaston Bachelard: Subversive Humanist.
  Madison: Univ. of Wisconsin Press, 1990
Tiles, Mary
  Bachelard: Science and Objectivity.
  Cambridge: Cambridge Univ. Press, 1984

-Bacon, Francis, 1561-1626 *see also* Logic, History of

Paterson, Anoinette Mann
  Francis Bacon and Socialized Science.
  Springfield, IL: Thomas, 1974

-Bakhtin, Mikhail M., 1895-1975

Clark, Katerina, and Michael Holquist
  Mikhail Bakhtin. Cambridge, MA: Harvard Univ. Press, 1988

-Ban Zhao, c. 45 - c. 115

Swann, N.L. (Nancy Lee)
  Pan Chao, Foremost Woman Scholar of China, First
  Century AD. Background, Ancestry, Life and Writings of
  the Most Celebrated Chinese Woman of Letters.
  New York/London, diss., 1932

-Barthes, Roland, 1915-1980

Lavers, Annette
  Roland Barthes: Structuralism and After.
  London: Methuen, 1982

-Baumgarten, Alexander Gottlieb, 1714-1762

Franke, Ursula
  Kunst als Erkenntnis: Die Rolle der Sinnlichkeit in der
  Ästhetik des Alexander Gottlieb Baumgarten.
  Wiesbaden: Steiner, 1972

-Bayle, Pierre, 1647-1708

Labrousse, Elizabeth
> Pierre Bayle, I-II. The Hague: Nijhoff, 1963-64
> Bayle (trans. Denys Potts). New York: Oxford Univ. Press, 1983

-Beattie, James, 1735-1803

Forbes, Margaret
> Beattie and His Friends.
> London, 1904. Reprinted, Altrincham: J. M. Stafford, 1990

-Beauvoir, Simone de, 1908-1986

Appignanesi, Lisa
> Simone de Beauvoir (1908-1986).
> New York: Viking Penguin, 1988

Ascher, Carol
> Simone de Beauvoir: A Life of Freedom.
> Brighton: Harvester, 1981

Beauvoir, Hélène de
> Souvenirs. Receuillis par Marcelle Routier
> Paris: Séguier, 1987

Cayron, Claire
> La nature chez Simone de Beauvoir.
> Paris: Gallimard, 1973

Craig, Carol
> Simone de Beauvoir's The Second Sex in the Light of the
> Hegelian Master-Slave Dialectic and Sartrian Existentialism.
> Edinburgh: diss., 1979

Descubes, Madeleine
> Connaître Simone de Beauvoir. Paris, 1974

d'Eaubonne, Françoise
> Une Femme Nommée Castor mon amie Simone de Beauvoir.
> Paris: Encre, 1986

Evans, Mary
> Simone de Beauvoir - A Feminist Mandarin.
> Brighton: Harvester/London, Tavistock, 1981

Francis, Claude, and Fernande Gontier
> Les écrits de Simone de Beauvoir. La vie - l'écriture,
> avec en appendice textes inédits ou rétrouvés.
> Paris: Gallimard, 1979
> Simone de Beauvoir. Paris: Gallimard, 1985

Gennari, Geneviève
> Simone de Beauvoir.
> Paris: Éditions Universitaires, 1959
> Simone de Beauvoir (Dutch trans. and introduction by M. H.
> Mout-van Tooren). The Hague: Kruseman, 1960

Heath, Jane
    Simone de Beauvoir. London: Harvester Wheatsheaf, 1989
Lasocki, Anne-Marie
    Simone de Beauvoir ou l'entreprise d'écrire.
    The Hague: Nijhoff, 1971
Leighton, Jean
    Simone de Beauvoir on Woman. Rutherford, 1975
Lilar, Suzanne
    Le malentendu du Deuxième sexe. Paris: P.U.F., 1969
Marks, Elaine
    Simone de Beauvoir: Encounters with Death.
    New Brunswick, 1973
Moi, Toril
    Feminist Theory and Simone de Beauvoir.
    Oxford/Cambridge, MA: Blackwell, 1989
Moubachir, Chantal
    Simone de Beauvoir ou Le souci de la différence.
    Paris, 1972
Okely, Judith
    Simone de Beauvoir, A Re-Reading.
    London: Virago, 1986
Ross, Betty W.
    Simone de Beauvoir's Idea of Transcendence and its
    Applicability to Women who Work as Nurses.
Sætre, Solveig
    Kvinnen - det annet kjönn?
    En studie i Simone de Beauvoirs filosofi.
    Oslo: Gyldendal Norsk Forlag, 1969
Schwarzer, Alice
    Simone de Beauvoir heute.
    Reinbeck bei Hamburg: Rowohlt, 1983
    Simone de Beauvoir aujourd'hui. Six entretiens
    (trans. from German). Paris: Mercure de France, 1984
Simons, Margaret Ann
    A Phenomenology of Oppression: A Critical Introduction
    to 'Le Dexième Sexe' by Simone de Beauvoir.
    Lafayette, IN: Purdue Univ., 1977
Wagner, Cornelia
    Simone de Beauvoirs Weg zum Feminismus. Zur Wandlung
    und narrativen Umsetzung ihres Emanzipationskonzepts.
    Rheinfelden: diss., 1984
Whitmarsh, Anne
    Simone de Beauvoir and the Limits of Commitment.
    Cambridge: Cambridge Univ. Press, 1981

Willems, G.
Simone de Beauvoir - Ontmoetingen. Bruges, 1972
Winegarten, Renée
Simone de Beauvoir. A Critical View.
Oxford, etc.: Berg Women's Series, 1988

film:
Dayan, Josée, and Malka Ribowska
Simone de Beauvoir. Paris, 1979

collections:
Schwarzer, Alice
Gesprekken met Simone de Beauvoir: uit een periode van 10 jaar
1972/1982 (Dutch trans. from German). Amsterdam, 1983
Wenzel, Hélène Vivienne (ed.)
Simone de Beauvoir: Witness to a Century.
New Haven, CT: Yale French Studies, No. 72, 1986

-Beecher, Catharine Ward, 1800-1878

Sklar, Kathryn Kisch
Catharine Beecher: A Study in American Domesticity.
New Haven, CT and London: Yale Univ. Press, 1973

-Benjamin, Walter, 1892-1940

Arendt, Hannah
Walter Benjamin; Bertolt Brecht: zwei Essays.
Munich: Piper, 1971
Buci-Glucksmann, Christine
Walter Benjamin und die Utopie des Weiblichen.
Hamburg, 1984
Buck-Morse, Susan
The Dialectics of Seeing: Walter Benjamin and the
Arcades Project. Cambridge, MA: MIT Press, c. 1989
Wiesenthal, Liselotte
Zur Wissenschaftstheorie Walter Benjamins.
Frankfurt: Athenäum, 1973

-Bentham, Jeremy, 1748-1832 *see also* Law, Philosophy of -

Boralevi, Lea Campos
Bentham and the Oppressed. Berlin: Walter de Gruyter, 1984

-Bergson, Henri, 1859-1941

Austermann, Maria
Die Entwicklung der ethischen und religions-
philosophischen Gedanken bei Henri Bergson.
Frankfurt a.M.: R.G. Fischer, 1981 (1968)

Barthélémy-Madaule, Madeleine
    Bergson. Paris: P.U.F., 1967
Gallagher, Idella J.
    Morality in Evolution: The Moral Philosophy of Henri Bergson.
    The Hague: Nijhoff, 1971
Hoffmann, Margarete
    Bergsons Intuitives Erkennen. Vienna: diss., 1923
Kennedy, Ellen
    Freedom and the Open Society.
    New York: Garland Publishers, 1987

-Berkeley, George, 1685-1753

Atherton, Margaret
    Berkeley's Revolution in Vision.
    Ithaca, NY: Cornell Univ. Press, 1990
Brykman, Geneviève
    Berkeley: Philosophie et apologetique.
    Paris: Vrin, 1984
Park, Désirée
    Complementary Notions: A Critical Study of Berkeley's
    Theory of Concepts. The Hague: Nijhoff, 1972
    The Notebooks of George Berkeley, Bishop of Cloyne, 1658-1753.
    Oxford: Alden Press, 1984

-Bernstein, Eduard, 1850-1932

Huygens, Cornélie
    Darwin-Marx. Bernstein als bestrijder van eene natuur-
    philosophische leer. Amsterdam, 1901

-Birgitta of Sweden, 1302-1373

Adelsten, Karola
    Licht aus dem Norden.
    Freiburg im Bresgau
    Germany: Lambertus Verlag, 1951

-Blackwell, Antoinette Louisa Brown, 1825-1921

Cazden, Elizabeth
    Antoinette Brown Blackwell. A Biography.
    Old Westbury, NY: The Feminist Press, 1983

-Bloch, Ernst, 1885-1977

Asperen, G. M. van
    Hope and History: A Critical Inquiry Into the
    Philosophy of Ernst Bloch.
    Utrecht: Utrecht Univ., diss., 1973

-Boethius, Anicius Manlius Severinus, c.480-524

Stump, Eleonore (trans., with notes and essays on the text)
  Boethius's De topicis differentiis.
  Ithaca, NY: Cornell Univ. Press, 1978

-Bolzano, Bernard, 1781-1848

Bodnar, Joanne
  Bolzano and Husserl: Logic and Phenomenology.
  Buffalo, NY: State Univ. of New York, diss., 1976
Neemann, Ursula
  Bernard Bolzanos Lehre von Anschauung und Begriff.
  Paderborn: Schönigh, 1972

-Bonaventure, St. (Giovanni di Fidanza), 1221-1274

Healy, Emma Theresa
  Woman According to St. Bonaventura.
  Erie, PA: 1956
Wiegels, Margot
  Die Logik der Spontaneität: Zum Gedanken der Schöpfung
  bei Bonaventura. Freiburg: Alber, 1969

-Bonnevie, Margarete, 1884-1970

Cf. Ottesen, Clara; in: Schröder (ed.), 1988

-Bosanquet, Bernard, 1848-1923

Bosanquet, Helen
  Bernard Bosanquet - A Short Account of His Life.
  1924. To be reissued

-Boulainvillier, Henry de, 1658-1722

Simon, Renée
  Henry de Boulainvillier. The Hague: Nijhoff, 1973

-Brentano, Franz von 1838-1917

Mayer-Hillebrand, Franziska
  (editions of works by Brentano)
McAlister, Linda
  The Development of Franz von Brentano's Ethics.
  Atlantic Highlands, NJ: Humanities Press, 1982

-Bridgman, Percy Williams, 1882-1961

Walter, Maila L.
  Science and Cultural Crisis: An Intellectual Biography
  of Percy William Bridgman (1882-1961).
  Stanford, CA: Stanford Univ. Press, c. 1990

-Bruggen, Carry van, 1881-1932

Jacobs, M.A.
C. van Bruggen, haar leven en literair werk.
Gent: Secretarie der Academie, 1962

Wolf, Ruth
Van alles het middelpunt.
Amsterdam: Querido, 1980

-Bruno, Giordano, 1548-1600

see also Renaissance; Philosophical Traditions

Paterson, Antoinette Mann
The Infinite Worlds of Giordano Bruno.
Springfield, IL: Thomas, 1970

Vedrine, Hélène
La conception de la nature chez Giordano Bruno.
Paris: Vrin, 1967

-Buber, Martin, 1878-1965

Schaeder, Grete
The Hebrew Humanism of Martin Buber. (Trans. N. J. Jacobs.)
Detroit: Wayne State Univ. Press, 1973

Sutter, Gerda
Wirklichkeit als Verhältniss: Der dialogische Austeig
bei Martin Buber. Munich: Pustet, 1972

Vermes, Pamela
Buber on God and the Perfect Man.
Decatur, GA: Scholars Press, 1981

-Buchler, Justus, 1914-1991

Singer, Beth J.
Ordinal Naturalism -
An Introduction to the Philosophy of Justus Buchler.
Lewisburg, PA: Bucknell Univ. Press, 1983

-Campanella, Tommaso, 1568-1639

Bock, Gisela
Thomas Campanella: Politisches Interesse und
philosophische Spekulation.
Tübingen: Niemeyer, 1974

-Camus, Albert, 1913-1960

Pieper, Annemarie
Albert Camus. Munich: Beck, 1984

Schaub, Karin
Albert Camus und der Tod. Basel: Edito Academica, 1968

-Carnap, Rudolf

Janovskaja, Sof'ja Aleksandrovna (ed.)
R. Karnap: Znâcenie i neobchodimost'.
Issledovanie po semantike i modal' - noj logike.
[Per. s anglijskogo N.V. Vorob'eva.
R.D.A. Bôcvar. Pred. S.A. Janovskaja].
Moskva:Izd. inostrannoj literatury, 1959

-Catherine of Siena (Caterina Benincasa), 1347-1380

Curtayne, Alice
St. Catherine of Siena. New York: Macmillan, 1930

Drane, Augusta Theodosia
The History of St. Catherine of Siena and Her Companions
London, 1880, 1890

Mignaty, Margarita Albana
Caterina de Siena e la parte che ebbe negli avvenimenti
d'Italia nel secolo XIV. Firenze, 1844

Seckendorf, Eleonore von
Die Kirchenpolitische Tätigkeit der heiligen Katharina
von Siena unter Papst Gregor XI. Berlin, 1917

-Châtelet, Marquise du, (Gabrielle Emilie le Tonnelier de Breteuil) 1706-1749 *see also* Empirical Sciences: Physical Sciences; Newton

Ehrman, Esther
Madame du Châtelet: Scientist, Philosopher and Feminist of the
Enlightenment. Oxford: Berg Publishers, 1986

editions:
Lettres inédites de Madame la Marquise Du Châtelet á M.
le Comte D'Argental. Paris, 1806

Wade, Ira O.
Studies on Voltaire With Some Unpublished Papers of Mme
du Châtelet. New York: Russell & Russell, 1947

-Cicero, 106-43 B.C.

Foà, Virginia Guazzoni
I fondamenti filosofici della teologia ciceroniana.
Milan: Marzorati, 1970

-Comte, Auguste, 1798-1857 *see also* Michelet

Kofman, Sarah
Aberrations: Le devenir-femme d'Auguste Comte.
Paris: Flammarion, 1978

Martineau, Harriet
Positive Philosophy of Auguste Comte.
New York and London, 1858

-Condillac, Etienne Bonot de (Abbé de Condillac), 1715-1780

Knight, Isabel F.
>The Geometric Spirit: The abbé de Condillac and the
>French Enlightenment.
>New Haven, CT: Yale Univ. Press, 1968

collections:

Chouillet, Anne-Marie (ed.)
>Condillac: La langue des calculs.
>Lille: Presses Univ. de Lille, 1981

-Condorcet, Marie-Jean A.N.C., Marquis de, 1743-1794

collections:

Rosenfield, Leonora Cohen (ed.)
>Condorcet Studies I.
>Atlantic Highlands, NJ: Humanities Press, 1984

-Croce, Benedetto, 1866-1952

Lamanna, E. Paola
>Introduzione alla lettura di Croce.
>Florence: Le Monnier, 1969

-Cruz, Sor Juana Inés de la, 1648-1695

Arroyo, Anita
>Razón y pasión de Sor Juana.
>Mexico City: Porrua, 1971

Perez, Maria Esther
>Lo americano en el teatro de Sor Juana inés de la Cruz.
>Eastchester, NY: Eliseo Torres, 1975

Sabat de Rivera, Georgina
>El Sueño de Sor Juana Inés de la Cruz: tradiçiones
>literarias y originalidad. London: Tamesis, 1976

Schons, Dorothy
>Bibliografía de Sor Juana Inés de la Cruz.
>Bibliográficas Méxicanas, Monograph 7. x
>Mexico City: Seria de Relaçciones Exteriores, 1927

Zamora Pallares, Dionisia
>Sor Juana Inés de la Cruz y la educacion de la mujer.
>Mexico City: Seminaria de Cultura Mexicana, 1963

-Darwin, Charles, 1809-1882 *see also* Modern and Contemporary
Philosophy; Empirical Sciences: Biology and Medicine;
Bernstein

Beer, Gillian
>Darwin's Plots.
>London: Routledge, 1983

Bulhof, Ilse Nina
Darwins Origin of Species: Betoverende Wetenschap -
een onderzoek naar de relatie tussen literatuur en
wetenschap. Baarn: Ambo, 1988
Himmelfarb, Gertrude
Darwin and the Darwinian Revolution. London, 1959

-Derrida, Jacques, 1930-
Kofman, Sarah
Lectures de Derrida. Paris: Galilée, 1984

-Descartes, René, 1596-1650
see also Epistemology and History of -
Behn, Irene
Der Philosoph und die Königin - Renatus Descartes und
Christina Wasa. Briefwechsel und Begegnung.
Freiburg and Munich: Alber, 1957
Grene, Marjorie
Descartes. Brighton: Harvester Press, 1985
Judovitz, Dalia
Subjectivity and Representation in Descartes -
The Origins of Modernity.
Cambridge: Cambridge Univ. Press, 1988
Rodis-Lewis, Geneviève
L'ordre chronologique, l'ordre des raisons, leur interaction
ou "L'oeuvre de Descartes."
Paris: Vrin, 1971
Descartes. Paris: Hachette, 1984
Romanowski, Sylvie
L'illusion chez Descartes: La structure du discours
cartésien. Paris: Klinksieck, 1974
Rorty, Amélie Oksenberg (ed.)
Essays on Descartes' "Meditations."
Berkeley: Univ. of California Press, 1986
Wilson, Margaret Dauler
Descartes.
London: Routledge & Kegan Paul, 1978

-Dewey, John, 1859-1952
Boydston, Jo Ann (ed.)
The Poems of John Dewey.
Carbondale: Southern Illinois Press, 1977
John Dewey: The Middle Works, 1899-1924 (Vol. 3, 4).
John Dewey: The Middle Works, 1899-1924 (Vol. 6).
John Dewey: The Later Works, 1925-1953 (Vol. 1-7).
Carbondale: Southern Illinois Press, 1978-1985

-Diderot, Denis, 1713-1784

Blum, Carol
Diderot: The Virtue of a Philosopher.
New York: Viking Press, 1974

-Dilthey, Wilhelm, 1833-1911

Bulhof, Ilse N.
Wilhelm Dilthey: A Hermeneutic Approach to the Study of
History and Culture. The Hague, etc.: Nijhoff, 1980

Kremer-Marietti, Angele
Wilhelm Dilthey et l'anthropologie historique.
Paris: Seghers, 1971

Schultz, Christa
Welt und Wissenschaft des jungen Dilthey.
Vienna: diss., 1947

Wassiliko, Theophila
Wilhelm Dilthey als Geschichtsphilosoph.
Vienna: diss., 1933

-Eckhart, Johannes (Meister Eckhart), 1260-1327/1328

Degenhart, Ingeborg
Studien zum Wandel des Eckhartbildes.
Leiden: Brill, 1967

-Eliot, George, (Mary Ann Evans), 1819-1880

Atkins, Dorothy
George Eliot and Spinoza. Salzburg: Univ. Salzburg,
Institut für Englische Sprache und Literatur, 1978

Guidacci, Margherita
Studi su Eliot. Milan: Inst. Propag. Libraria, 1975

Uglow, Jennifer
George Eliot.
New York: Pantheon, 1987

-Empedocles, 5th cent. B.C.

Millerd, Clara Elizabeth
On the Interpretation of Empedocles.
Chicago: Univ of Chicago Press, 1901;
New York: Garland Publishers, 1980

-Engels, Friedrich, 1820-1895 *see also* Kant

Fiorani, Eleonora
Friedrich Engels e il materialismo dialettico.
Milan: Feltrinelli, 1971
Engels Revisited. New Feminist Essays.
London and New York: Tavistock, 1987

-Epicurus, 342-270 B.C.

Asmis, Elizabeth
    Epicurus' Scientific Method.
    Ithaca, NY: Cornell Univ. Press, 1984
Rodis-Lewis, Geneviève
    Epicure et son école. Paris: Gallimard, 1975

-Erasmus, Desiderius, 1467-1536

Phillips, Margaret Mann
    Erasmus and the Northern Renaissance.
    Totowa, NJ: Rowman & Littlefield, 1981
Thompson, Sister Geraldine
    Under Pretext of Praise: Satiric Mode in Erasmus
    Fiction. Toronto: Univ. of Toronto Press, 1973

translations:

Roper, Margaret More
    Treatise Upon the Pater Noster by Erasmus. 16th cent.

editions:

Grimm, Laura (ed.)
    Erasmus Roterodamus: Fortrolige samtaler (i utvalg)
    (Norwegian trans. E. Grimm). Oslo: Aschehoug with
    Thorleif Dahls Kulturbibliotek, 1983
Reeve, Anne (ed.)
    Erasmus's Annotations on the New Testament.
    The Gospels: Facsimile of the final Latin Text with
    all earlier versions. London: Duckworth, 1989
Rummel, Erika (ed.)
    The Erasmus Reader.
    Toronto, etc.: Univ. of Toronto Press, 1990

-Farabi, al, c. 873-950

Galston, Miriam
    Politics and Excellence. The Political Philosophy of
    Alfarabi. Princeton, NJ: Princeton Univ. Press

-Ferrari, Giuseppe, 1812-1876

Ghibaudi, Silvia Rota
    Giuseppe Ferrari: L'evoluzione del suo pensiero.
    Florence: Olschki, 1969

-Feuerbach, Ludwig Andreas, 1804-1872

Debus, Ilse
    Individuum und Gattung. Die Frau im Denken Feuerbachs.
    Düsseldorf, 1984

-Fichte, Johann Gottlieb, 1762-1814 *see also* Social Philosophy; Herder
Bäumer, Gertrud
    Fichte und sein Werk. Berlin, 1921
Schröder, Hannelore
    Die Rechtlosigkeit der Frau im Rechtsstaat.
    Frankfurt: Campus, 1975

-Finch (Vicountess Conway), Anne, 1631-1679
Nicolson, Marjorie Hope
    Conway Letters. New Haven, CT: Yale Univ. Press, 1930

-Fontenelle, Bernard le Bovier de, 1657-1757
Marcialis, Maria Teresa
    Fontenelle: Un filosofico mondano.
    Sassari: Galizzi, 1978

-Foucault, Michel, 1926-1984
Guédez, Annie
    Foucault. Paris: Édition Delarge, 1972
Kremer-Marietti, Angèle
    Foucault. Paris: Seghers, 1974
    M. Foucault - der Archäologe des Wissens.
    Frankfurt/Berlin/Vienna, 1976
Major-Poetzl, Pamela
    Michel Foucault's Archaeology of Western Culture.
    Towards a New Science of History.
    Brighton: Harvester/Univ. of North Carolina Press, 1983
O'Farrell, Clare
    Foucault: Historian or Philosopher?
    London: Macmillan, 1989

collections:
Diamond, Irene, and Lee Quinby (eds.)
    Feminism and Foucault - Reflections on Resistance.
    London: Academic & University Publishers Group, 1988

-Frege, Gottlob, 1848-1925
De Monticelli, Roberta
    Dottrine dell'intelligenza. Saggio su Frege e
    Wittgenstein.
    Bari: De Donato, 1982
Egidi, Rosaria
    Ontologia e conoscenza matematica: Un saggio su
    Gottlieb Frege.
    Florence: Sansoni, 1963

Haaparanta, Leila
    Frege's Doctrine of Being.
    Helsinki: Acta Philosophica Fennica, 1985
Weiner, Joan
    Frege in Perspective.
    Ithaca, NY: Cornell Univ. Press, 1990

collections:
Haaparanta, Leila, and Jaakko Hintikka (eds.)
    Frege Synthesized.
    Dordrecht, etc.: Reidel, 1986

-Freud, Sigmund, 1856-1939 *see also* Anthropology; Epistemology,
    History of
Cavé, Madeleine
    L'Oeuvre paradoxale de Freud. Paris: P.U.F., 1945
Kofman, Sarah
    L'enigme de la femme: la femme dans les textes de Freud.
    Paris: Galilée, 1980
    The Enigma of Women: Women in Freud's Writings
    (trans. Catherine Porter).
    Ithaca, NY, etc.: Cornell Univ. Press, 1985
    L'enfance de l'art: une interpretation de l'esthetique
    freudienne. Paris: Galilée, 1985
    Pourquoi rit-on?. Freud et le mot d'esprit.
    Paris: Galilée, 1986
Krüll, Marianne
    Freud und sein Vater. Die Entstehung der Psychoanalyse
    und Freuds ungelöste Vaterbindung.
    Munich: Beck, 1979
Schlesinger, Renate
    Konstruktionen der Weiblichkeit bei S. Freud:
    zum Problem von Entmythologisierung und
    Remythologisierung in der psychoanalytischen Theorie.
    Frankfurt a. M.: Europäische Verlagsanstalt, 1981
Seifert, Edith
    Was will das Weib? Zu Begehren und Lust bei Freud und Lacan.
    Weinheim/Berlin: Quadriga, 1987

-Fry, Roger Eliot, 1866-1934
Falkenheim, Jacqueline V.
    Roger Fry and the Beginnings of Formalist Art Criticism.
    Ann Arbor, MI: UMI Research Press, 1980

Spalding, Frances
> Roger Fry: Art and Life.
> Herts: Granada, 1980

Woolf, Virginia
> Roger Fry. A Biography.
> London, 1969

-Fuller, (Sarah) Margaret, Marchioness Ossoli, 1810-1850

Blanchard, Paula
> Margaret Fuller: From Transcendentalism to Revolution.
> Reading, MA: Addison-Wesley, 1987

Chevigny, Bell Gale
> The Woman and the Myth: Margaret Fuller's Life and
> Writings. Bloomington: Indiana Univ. Press, 1987 or earlier

Copperfield, Faith
> In Quest of Love: The Life and Death of Margaret Fuller. 1957

Stern, Madeleine B.
> The Life of Margaret Fuller, 1942

Wade, Mason
> Margaret Fuller: Whetstone of a Genius, 1940

-Gadamer, Hans-Georg, 1900-

collections:

Wright, Kathleen (ed.)
> Festivals of Interpretation: Essays on Hans-Georg
> Gadamer's Work.
> Ithaca, NY: State Univ. of New York Press, 1990

-Gandhi, Mahatma Karamtsjandra, 1869-1948

Chatterjee, Margaret
> Gandhi's Religious Thought. London: Macmillan, 1983

Richards, Glyn
> The Philosophy of Gandhi: A Study of His Basic Ideas.
> New York: Barnes & Noble, 1982

-Gassendi, Pierre, 1592-1655

Joy, Lynn S.
> Gassendi the Atomist - Advocate of History in an Age of Science.
> Cambridge: Cambridge Univ. Press, 1988

-Genovesi, Antonio, 1712-1769

Zambelli, Paola
> La formazione filosofica di Antonio Genovesi.
> Napels: Morano, 1972

-Goldman, Lucien, 1913-1970

Evans, Mary
    Lucien Goldman: An Introduction.
    Atlantic Highlands, NJ: Humanities Press, 1981

-Gournay, Marie le Jars de, 1565-1645

Holmes, Peggy Preston
    The Life and Literary Works of Marie de Jars de Gournay.
    London: Univ. of London, diss., 1952
Ilsley, Marjorie Henry
    A Daughter of the Renaissance: Marie le Jars de
    Gournay. Her Life and Works. The Hague: Mouton, 1963
Schiff, Mario
    La Fille d'Alliance de Montaigne: Marie de Gournay
    (with reprints of her works). Paris: Honoré Champion, 1910

-Gramsci, Antonio, 1891-1937

Buci-Glucksmann, Christine
    Gramsci e lo stato. Rome: Riuniti, 1976
    Gramsci and the State.
    London: Lawrence and Wishart, 1980
Macciocchi, Maria Antonietta
    Per Gramsci. Bologna: Il Mulino, 1974
Williams, Gwyn A.
    Proletarian Order: Antonio Gramsci, Factory Councils
    and the Origins of Communism in Italy, 1911-1921.
    London: Pluto, 1975

-Green, Thomas Hill, 1836-1882

Cacoullos, Ann R.
    Thomas Hill Green: Philosopher of Rights.
    New York: Twayne, 1974

-Gregory of Nazianzus, c. 329-c. 389

Radford-Ruether, Rosemary
    Gregory of Nazianzus: Rhetor and Philosopher.
    Oxford: Clarendon Press, 1969

-Halévy, Elie, 1870-1937

Bramsen, Michèle Bo
    Portrait d'Elie Halévy.
    Amsterdam: B.R. Grüner, 1978
Chase, Myrna
    Elie Halévy: An Intellectual Biography.
    New York: Columbia Univ. Press, 1980

-Hamann, Johann Georg, 1730-1788

Piske, Irmgard
Offenbarung und Sprache. Zur Auseinandersetzung
Hamanns mit Kant.
Frankfurt am Main, etc.: Peter Lang, 1989

-Hamilton, Edith, c. 1865-1963

Reid, D.
Edith Hamilton: an Intimate Portrait. 1967

-Hartmann, Nicolai, 1882-1950

Cadwallader, Eva Hauel
Searchlight on Values -
Nicolai Hartmann's Twentieth-century Value Platonism.
Lanham, MD: Univ. Press of America, 1985

-Hegel, Georg Wilhelm Friedrich, 1770-1831 *see also* de Beauvoir;
Kant; Logic, History of; Ethics and Morality, History of;
Modern and Contemporary Philosophy

Aamodt Sveen, Sissel
Frihet og familie. En analyse av Hegels familiefilosofi.
Bergen: Filosofisk Institutt, 1983

Abbiero, Marcella d'
"Alienazione" in Hegel. Rome: Ateneo, 1970

Cavarero, Adriana
L'interpretazione hegeliana di Parmenide. Trento: Verifiche, 1984

Cordua, Carla
Idea y figura: El concepto Hegeliana del arte.
Puerto Rico: Editorial Universitaria, 1979

Görland, Ingtraud
Die Kantkritik des jungen Hegel. Frankfurt: Klostermann, 1966
Die konkrete Freiheit des Individuums bei Hegel und
Sartre. Frankfurt: Klostermann, 1978

Janicaud, Dominique
Hegel et le destin de la Grèce. Paris: Vrin, 1975

Langan, Janine D.
Hegel and Mallarmé. Lanham, MD: Univ. Press of America, 1986

Mercier-Josa, Solange
Pour lire Hegel et Marx. Paris: Sociales, 1980

Motroschilova, N.V. (Nelli Vasilevna)
Put Gegeliu k "Nauke logiki."
Moscow: Idz.vo "Nauke," 1984

Peres, Constanze
Empfindung und Reflexion: Ein Problem des 18.
Jahrhunderts. Hildesheim, etc.: Olms, 1986

Rose, Gillian
Hegel Contra Sociology.
Atlantic Highlands, NJ: Humanities Press, 1981
Schrader-Klebert, Karin
Das Problem des Anfangs in Hegels Philosophie.
Munich: Oldenbourg, 1969
Shklar, Judith N.
Freedom and Independence - A Study of the Political
Ideas of Hegel's Phenomenology of Mind.
New York: Cambridge Univ. Press, 1976

-Heidegger, Martin, 1889-1976 *see also* Ethics and Morality,
History of; Hegel; Nietzsche
Andia, Ysabel de
Présence et eschatologie de Martin Heidegger.
Paris: Univ. de Lille III, 1975
Cavaliere, Renata Viti
Heidegger e la storia della filosofia.
Napels: Giannini, 1979
Cecchi Duso, Gianna de
L'interpretazione Heideggeriana dei presocratici.
Padua: Cedam, 1970
Gethmann-Siefert, Annemarie
Das Verhältniss von Philosophie und Theologie im
Denken Martin Heideggers. Freiburg: Alber, 1974
Görland, Ingtraud
Transzendenz und Selbst: eine Phase in Heideggers Denken.
Frankfurt: Klostermann, 1981
Irigaray, Luce
L'oubli de l'air chez Martin Heidegger.
Paris: Minuit, 1983
Laffoucrière, Odette
Le destin de la pensée et "La mort de Dieu" selon Heidegger.
The Hague: Nijhoff, 1968

-Heloïse, c.1100-?
Charrier, Charlotte
Héloïse dans l'Histoire et dans la Légende.
Paris: Honoré Champion, 1933
Hamilton, Elizabeth
Heloïse.
London: Hodder and Stoughton, 1966
Jeander, Yvette
Héloïse: L'amour et l'absolu.
Lausanne: Éditions Rencontres, 1966

-Henry, Michael, fl. after WWII

Dufour-Kowalska, Gabrielle
Michael Henry, un philosophe de la vie et de la praxis.
Paris: Vrin, 1980
Chicago: Univ. of Chicago Press, 1982

-Herder, Johann Gottfried, 1744-1803

Freisinger, Editha
Die Erweckung des nationalen Gedankens bei den
deutschen idealisten herder und Fichte.
Vienna: diss., 1940

-Hilbert, David, 1862-1943

Reid, Constance
Hilbert.
New York/Heidelberg/Berlin: Springer, 1970

-Hildegard of Bingen, 1098-1179

Flanagan, Sabina
Hildegard of Bingen, 1098-1179 - A Visionary Life.
London: Routledge, 1989

Führkötter, Adelgundis
Hildegard von Bingen. Eine Biographie.
Salzburg: Otto Müller Verlag, 1979

Maurman, B.
Die Himmelrichtungen im Weltbild des Mittelalters.
Hildegard von Bingen, Honorius Augustodunensis und
andere Autoren. Munich: Wilhelm Fink, 1976

Newman, Barbara
Sister of Wisdom: St. Hildegard's Theology of the Feminine.
Berkely: Univ. of California Press, 1987

Schrader, Marianna
Die Herkunft des Hl. Hildegard.
Revised ed. by Adelgundis Führkötter: Quellen u.
Abhandlungen zur mittelrheinischen Kirchengeschichte, vol. 43.
Mainz: Isnard Frank, 1981

Schrader, Marianna, and Adelgundis Führkötter
Die Echtheit des Schrifttums der hl. Hildegard von Bingen.
Cologne and Graz, 1956

Walker-Moskop, Ruth M.
Health and Cosmic Continuity in Hildegard of Bingen.
Austin: Univ. of Texas at Austin, diss., 1984

Widmer, Bertha
Heilsordnung und Zeitgeschehen in der Mystik Hildegards
von Bingen. Basel and Stuttgart, 1955

collections:

Brück, A.P. (ed.)
    Hildegard von Bingen -
    Festschrift zum 800. Todestag der Heiligen
    (Quellen und Abhandlungen zur mittelrheinischen
    Kirchengeschichte 33).
    Mainz: Selbstverlag der Ges. für mittelrheinische
    Kirchengeschichte, 1979

-Hippocrates, 5th cent. B.C.

Duminil, Marie-Paule
    Le sang, les vaisseaux, le coeur dans la collection Hippocratique.
    Paris: Belles, 1983

-Hobbes, Thomas, 1588-1679

Baumgold, Deborah
    Hobbes' Political Theory.
    Cambridge: Cambridge Univ. Press, 1988

Goyard-Fabre, Simone
    Le droit et la loi dans la philosophie de Thomas Hobbes.
    Paris: Klincksieck, 1975

Hampton, Jean
    Hobbes and the Social Contract Tradition.
    Cambridge: Cambridge Univ. Press, 1987; paper, 1988

Macauley-Graham, Catharine Sawbridge
    Loose Remarks on Certain Positions to be found in Mr. Hobbes's
    Philosophical Rudiments of Government and Society, with a
    Short Sketch of a Democratical form of Government in a
    letter to Signior Paoli. London: T. Davies, 1767

Reik, Miriam M.
    The Golden Lands of Thomas Hobbes.
    Detroit: Wayne State Univ. Press, 1977

-Horney, Karen, 1885-1952

Quinn, Susan
    A Mind of Her Own: The Life of Karen Horney.
    Summit Books, 1987; London: Macmillan, 1988

Westkott, Marcia
    The Feminist Legacy of Karen Horney.
    New Haven, CT: Yale Univ. Press, 1989

-Hume, David, 1711-1766 *see also* History of Anthropology; Mathematics

Baier, Annette
    A Progress of Sentiments. Reflections on Hume's Treatise.
    Cambridge, MA: Harvard Univ. Press, 1991

Kydd, Rachael Mary
Reason and Conduct in Hume's Treatise.
London, etc.: Oxford Classical and Philosophical Monographs,
1946. Reprinted, Bristol: Thoemmes Press, 1990
Merleker, Margarete
Humes Begriff der Realität.
Halle: Niemeyer, 1920

-Husserl, Edmund, 1859-1938 *see also* Logic, History of
Bello, Angela Ales
Edmund Husserl e la storia.
Parma: Studium Parmense, 1972
Husserl e le scienze. Rome: Goliarda, 1980
Cunningham, Suzanne
Language and the Phenomenological Reductions of Edmund
Husserl. The Hague: Nijhoff, 1976
Saraiva, Maria Manuela
L'imagination selon Husserl. The Hague: Nijhoff, 1970
Souche-Dagues, Denise
Le développement de l'intentionalité dans la
phénomenologie Husserlienne. The Hague: Nijhoff, 1972
Ströker, Elisabeth
Lebenswelt und Wissenschaft in der Philosophie Edmund
Husserls. Frankfurt: Klostermann, 1979

editions:
Tymieniecka, Anna-Teresa (ed.)
The later Husserl and the Idea of Phenomenology: Idealism-
Realism, Historicity and Nature. Analecta Husserliana 2.
Dordrecht: Reidel, 1972

-Ingarden, Roman, 1893-1970
Tymieniecka, Anna-Teresa (ed.)
Analecta Husserliana IV: Ingardeniana. Dordrecht: Reidel, 1976

-James, William, 1842-1910
Bellatalla, Luciana
Uomo e ragione in William James. Turin: Univ. di Pisa, 1979
Seigfried, Charlene Haddock
Chaos and Content: A Study in William James.
Athens: Ohio Univ. Press, 1978
William James's Radical Reconstruction of Philosophy.
Ithaca, NY: State Univ. of New York Press, 1990
Suckiel, Ellen Kappy
The Pragmatic Philosophy of William James
Notre Dame, IN: Univ. of Notre Dame Press, 1982

-Jaspers, Karl, 1883-1969

Arendt, Hannah (ed.)
    Karl Jaspers. The great Philosophers I-II
    Trans. from German by Ralph Manheim.
    London: Hart-Davis, 1962-1966

Young-Bruehl, Elizabeth
    Freedom and Karl Jaspers' Philosophy.
    New Haven, CT: Yale Univ. Press, 1981

-Jefferson, Thomas, 1743-1826

Koch, Adrienne
    The Philosophy of Thomas Jefferson.
    New York: Columbia Univ. Press, 1943
    Jefferson and Madison: The Great Collaboration.
    New York: Gallaxy Book, 1964

-Jung, Carl Gustav, 1875-1961

Franz, Marie-Louise von
    Jung's Typology. Zürich, 1971

collections:

Laszlo, Violet de (ed., with an introduction)
    The Basic Writings of C.G. Jung.
    Princeton, NJ: Princeton Univ. Press, 1990?

Lauter, Estella and Carol Schreier Ruprecht (eds.)
    Feminist Archetypal Theory:
    Interdisciplinary Revisions of Jungian Thought.
    Knoxville: Univ. of Tennessee Press, 1985

-Kant, Immanuel, 1724-1804 *see also* Aesthetics; History of:
    Epistemology; Logic; Mathematics; Political Philosophy

Arendt, Hannah
    Lectures on Kant's Political Philosophy
    (Trans. R. Breiner.). Chicago: Univ. of Chicago Press, 1982

Bertoni, Enrica
    Kant. Florence: Vallecchi, 1974

Buroker, Jill Vance
    Space and Incongruence: The Origins of Kant's Idealism.
    Dordrecht: Reidel, 1981

Falkenburg, Brigitte
    Die Form der Materie. Zur Metaphysik der Natur bei
    Kant und Hegel. Frankfurt a.M.: Athenäum, 1987 (1985)

Ginsberg, Hannah
    The Role of Taste in Kant's Theory of Cognition.
    New York: Garland Publishers, 1990 (diss. ,1988)

Goyard-Fabre, Simone
    Kant et le problème du droit. Paris: Vrin, 1975
Herman, Barbara
    Morality as Rationality. A Study of Kant's Ethics.
    New York: Garland Publishers, 1990 (diss., 1976)
Jauch, Ursula Pia
    Immanuel Kant zur Geschlechtsdifferenz:
    Aufklärerische Vorurteilskritik und bürgerliche
    Geschlechtsvormundschaft. Vienna: Passagen Verlag, 1988
Kitcher, Patricia
    Kant's Transcendental Psychology.
    Oxford and New York: Oxford Univ. Press, 1990
Klinger, Cornelia
    Die politische Funktion der transcendentalphilosophischen
    Theorie der Freiheit:
    Sinn und Grenzen der Hegelschen Kritik der
    Freiheitstheorie Kants. Cologne: diss., 1981
Korsgaard, Christine Marion
    The Standpoint of Practical Reason.
    New York: Garland Publishers, 1990 (diss., 1981)
Krobath, Elisabeth
    Das Problem der Affinität bei Kant und im deutschen
    Idealismus. Vienna: diss., 1934
Lamacchia, Ada
    La filosofia della religione in Kant.
    Vol. I: Dal dogmatismo teologico al teismo morale.
    Manduria: Lacaita, 1969
Laurentiis, Alegra de
    Marx's und Engels' Rezeption der Hegelschen Kantkritik.
    Frankfurt: Lang, 1983
McCloskey, Mary
    Kant's Aesthetic. London: Macmillan, 1987
Meld, Susan Shell see Shell
Mertens, Helga
    Kommentar zur ersten Einleitung in Kants Kritik der
    Urteilskraft. Munich: Berchmanskolleg, 1973
Nerheim, Hjördis
    Estetisk rasjonalitet: en analyse av konstitusjons-
    begrepet i Kants "Kritik der ästhetischen Urteilskraft."
    Oslo: H. Nerheim, 1985 (diss., Univ. Oslo, 1986)
O'Neill, Onora
    Acting on Principle: An Essay in Kantian Ethics.
    New York: Columbia Univ. Press, 1975
    Constructions of Reason: Exploration of Kant's
    Practical Philosophy. Oxford: Blackwell, 1990

Orts, Adela Cortina
Dios en la filosofia trascendental de Kant.
Salamanca: Univ. Pontificia, 1981

Pagano, Giacoma M.
La teoria del giudizio in Kant.
Napels: La Nuova Cultura, 1976

Palumbo, Margherita
Immaginazione e matematica in Kant.
Laterza: Rome/Bari, 1985

Panova, Elena
Kant i analitichnata metafizika
Sofia: idz-vo na Bulgarskata akademiia na naukite, 1986.

Rovighi, Sofia Vanni
Introduzione allo studio di Kant.
Brescia: La Scuola Ed., 1968

Shaw, Gisela
Das Problem des Dinges an Sich in der Englischen Kant-
interpretation. Bonn: Bouvier, 1969

Shell, Susan Meld
The Rights of Reason: A Study of Kant's Philosophy and Politics.
Toronto: Univ. of Toronto Press, 1980

Thom, Martina
Immanuel Kant. Leipzig: Urania, 1974

Wentscher, Else
Englische Wege zu Kant. Leipzig: Tauchnitz 1931

Wike, Victoria S.
Kant's Antinomies of Reason - Their Origin and
Resolution. Washington, DC: Univ. Press of America, 1982

Zdansky, Rossina
Über das Problem der Zeit und des Raumes bei Kant.
Vienna: diss., 1938

editions:

Heidemann, Ingeborg (ed.)
Immanuel Kant, Kritik der reinen Vernunft.
Stuttgart: Philipp Reclam, 1978

-Kierkegaard, Sören, 1813-1855

Anderson, Barbara
Kierkegaard: A Fiction. Syracuse, NY: Syracuse Univ. Press, 1974

Kuhnhold, Christa
Der Begriff des Sprunges und der Weg des Sprachdenkens:
Eine Einführung in Kierkegaard.
Berlin: De Gruyter, 1975

Stendahl, Brita K.
Sören Kierkegaard. Boston: Twayne, 1976
Tielsch, Elfriede Walesca
Kierkegaards Glaube:
der Aufbruch des frühen 19. Jahrhunderts in das
Zeitalter moderner, realistischer Religionsauffassung.
Göttingen: Vandenhoeck & Ruprecht, 1964
Viallaneix, Nelly
Écoute, Kierkegaard: Essai sur la communication de la
parole. Paris: Cerf, 1979

collections:

Watkins, Julia (ed., trans.)
Sören Kierkegaard. Early Polemical Writings.
Princeton, NJ: Princeton Univ. Press, 1900

-Klages, Ludwig von, 1872-1956

Breukers, Eugenie Marie Josephine
De bijdrage van Ludwig Klages tot de algemene psychologie.
Roermond: Romen, 1941

-Kotarbinski, Tadeusz, 1886-

Rand, Rosalia (Rose)
T. Kotarbinski's Philosophie. Vienna: diss., 1937

-Lacan, Jacques, 1901-1981 *see also* Freud; The Psychoanalytical
Tradition

Andrès, Mireille
Lacan et la question du métalangue.
Paris: Point Hors Ligne, 1984
Felman, Shoshana
Jacques Lacan and the Adventure of Insight.
Cambridge, MA: Harvard Univ. Press, 1987
Grosz, Elizabeth
Jacques Lacan: a Feminist Introduction.
London, etc.: Routledge, 1990
Kremer-Marietti, Angèle
Lacan ou la rhétorique de l'inconscient.
Paris: Aubier, 1978
Lemaire, Anika
Jacques Lacan. Brussels: Mardaga, 1977
MacCannell, Juliet Flower
Figuring Lacan: Criticism and the Cultural Unconscious.
London: Croom Helm, c. 1986
Lincoln: Univ. of Nebraska Press, 1986

collections:
Mitchell, Juliet, and Jacqueline Rose (eds.)
 Feminine Sexuality, Jacques Lacan and the École Freudienne.
 London, etc.: Macmillan, 1982

-Lavelle, Louis, 1883-1951
Maria, Amalia de
 L'antropologia di Lavelle. Turin: Giappichelli, 1976

-Leibniz, Gottfried Wilhelm, 1646-1716 *see also* Metaphysics;
 Logic, History of
Becco, Annes
 Le simple selon G.W. Leibniz. Paris: Vrin, 1975
Dumas, Marie-Noëlle
 La pensée de la vie chez Leibniz. Paris: Vrin, 1976
Elsinger, Bertha
 Das "Vinculum substantiale" im System Leibniz.
 Vienna: diss., 1918
Frémont, Christiane
 L'être et la relation -
 Avec trente-cinq lettres de Leibniz. Paris: Vrin, 1981
Ishiguro, Hidé
 Pre-established Harmony Versus Constant Conjunction.
 Oxford: Oxford Univ. Press, 1978
Johannsen, Christa
 Leibniz: Roman seines Lebens. Berlin: Union, 1966
Saw, Ruth Lydia
 Leibniz. Harmondsworth:
 Penguin Books, 1954
Schulenburg, Sigrid von der
 Leibniz als Sprachforscher.
 Frankfurt am Main: Klostermann, 1973
Simonovits, Anna
 Dialektisches Denken in der Philosophie von Gottfried
 Wilhelm Leibniz.
 Budapest: Akademiai Kiado, 1968
Tymieniecka, Anna-Teresa
 Leibniz' Cosmological Synthesis.
 Assen: Van Gorcum 1964
Wilson, Catherine
 Leibniz's Metaphysics - A Historical and Comparative Study.
 Manchester: Manchester Univ. Press, 1989
Wilson, Margaret Hodge Dauler
 Leibniz' Doctrine of Necessary Truth.
 New York: Garland Publishing, 1990 (diss., 1965)

editions:

Okruhlik, Kathleen, and James Robert Brown (eds.)
The Natural Philosophy of Leibniz.
[Univ. of Western Ontario Series in the Philosophy of Science 29]
Dordrecht: Reidel, 1985

-Leporin-Erxleben, Dorothea Christiane, 1715-1762

Böhm, Heinz
Dorothea Christiane Erxleben. Quedlinburg, 1965

-Lessing, Gotthold Ephraim, 1729-1781

Arendt, Hannah
Von der Menschlichkeit in finsteren Zeiten:
Rede über Lessing. Munich: Hauswedell, 1960

-Levinas, Emmanuel, 1906-

Chalier, Catharine
Figures du féminin: Lecture d'Emmanuel Levinas.
Paris: La Nuit Surveillé, 1982

Wyschogrod, Edith
Emmanuel Levinas: The Problem of Ethical Metaphysics.
The Hague: Nijhoff, 1974

collections:

Aronowicz, Anette (ed., trans., Introduction)
Nine Talmudic Readings by Emmanuel Levinas.
Bloomington: Indiana Univ. Press, 1990

-Lewis, Clarence Irving, 1883-1964

Du Bose, Louisa Shannon
The Concept of Possibility in C.I. Lewis' Epistemology.
Bryn Mawr, PA: Bryn Mawr College, diss., 1917

Rosenthal, Sandra B.
The Pragmatic A Priori: A Study in the Epistemology of
C.I. Lewis. St. Louis: Green, 1976

-Locke, John, 1632-1704 *see also* History of: Anthropology;
Epistemology

Cavarero, Adriana
La teoria politica di John Locke. 1984

Cockburn, Catharine Trotter
Defence of Locke. 1701. In:
The Works of Mrs. Catharine Cockburn, Theological,
Moral, Dramatic, and Poetical, Vol. I
Ed., with biography, by Thomas Birch. London, 1751

Grant, Ruth W.
John Locke's Liberalism.
Chicago: Univ. of Chicago Press, 1987
Squadrito, Kathleen M.
Locke's Theory of Sensitive Knowledge.
Washinton, DC: Univ. Press of America, 1978
John Locke. Boston: Twayne, 1979
Vaughn, Karen Iversen
John Locke: Economist and Social Scientist.
Chicago: Univ. of Chicago Press, 1980

collections and editions:
Yolton, Jean S., and John W. Yolton (eds.)
Locke: A Reference Guide. Boston: G.K. Hall, 1985
John Locke: "Some Thoughts Concerning Education."
Oxford: Clarendon, 1989
Yolton, Jean S. (ed.)
A Locke Miscellany - Locke Biography and Criticism for All.
Bristol: Thoemmes, 1990

-Lukács, Georg, 1885-1971
Marcus, Judith
Georg Lukács and Thomas Mann.
Amherst: Univ. of Massachusetts Press, 1986

collections:
Heller, Agnes (ed.)
Lukács Revalued.
Oxford: Blackwell, 1983

-Luxemburg, Rosa, 1870-1919
Dunayevskaya, Raya
Rosa Luxemburg, Women's Liberation, and Marx's Philosophy.
Atlantic Highlands, NJ: Humanities Press, 1982
Ettinger, Elzbieta
Rosa Luxemburg: A Life.
New York: Beacon Press, 1987
Roland Holst-van der Schalk, Henriëtte
Rosa Luxemburg. Haar leven en werken.
Rotterdam, 1935

-Mach, Ernst, 1838-1916
Weinländer, Maria
Das Naturgesetz bei Ersnt Mach und den Modernen.
Vienna: diss., 1936

-Machiavelli, Niccolò, 1469-1527 see also Political Philosophy,
    History of; Spinoza

collections:
Bock, Gisela (ed.)
    Machiavelli and Republicanism.
    Cambridge: Cambridge Univ. Press, 1990

-Maine de Biran, Marie François Pierre Gonthier, 1766-1824
Drevet, Antoinette
    Maine de Biran. Paris: P.U.F., 1968

-Malebranche, Nicolas, 1638-1715
Maria, Amalia de
    Antropologia e teodicea di Malebranche.
    Turin: Accademia delle Scienze, 1970

-Malthus, Thomas Robert, 1776-1834
Blackwell, Elizabeth
    A Medical Address on the Benevolence of Malthus, contrasted
    with the Corruptions of Neo-Malthusianism. London, 1888

-Marsilius of Padua, c.1275-c.1342
Quillet, Jeannine
    Marsile de Padoue, le défenseur de la paix.
    Paris: Vrin, 1968
    La philosophie politique de Marsile de Padoue.
    Paris: Vrin, 1970

-Martineau, Harriet, 1802-1876
Rivlin, Joseph
    Harriet Martineau: A Bibliography of her Separately
    Printed Books.
    New York: The New York Public Library, 1947

-Marx, Karl, 1818-1883 *see also* Modern and Contemporary
    Philosophy; Bernstein; Hegel; Kant; Luxemburg;
    European Traditions
Beetz, Manuela
    Die Produktion- und Reproduktion des unmittelbaren
    Lebens. Das Familien- und Geschlechtsverhältnis bei
    Karl Marx und Friedrich Engels.
    Cologne: Pahl-Rugenstein, 1989
Bologh, Roslyn Wallach
    Dialectical Phenomenology: Marx's Method.
    London: Routledge & Kegan Paul, 1979

Comoth, Katharina
  Die "Verwirklichung der Philosophie," Subjektivierung
  im Denken des jungen Marx. Bonn: Bouvier, 1975
Gould, Carol C.
  Marx's Social Ontology. Cambridge, MA: MIT Press, 1978
Heller, Agnes
  Theorie der Bedürfnisse bei Marx
  (introduction by Pier Aldo Rovatti). Hamburg, etc.: VSA, 1976
  The Theory of Needs in Marx.
  London: Allison & Busby, 1976
Sherover-Marcuse, Erica
  Emancipation and Consciousness -
  Dogmatic and Dialectical Perspectives in the Early Marx.
  Oxford, etc.: Blackwell, 1986

  collections:
Meier, Olga [and Emile Bottigelli] (ed.)
  Les filles de Karl Marx. Lettres inédites.
  Paris: Édition Albin Michel, 1979

-Mauthner, Fritz, 1849-1923
Albertazzi, Liliana
  Fritz Mauthner: La critica della lingua.
  Lanciano: Rocca Caraba, 1986

-Mechthild of Magdeburg, c.1207-c.1282
Woodruff, Sue
  Meditations with Mechthild of Magdeburg.
  Santa Fe, NM: Bear and Co., n.d.

-Meinong, Alexius, 1853-1920
Kalsi, Marie-Luise Schubert
  Alexius Meinong. The Hague: Nijhoff, 1978

-Merleau-Ponty, Maurice, 1908-1961
Kruks, Sonia
  The Political Philosophy of Merleau-Ponty.
  Atlantic Highlands, NJ: Humanities Press/Brighton:
  Harvester Press, 1981
Langer, Monika M.
  Merleau-Ponty's Phenomenology of Perception - A Guide
  and Commentary. London: Macmillan, 1989
Whitford, Margaret
  Merleau-Ponty's Critique of Sartre's Philosophy.
  Lexington: French Forum, 1982

-Michelet, Jules, 1798-1874

d'Héricourt, Jenny
    La femme affranchie: réponse à MM. Michelet, Proudhon,
    E. de Giradin, A. Comte et aux autres novateurs
    modernes. Brussels: A. Lacroix, Van Meenen & Cie., 1860

Moreau, Thérèse
    Le Sang de l'histoire: Michelet, l'histoire et l'idée
    de la femme au XIXe siècle.
    Paris: Flammarion, 1982

Orr, Linda
    Jules Michelet: Nature History and Language.
    Ithaca, NY: Cornell Univ. Press, 1976

-Mill, John Stuart, 1806-1873

Borchard, Ruth
    John Stuart Mill. The Man. London: Watts, 1957

Freundlich, Elsa
    John Stuart Mills Kausaltheorie.
    Dusseldorf: Schwann, 1914

Himmelfarb, Gertrude
    On Liberty and Liberalism: The Case of John Stuart Mill.
    New York: Knopf, 1974

Kamm, Josephine
    John Stuart Mill in Love.
    London: Gordon & Cremonesi, 1977

Leon-Morera, Maria Luisa
    Estudio sobre los aspectos mas representativos en las filosofias
    de la ciencia de William Whewell y John Stuart Mill.
    Barcelona: diss., 1978

Mansfield, Sue
    John Stuart Mill: The Subjection of Women.
    AHM Publishing Corp., 1980

Tulloch, Gail
    Mill and Sexual Equality.
    Brighton: Wheatsheaf Books, 1989

collections and editions:

Rossi, Alice S. (ed.)
    Essays on Sex Equality by John Stuart Mill and
    Harriet Taylor Mill.
    Chicago: Univ. of Chicago Press, 1970

Schröder, Hannelore (ed., with introduction)
    John Stuart Mill, Harriet Taylor Mill, Helen Taylor:
    Die Hörigkeit der Frau. Texte zur Frauenemanzipation.
    Frankfurt am Main: Syndikat, 1976

-Montaigne, Michel Eyquem de, 1533-1592

Favre, Julie Velten
Montaigne, moraliste et pédagogue.
Paris: Fischbacher, 1887 or earlier
Gournay, Marie de
Le Proumenoir de Monsieur de Montaigne, par sa fille
d'alliance. Paris: Abel l'Angelier, 1594
McGowan, Margaret
Montaigne's Deceit. Philadelphia: Temple Univ. Press, 1974
Sichel, Edith
Michel de Montaigne. New York: Dutton, 1911

-Montesquieu, Charles Louis de Secondat Baron de, 1689-1755

Guyard-Fabre, Simone
La philosophie du droit de Montesquieu. Paris: Klincksieck, 1973
Mason, Sheila M.
Montesquieu's Idea of Justice. The Hague: Nijhoff, 1975
Rosso, Jeanette Geffriaud
Montesquieu et la fémininité.
Pisa: Libreria Goliardica, 1977

-Montessori, Maria, 1870-1952

Kramer, Rita
Maria Montessori: A Biography. New York: Putnam, 1976

-Murdoch, Iris, 1919-

Dipple, Elizabeth
Iris Murdoch: Work for the Spirit. London: Methuen, 1982

-Natorp, Paul, 1854-1924

Saltzman, Judy Deane
Paul Natorp's Philosophy and Religion Within the
Marburg Neokantian Tradition.
Hildesheim: Georg Olms Verlag, 1981

-Neurath, Otto, 1882-1945

Nemeth, Elisabeth
Otto Neurath und der Wiener Kreis. Revolutionäre
Wissenschaftlichkeit als politischer Anspruch.
Frankfurt am Main and New York: Campus Verlag, 1981

editions:

Neurath, Marie, and Robert S. Cohen (eds. and trans.)
Otto Neurath: Philosophical Papers 1913-1946.
Dordrecht: Reidel, 1983

-Newton, Isaac, 1642-1727
see also Modern and Contemporary Philosophy

Châtelet-de Breteuil, Gabrielle Emilie le Tonnelier, du.
First French translation of Isaac Newton's
Philosophiae Naturalis Principia Mathematica.
"Principes Mathématiques de la Philosophie Naturelle."
Paris: Desaint & Saillant, 1759
Institutions de physique. Paris: Prault fils, 1740

Hall, Maria Boas, A. Rupert Hall, and - (eds.)
Unpublished Scientific Papers of Isaac Newton.
Cambridge: Cambridge Univ. Press, 1962

-Nicholas of Cusa, 1401-1464
Börresen, Kari Elisabeth (ed.)
Nicolaus Cusanus' dialog De pace fidei. Om trosfreden
(Introduction, Norwegian trans. and commentary by
K.E. Börresen.) Oslo: Solum, 1983

Pechowitz, Hilda
Die Stellung des Menschen in der Philosophie des
Nicolaus Cusanus. Vienna: diss., 1938

-Nietzsche, Friedrich, 1844-1900 see Political Philosophy, History of
Andreas-Salomé, Lou
Friedrich Nietzsche in seinen Werken.
Vienna: Konegen, 1911

Bulhof, Ilse Nina
Apollos Wiederkehr: eine Untersuchung der Rolle des
Kreises in Nietzsches Denken über Geschichte und Zeit.
The Hague: Nijhoff, 1969

Clark, Maudemarie
Nietzsche on Truth and Philosophy.
New York: Cambridge Univ. Press, 1900

Funke, Monika
Ideologiekritik und ihre Ideologie bei Nietzsche.
Stuttgart: Fromann, 1974

Goyard-Fabre, Simone
Nietzsche et la conversion métaphysique.
Paris: Pensées Universitaires, 1972
Nietzsche et la question politique. Paris: Sirey, 1977

Graybeal, Jean
Language and "the Feminine" in Nietzsche and Heidegger.
Bloomington: Indiana Univ. Press, 1990

Higgins, Kathleen Marie
Nietzsche's Zarathustra.
Philadelphia: Temple Univ. Press, 1987

Irigaray, Luce
Amante marine de Friedrich Nietzsche.
Paris: Editions de Minuit, 1980

Kofman, Sarah
Nietzsche et la métaphore.
Paris: Payot (Bibliothèque scientifique), 1972
Nietzsche et la scène philosophique.
Paris: Galilée, 1986

Pfeffer, Rose
Nietzsche: Disciple of Dionysus.
Lewisburg, PA: Bucknell Univ. Press, 1972

Schutte, Ofelia
Beyond Nihilism: Nietzsche Without Masks.
Chicago: Univ. of Chicago Press, 1984

Strambauch, Joan
Nietzsche's Thought of Eternal Return.
Baltimore: Johns Hopkins Univ. Press, 1972

collections:

Higgins, Kathleen Marie, and Robert C. Solomon (eds.)
Reading Nietzsche.
Oxford: Oxford Univ. Press, 1988

-Origen, c. 185-c. 254
Harl, Marguerite et al.
Origene: Traité des principes (Peri archon).
Paris: Augustiniennes, 1976

-Pardo Bazán, Emilia condesa de, 1851-1921
Pattison, W.(Walter) T.
Emilia Pardo Bazán.
New York: Twayne Publishers, 1971

-Parmenides, *see* Plato; Hegel

-Pascal, Blaise, 1623-1662 *see also* Physical Sciences, History of
Canilli, Adele
Pascal: La struttura dell'uomo.
Padua: Liviana, 1978

Kummer, Irene Elisabeth
Blaise Pascal: Das Heil im Widerspruch.
Berlin: De Gruyter, 1978

-Paul of Venice, *see* Logic, History of

-Peirce, Charles Sanders 1839-1914

see also Logic, History of; Mathematics, History of

Kevelson, Roberta
Charles Peirce's Method of Methods.
Amsterdam: John Benjamins
(Foundations of Semiotics Series), 1987

collections:

Eisele, Carolyn (ed.)
Historical Perspectives on Peirce's Logic of Science,
A History of Science, I-II. Berlin: Mouton, 1985

Eisele, Carolyn (ed.)
Peirce, Charles Sanders. The new elements of mathematics.
The Hague, etc.: Mouton etc., 1976
[1. Arithmetic. 2. Algebra and geometry 3. Mathematical
miscellanea. 4. Mathematical philosophy]

-Philodemus, 1st cent. B.C.

DeLacy, Estelle A., and Philip H. DeLacy
Philodemus. Philadelphia: 1941

-Piaget, Jean, 1896-1980

Boden, Margaret A.
Jean Piaget. New York: Penguin Books, 1980

Gallagher, Jeanette McCarthy, and D. Kim Reid
The Learning Theory of Piaget and Inhelder.
Monterey, CA: Brooks/Cole, 1981

Lafuente, Maria Isabel
Casualidad y conocimiento según Piaget.
Léon: Colegio Universitario de Léon, Univ. ETC, 1977

collections:

Campbell, Sarah (ed.)
Piaget Sampler. New York: Wiley, 1976

-Pisan, Christine de, 1364-c. 1430

Laigle, Mathilde
Le Livre des Trois Vertus de Christine de Pisan et Son
Milieu Historique et Litteraire.
Paris: Honoré Champion, 1912

Pernoud, Régine
Christine de Pisan. Paris: Calmann-Lévy, 1982

Pinet, Marie-Josephe
Christine de Pisan 1364-1430.
Paris, 1927

Rigaud, Rose
Les Idées féministes de Christine de Pisan.
Neuchatel, 1911

Solente, Suzanne
Le Livre de la Mutacion de Fortune par Christine de
Pisan (trans., introduction and analysis of de Pisan (1404)).
Paris: Éditions A. & C. Picard & Cie, 1959

Willard, Charity Cannon
Christine de Pisan: Her Life and Works. A Biography.
New York: Persea Books, 1984

-Plato, 428-348 B.C.
see also Classical Philosophy; Anthropology, History of
Philosophical; Logic, History of

Annas, Julia
An Introduction to Plato's "Republic."
Oxford and Don Mills: Clarendon Press, 1981

Billings, Grace
The Art of Transition in Plato.
New York: Garland Publishers, 1979

Bluestone, Natalie Harris
Women and the Ideal Society:
Plato's 'Republic' and Modern Myths of Gender.
Berg Publishers Ltd. (via Blackwell, Oxford), 1987

Burger, Ronna
Plato's Phaedrus: A Defense of a Philosophical Art of
Writing. University: Univ. of Alabama Press, 1980
The Phaedo - A Platonic Labyrinth.
New Haven, CT: Yale Univ. Press, 1984

Cavarero, Adriana
Dialettica e politica in Platone. Padua: CEDAM, 1974
Platone: Il filosofo e il problema politico. La lettera
VII e l'epistolario. 1976

Chanteur, Janine
Platon, le desir et la cité. Paris: Sirey, 1979

Desjardins, Rosemary
The Rational Enterprise - Logos in Plato's Theaetetus.
New York: State Univ. of New York Press, 1990

Hellwig, Antje
Untersuchungen zur Theorie der Rhetorik bei Platon und
Aristoteles.
Göttingen: Vandenhoeck & Ruprecht, 1973

Hentschke, Ada Babette
Politik und Philosophie bei Platon und Aristoteles.
Frankfurt: Klostermann, 1971

Isnardi Parente, Margherita
  Filosofia e politica nelle lettere di Platone.
  Napels: Guida, 1970
  Studio sull'Academia platonica antica.
  Firenze: Olschki, 1979
Keuls, Eva C.
  Plato and Greek Painting. Leiden: Brill, 1978
Mackenzie, Mary Margaret
  Plato on Punishment. Berkeley: Univ. of California Press, 1981
Meinwald, Constance C.
  Plato's Parmenides.
  Oxford and New York: Oxford Univ. Press, 1990
Murdoch, Iris
  The Fire and the Sun: Why Plato Banished the Artists.
  Oxford: Clarendon Press, 1977
Pellikaan-Engel, M.E.
  Hesiod and Parmenides -
  A New View on their Cosmologies and on Parmenides'.
  Proem. Amsterdam: 1974, 1978
Songe-Möller, Vigdis
  Zwiefältige Wahrheit und zeitliches Sein:
  eine Interpretation des parmenideischen Gedichts.
  Würzburg: Verlag Neumann & Könighausen, 1980
Sprague, Rosamond Kent
  Plato's Philosopher-Kind: A Study of the Theoretical
  Background. Columbia: Univ. of South Carolina Press, 1976
Vogel, C.J. de
  Plato, de filosoof van het transcendente.
  Baarn: Het Wereldvenster, 1968
  Rethinking Plato and Platonism. Leiden: Brill, 1986

  editions:

Hamilton, Edith, and Huntington Cairns (eds.)
  The Collected Dialogues of Plato.
  Princeton, NJ: Princeton Univ. Press, 1961

-Plotinus, 205-270
Essen-Zeeman, C.W. van
  De Plaats van de Wil in de Philosophie van Plotinus.
  Arnhem: Slaterus, 1946
Gatti, Maria Luisa
  Plotino e la metafisica della contemplatione.
  Milan: CUSL, 1982
Isnardi Parente, Margherita
  Introduzione a Plotino. Bari: Laterza, 1989

-Popper, Karl, 1902-
Bouveresse, Renée
    Karl Popper, Ou le rationalisme critique.
    Paris: Vrin, 1978

-Priestley, Joseph, 1733-1804
Holt, Anne
    A Life of Joseph Priestley (Introduction by F. W. Hirst).
    Oxford: Univ. Press 1931

-Proudhon, Pierre-Joseph, 1809-1965 *see also* Michelet
Lambert (Adam), Juliette
    Idées anti-proudhonniennes sur l'amour, la femme et le mariage.
    Paris: Dentu, 1861

-Pythagoras, c. 575-500 B.C.
Vogel, C.J. de
    Pythagoras and Early Pythagoreanism. An Interpretation
    of Neglected Evidence on the Philosopher Pythagoras.
    Assen: Van Gorcum, 1966

-Quine, Willard Van Orman, 1908-
Siegel, Judith F. Bell
    Logic Without Mentalism: A Study of Quine's Views.
    Chicago: Univ. of Chicago, diss., 1975

collections:
Harding, Sandra (ed.)
    Can Theories be Refuted? -
    Essays on the Duhem-Quine Thesis.
    Dordrecht: Reidel, 1976

-Ramée, Pierre de la (Petrus Ramus), 1515-1572
Bruyère, Nelly
    Méthode et dialectique dans l'oeuvre de La Ramée.
    Paris: Vrin, 1984

-Reid, Thomas, 1710-1796
Griffin-Collart, Evelyne
    La philosophie écossaise du sens commun:
    Thomas Reid et Dugald Stewart.
    Brussels: Academies, 1980
Marcil-Lacoste, Louise
    Claude Buffier and Thomas Reid -
    Two Common-sense Philosophers.
    Montreal: McGill-Queen's Univ. Press, 1982

-Reinach, Adolf, 1883-1917

Bretter-Vandervort, Lucinda
The Phenomenology of Adolf Reinach: Chapters in the
Theory of Knowledge and Legal Philosophy.
Montreal: McGill Univ., 1973

-Richard of Kilvington, fl. c.1325

Kretzmann, Barbara Ensign, Norman Kretzmann (eds. and trans.)
The Sophismata of Richard Kilvington.
Cambridge: Cambridge Univ. Press, 1990

-Rosenzweig, Franz, 1886-1929

Freund, Else-Rahel
Die Existenzphilosophie Franz Rosenzweigs: Ein Beitrag
zur Analyse seines Werkes "Der Stern der Erlösung."
Hamburg: Meiner, 1959 (first ed. 1933 not distributed
for reasons of politics)

-Rousseau, Jean-Jacques, 1712-1778
see also Anthropology, History of Philosophical

Airaghi, Maria Adelia
Rousseau. Florence: Vallecchi, 1974

Carter, Christine Jane
Rousseau and the Problem of War.
New York: Garland Publishers, 1987 (diss., 1985)

Hartle, Ann
The Modern Self in Rousseau's Confessions: A Reply to
St. Augustine.
Notre Dame, IN: Univ. of Notre Dame Press, 1983

Lallo, Carmela Metelli di
Componenti anarchiche nel pensiero di J.J. Rousseau.
Florence: Nuova Italia, 1970

Lee, Dug-Soo
Zum Begriff der Weiblichkeit in Rousseaus
Erziehungstheorie. Göttingen: Master's Thesis, 1976

Roland Holst-van der Schalk, Henriëtte
Jean Jacques Rousseau: een beeld van zijn leven en
werken. Amsterdam: Maatschappij voor goede en goedkope
lectuur, 1912

Roosevelt, Grace G.
Reading Rousseau in the Nuclear Age.
Philadelphia: Temple Univ. Press, 1990

Shklar, Judith
Men and Citizens: A Study of Rousseau's Social Theory.
Cambridge: Cambridge Univ. Press, 1969

-Ruskin, John, 1819-1900
Garrigan, Kristine Ottesen
Ruskin on Architecture: His Thought and Influence.
Madison: Univ. of Wisconsin Press, 1973

-Russell, Bertrand Arthur William, 1872-1970
see also History of Modern Logic
Eames, Elizabeth Ramsden
Bertrand Russell's Theory of Knowledge.
London: Allen & Unwin, 1969
Bertrand Russell's Dialogue with his Contemporaries.
Carbondale, Edwardsville: Southern Illinois Univ. Press, 1989
Jackson, Marie-Louise
Style and Rhetoric in Bertrand Russell's Work.
Frankfurt: Lang, 1983
Rheinwald, Rosemarie
Semantische Paradoxien, Typentheorie und Ideale Sprache.
- Studien zur Sprachphilosophie Bertrand Russells
Berlin: De Gruyter, 1989

collections and editions:

Eames, Elizabeth Ramsden, and Kenneth Blackwell (eds.)
The Collected Papers of Bertrand Russell:
Vol. 7 - Theory of Knowledge: The 1913 Manuscript.
Oxford: Blackwell, 1984
Moran, Maragaret, Richard A. Rempel and - , (eds.)
Vol. 12 - Contemplation and Action, 1902-14.
Vol. 13 - Prophesy and Dissent, 1914-16.

-Sartre, Jean-Paul, 1905-1980 *see also* Hegel; Merleau-Ponty
Boschetti, Anna
Sartre et 'Les Temps Modernes':
Une entreprise intellectuelle. Paris: Minuit, 1985
Barnes, Hazel E.
Sartre. Philadelphia: Lippincott, 1973
Cannon, Betty
Sartre & Psychoanalysis
An Existentialist Challenge to Clinical Metatheory.
Lawrence: Univ. Press of Kansas
Cohen-Solal, Anne
Sartre 1905-1980. Paris: Gallimard, 1985
Sartre: A Life. New York: Pantheon, 1987
Grene, Marjorie
Sartre. New York: New Viewpoints, 1973. Washington, DC:
Center for Advanced Research & Univ. Press of America, 1983

Howells, Christina
> Sartre's Theory of Literature.
> London: Modern Humanities Research Association, 1979

McCall, Dorothy
> The Theatre of Jean-Paul Sartre.
> New York: Columbia Univ. Press, 1969

Morris, Phyllis Sutton
> Sartre's Concept of a Person: An Analytic Approach.
> Amherst: Univ. of Massachusetts Press, 1976

Murdoch, Iris
> Sartre: A Romantic Rationalist.
> London: Bowes and Bowes, 1953
> London: Chatto & Windus, 1987

Pagano, Giacoma M.
> Sartre e la dialettica. Napels: Giannini, 1970

Papone, Annagrazia
> Esistenza e corporeita in Sartre.
> Florence: Monnier, 1969

Warnock, Mary
> Sartre: A Collection of Critical Essays.
> London: Hutchinson/New York: Anchor, 1965

-Schelling, Friedrich Wilhelm Joseph von, 1775-1854

Loer, Barbara
> Das Absolute und die Wirklichkeit in Schellings
> Philosophie. Berlin: De Gruyter, 1974

-Schlegel, Friedrich von, 1772-1829

Dieschner, Caroline
> Friedrich Schlegels Lucinde und Materialien zu einer
> Theorie des Müssiggangs.
> Hildesheim: Gerstenberg, 1980

-Schleiermacher, Friedrich, 1768-1834

Keller-Wentorf, Christel
> Schleiermachers Denken. Berlin: De Gruyter, 1984

-Schlözer, Dorothea, 1770-1825

Küssner, Martha
> Dorothea Schlözer. Göttingen: Musterschmidt, 1976

-Schopenhauer, Arthur, 1788-1860

Pott, H.J.
> Pessimisme als filosofie. Inleiding tot het denken van
> Arthur Schopenhauer. Baarn: Ambo, 1988

-Schreiner, Olive, 1855-1920

First, Ruth, and Ann Scott
Olive Schreiner: A Biography.
New York: Schocken Books, 1980

-Schütz, Alfred, 1899-1959

List, Elisabeth, and Ilja Srubar (eds.)
Alfred Schütz. Neue Beiträge zur Rezeption seines Werkes.
Amsterdam: Rodopi, 1988

-Schuurman (or Schurman), Anna Maria van, 1607-1678

Birch, Una Pope-Hennessy
Anna Van Schurman: Artist, Scholar, Saint.
London: Longmans, Green and Co., 1909

-Schweizer, Albert, 1875-1965

Schur, Rosa
Albert Schweizers Ethik.
Vienna: diss., 1933

-Seghers, Anna, 1900-1988

Maag, Regula
Den Faschismus überwunden.
Zürich: ADAG, 1984

-Seneca, c. 4 B.C.- A.D. 65.

Bellincioni, Maria
Educazione alla sapientia in Seneca.
Brescia: Paideia, 1978
Fillion-Lahille, Janine
Le "De ira" de Sénèque et la philosophie Stoïcienne
des passions.
Paris: Klincksieck, 1984
Hadot, Ilsetraut
Seneca und die griechisch-römische Tradition der
Seelenleitung.
Berlin: De Gruyter, 1969

-Shelley, Mary, 1797-1851

Spark, Muriel
Child of Light: A Reassessment of Mary Shelley.
London: Tower Bridge Publications Ltd., 1951
Mary Shelley (revised ed. of Child of Light).
New York and Scarborough, Ontario: New American Library
(A Meridian Book), 1987
New York: NAL Penguin Inc., 1987

-Smith, Adam, 1723-1790

Robbins, Caroline
The Eighteenth-Century Commonwealthsman.
Cambridge, MA, 1959

-Socrates, c. 470-399 B.C. *see also* Logic, History of

Kofman, Sarah
Socrate(s).
Paris: Galilée, 1989
Raschini, Maria A.
Interpretazione Socratiche. Milan: Marzorati, 1970

-Solovyov, Vladimir Sergeyevich, 1853-1900

Bosco, Nynfa
Vladimir Soloviev: Esperienza religiosa e ricerca filosofic.
Turin: Giappichelli, 1976

-Somerville, Mary Fairfax, 1780-1872

Patterson, Elizabeth Chambers
Mary Somerville and the Cultivation of Science, 1815-1840.
International Archives of the History of Ideas 102.
Dordrecht: Martinus Nijhoff, 1983
Somerville, Martha
Mary Somerville. Personal Recollections. From Early
Life to Old Age: With Selections from her Correspondence.
London: John Murray, 1873

-Spinoza, Baruch de, 1632-1672

Bertrand, Michèle
Spinoza et l'imaginaire.
Paris: P.U.F., 1983
Brykman, Genevieve
La judéité de Spinoza.
Paris: Vrin, 1972
Calvetti, Carla Gallicet
Spinoza lettore del Machiavelli.
Milan: Universitá Cattolica del Sacro Cuore, 1972
Grene, Marjorie
Spinoza.
New York: Doubleday, 1973

collections:

Grene, Marjorie, and Debra Nails (eds.)
Spinoza and the Sciences.
Dordrecht, etc.: Reidel, 1986

-Stebbing, L. Susan, 1885-1943
Wisdom, John (ed.)
Philosophical Studies -
Essays in Memory of L. Susan Stebbing.
London, 1948 (The Aristotelian Society)

-Strauss, Leo, 1899-1973
Drury, Shadia B.
The Political Ideas of Leo Strauss.
London: Macmillan, 1988

-Suarez, Francisco, 1548-1617
Gemmeke, Elisabeth
Die Metaphysik des sittlichen Guten bei Franz Suarez.
Freiburg: Herder, 1965
Kellner, Aloisia
Die Gottesbeweise bei Franz Suarez.
Vienna: diss., 1933

-Teilhard de Chardin, Pierre, 1881-1955 *see also* Asian Traditions
King, Ursula
Towards a New Mysticism: Teilhard de Chardin and
Eastern Religions.
London: Collins, 1980

-Teresa of Avila, 1515-1582
Lincoln, Victoria
Teresa: A Woman. A Biography of Teresa of Avila.
Albany: State Univ. of New York Press, 1984

-Thomas Aquinas, 1225-1274
see also Anthropology, History of Philosophical
Edwards, Sandra (trans.)
St. Thomas Aquinas, Quodlibetal Questions 1 and 2.
Toronto: Pontifical Institute of Medieval Studies, 1983
Welp, Dorothée
Willensfreiheit bei Thomas von Aquin.
Freiburg, CH: Univ. Fribourg, 1979
Wheeler, Mary Cecilia
Philosophy and the Summa Theologica of Saint Thomas Aquinas.
Washington, DC: Catholic Univ. American Press, 1956
Zelder, Beatrice (transl.)
Saint Thomas Aquinas - On the Unity of the Intellect
Against the Averroists.
Milwaukee: Marquette Univ. Press, 1968

-Thoreau, Henry David, 1817-1862

Flak, Micheline
Thoreau ou la sagesse au service de l'action.
Paris: Seghers, 1973

-Tillich, Paul, 1886-1965

Manferdini, Tina
La filosofia della religione in Paul Tillich.
Bologna: Dehoniane, 1977
Scabini, Eugenia
Il pensiero di Paul Tillich.
Milan: Vita e Pensiero, 1967

-Valgimigli, Manara, 1876-1965

Ghezzo, Maria Vittoria
Manara Valgimigli (1876-1965): Studi e Ricordi.
Milan: SPES, 1977
Marcelli, Maria Antonietta
Manara Valgimigli scrittore. Milan: SPES, 1964
Ruffino, Rita Lucia
Manara Valgimigli filologopoeta.
Milan: Sicilia Nuova, 1974

-Vico, Giambattista, 1688-1744

Mondolfo, Rodolfa
Il - verum-factum - prima di Vico.
Naples: Guida, 1969

-Vives, Juan Luis, 1492-1540

Guerlac, Rita
Juan Louis Vives against the Pseudodialecticians:
A Humanist Attack on Medieval Logic. Milan: Unicopli, 1981

-Wang Fu-Chih, 1619-1692

Black, Alison H.
Man and Nature in the Philosophical Thought of Wang
Fu-chi. London: Univ. of Washington Press, 1988

-Weber, Max, 1868-1958

Bologh, Roslyn Wallach
Love or Greatness. Max Weber and Masculine Thinking -
A Feminist Inquiry. London: Unwin & Hyman, 1990
Weber, Marianne
Max Weber: A Biography (ed. and trans. by Harry Zohn).
New York: Wiley, 1975

-Weil, Simone, 1909-1943

Davy, Marie-Magdeleine
Simone Weil. Paris: P.U.F., 1966
Fiori, Gabriella
Simone Weil: An Intellectual Biography.
Athens: Univ. of Georgia Press, 1989
Pérez, Bea
Antropologia y filosofia en Simone Weil.
Diss: València, 1990
Petrement, Simone
Simone Weil: A Life.
New York: Pantheon, 1976

-Weizsäcker, Viktor von, 1886-1957

Kasanmoentalib, Soemini
De Dans van Dood en Leven. De Gestaltkreis van Viktor
von Weizsäcker in zijn wetenschapshistorische en
filosofische context.
Zeist (NL): Kerckenbosch, 1989

-Whitehead, Alfred North, 1861-1947

Emmet, Dorothy
Whitehead's Philosophy of Organism.
Westport, CT.: Greenwood Press, 1981
Fitzgerald, Janet
Alfred North Whitehead's Early Philosophy of Space and Time.
Washington, DC: Univ. Press of America, 1979
Kraus, Elizabeth M.
The Metaphysics of Experience -
A Companion to Whitehead's "Process and Reality."
Bronx, NY: Fordham Univ. Press, 1979
Parmentier, Alix
La philosophie de Whitehead et le problème de Dieu.
Paris: Beauchesne, 1968
Plamodon, Ann L.
Whitehead's Organic Philosophy of Science.
Albany: State Univ. of New York Press, 1979
Simonpietri-Moncfeldt, Fannie A.
Lo individual y sus relaciones internas en Alfred North
Whitehead. Pamplona: Edic. Univ. de Navarra, 1977

-Wilkins, John, 1614-1672

Shapiro, Barbara J.
John Wilkins, 1614-1672: An Intellectual Biography.
Berkeley: Univ. of California Press, 1969

-William of Ockham, c.1285-1349

Adams, Marilyn McCord
    William Ockham.
    Notre Dame, IN: University of Notre Dame Press, 1987

-Wittgenstein, Ludwig, 1889-1951 *see also* Mathematics, Philosophy of

Ambrose, Alice, and Morris Lazerowitz
    Essays in the Unknown Wittgenstein.
    Buffalo, NY: Prometheus Books, 1984

Hintikka, Merrill B., Jaakko Hintikka, and -
    Investigating Wittgenstein.
    Oxford, etc.: Blackwell, 1986

Novielli, Valeria
    Wittgenstein e la filosofia. Bari: Adriatica, 1969

Pitkin, Hanna Fenichel
    Wittgenstein and Justice.
    Berkeley: Univ. of California Press, 1972

Premo, Blanche Lillie Kolar
    Wittgenstein's Notion of Descriptions:
    From Logic to Grammar.
    Milwaukee, WI: Marquette Univ., diss., 1974

collections:

Ambrose, Alice (ed.)
    Wittgenstein's Lectures: Cambridge 1932-1935
    From the Notes of Alice Ambrose and Margaret MacDonald.
    Totowa, NJ: Rowman & Littlefield, 1979
    Oxford: Blackwell, 1980

Ambrose, Alice, and Morris Lazerowitz (ed.)
    Ludwig Wittgenstein: Philosophy and Language.
    London: Allen & Unwin, 1972

Diamond, Cora (ed.)
    Wittgenstein's Lectures on the Foundations of
    Mathematics. Ithaca, NY: Cornell Univ. Press, 1976

Klenk, Virginia H.
    Wittgenstein's Philosophy of Mathematics.
    The Hague: Nijhoff, 1976

Nagl-Docekal, Herta (ed.)
    Wittgenstein und die Philosophie des zwanzigsten
    Jahrhunderts. Vienna: 1989

-Wollstonecraft, Mary, 1759-1797

Flexner, Eleanor
    Mary Wollstonecraft.
    New York: Coward, McCann, and Geoghean, 1972

Penigault-Duchet, Paule
Mary Wollstonecraft-Godwin, 1759-1797.
Paris: Diffusion Didier-Erudition, 1984 [1975]
Sunstein, Emily W.
A Different Face, The Life of Mary Wollstonecraft.
New York: Harper & Row, 1975
Todd, Janet M.
Mary Wollstonecraft. London: Garland Publishers, 1976
Tomalin, Claire
The Life and Death of Mary Wollstonecraft.
Harmondsworth, etc.: Penguin, 1985 (1974)

-Woolf, Virginia, 1882-1841

Bowlby, Rachel
Feminist Destinations. Oxford, etc.: Blackwell, 1989
Gow, Kathleen M.
So Virginia is There Right and Wrong. Toronto: Wiley, 1980
Lehmann, J.
Virginia Woolf and her World.
London: Thames & Hudson, 1975
Marcus, Jane
Virginia Woolf and the Language of Patriarchy.
Bloomington: Indiana Univ. Press, 1987
Woolf, Virginia
Moments of Being: Unpublished Autobiographical Writings
(ed. and with introduction by Jeanne Schulkind).
New York: Harcourt Brace Jovanovich, 1976

-Wordsworth, William, 1770-1850 *see also* Epistemology, History of

Ferguson, Frances
Wordsworth: Language as Counter-Spirit.
New Haven, CT: Yale Univ. Press, 1977

-Zawirski, Zygmunt, 1882-1948

Lachman, Irena
Zygmunt Zawirski, his Life and his Work. Dordecht: Reidel, 1986

B7   Philosophical Traditions

B7.1   General Works, Surveys

Grene, Marjorie
Philosophy In and Out of Europe.
Berkeley: Univ. of California Press, 1976
Warnock, Mary
Schools of Thought. London: Faber & Faber, 1977

B7.2   **The Feminist Tradition**
see also Ideologies and Theories: Feminism; History:
Modern and Contemporary Philosophy

Albistur, Maïté; Daniel Armogathe
Histoire du féminisme français I-II. Paris: des Femmes, 1977

Berg, Barbara J.
The Remembered Gate: Origins of American Feminism, the
Woman and the City 1800-1860.
New York: Oxford Univ. Press, 1978

Browne, Alice
The Eighteenth Century Feminist Mind.
Brighton: Harvester/Detroit: Wayne State Univ. Press, 1987

Castro, Ginette
American Feminism. A Contemporary History.
New York: New York Univ. Press, 1990

Cott, Nancy
The Grounding of Modern Feminism.
New Haven, CT: Yale Univ. Press, 1989

Donovan, Josephine
Feminist Theory: The Intellectual Tradition of American
Feminism. New York: Ungar, 1985

Dubois, Ellen C.
Feminism and Suffrage. Ithaca, NY: Cornell Univ. Press, 1978

Duchen, Claire
Feminism in France From May '68 to Mitterand.
London: Routledge & Kegan Paul, 1986

Grimshaw, Jean
Feminist Philosophers:
Women's Perspectives on Philosophical Traditions.
Brighton: Harvester (Wheatsheaf Books), 1986

Hirsch, Marianne, and Evelyn Fox Keller
Conflicts in Feminism.
New York and London: Routledge, 1990

Leger, Danièle
Le Féminisme en France. Paris, 1982

Malmgreen, Gail
Neither Breado nor Roses: Utopian Feminists and the
English Working Class, 1800-1850. Brighton: Noyce, 1978

Moses, Claire Goldberg
French Feminism in the Nineteenth Century.
Albany: State Univ. of New York Press, 1984

Richardson, Lula McDowell
The Forerunners of Feminism in French Literature of the
Renaissance from Christine of Pisa to Marie Gournay.
Baltimore, and Paris, 1929

Rossi, Alice S.
  The Feminist Papers: from Adams to de Beauvoir.
  New York: Columbia Univ. Press, 1973
Smith, Hilda L.
  Reason's Disciples: Seventeenth-century English Feminists.
  Champaign: Univ. of Illinois Press, 1982
Spender, Dale
  Feminist Theories: Three Centuries of Women's
  Intellectual Traditions.
  London: The Women's Press/New York: Pantheon, 1983
Wawrytko, Sandra A.
  The Undercurrent of Feminine Philosophy in Eastern and
  Western Thought. Washington, DC: Univ. Press of America, 1975

  collections:
Boxer, Marilyn J., and Jean H. Quataert (eds.)
  European Socialist Feminism in the Nineteenth and Early
  Twentieth Centuries. New York: Elsevier, 1978
Finn, Geraldine, and Angela Miles (eds.)
  Feminism in Canada. Montreal: Black Rose, 1982
Jardine, Alice, and Paul Smith (eds.)
  Men in Feminism. New York: Methuen, 1987
Marks, Elaine, and Isabelle de Courtivron (eds.)
  New French Feminisms.
  Brighton: Harvester (Wheatsheaf Books), 1981
  Vienna/Munich: Oldenbourg, 1989
Moi, Toril (ed.)
  French Feminist Thought - A Reader.
  Blackwell, London, etc., 1988
Persall, Marilyn (ed.)
  Women and Values: Readings in Recent Feminist
  Philosophy. Belmont, CA: Wadsworth, 1986
Rogers, Katharine M.
  Feminism in 18th Century England.
  Brighton: Harvester (Wheatsheaf Books)/Urbana: Univ. of
  Illinois Press, 1982
Schissel, Lilian (ed.)
Young, Iris Marion, Jeffner Allen, and -
  The Thinking Muse: Feminism and Modern French Philosophy.
  Bloomington: Indiana Univ. Press, 1989

B7.3   **American Traditions** *see also* Ideologies and Theories
Curti, Merle
  Human Nature in American Historical Thought.
  Columbia: Univ. of Missouri Press, 1968

Jed, Stephanie H.
      Conscience in America. New York: Dutton, 1968
Russett, Cynthia Eagle
      The Concept of Equilibrium in American Social Thought.
      New Haven, CT: Yale Univ. Press, 1966

editions:

Flower, Elizabeth, and G. Murray Murphey (eds.)
      A History of Philosophy in America I-II.
      New York: Putnam, 1977

B7.4   Asian Traditions

Bruteau, Beatrice
      Evolution Toward Divinity: Teilhard de Chardin and the
      Hindu Traditions. Wheaton, IL: Theosophical House, 1974
Ching, Julia
      To Acquire Wisdom: The Way of Wang Yang-ming.
      New York: Columbia Univ. Press, 1976
Gluck, Carol
      Japan's Modern Myths. Ideology in the Late Meiji Period.
      Princeton, NJ: Princeton Univ. Press, 1986
Heimann, Betty
      Facets of Indian Thought. London: Allen & Unwin, 1964

collections:

Ching, Julia, with Chaoying Fang (eds.)
      The Records of Ming Scholars. Huang Tsung-hsi.
      Honolulu: Univ. Press of Hawaii, 1987
O'Flaherty, Wendy Doniger (ed.)
      Karma and Rebirth in Classical Indian Traditions.
      Berkeley: Univ. of California Press, 1980

B7.5   European Traditions *see also* Ideologies and Theories;
      Modern and Contemporary Philosophy; Psychoanalytical
      Tradition
Bäumer, Gertrud *see* Social Philosophy
Curti, Merle
      Le origini moderne della storiografia filosofica.
      Florence: La nuova Italia, 1976
Dunayevskaya, Raya
      Marxism and Freedom from 1776 until today.
      New York: Twayne Publishers, 1958
      London: Routledge and Kegan Paul, 1974
Isnardi Parente, Margherita
      Filosofia dell'ellenismo. Torino: Loescher, 1977

Laurenzi, M. Christina
Il "Socialismo Religioso" Svizzero: Leonhard Ragaz.
Assisi: Cittadella, 1976

Lavallard, Marie-Hélène
La philosophie marxiste. Paris: Sociales, 1982

Ornstein, Martha
The Role of Scientific Societies in the Seventeenth Century.
Chicago, 1938.

Rawson, Elizabeth
The Spartan Tradition in European Thought.
Oxford: Clarendon Press, 1969

Staël-Holstein, Anne-Louise Germaine Necker de
De l'Allemagne I-III. London, 1813. English trans.:
Germany I-II. New York, 1887

Thijssen-Schoute, C. Louise
Uit de republiek der Letteren: elf studien op het
gebied der ideeëngeschiedenis van de Gouden Eeuw.
The Hague: Nijhoff, 1967
Nederlands Cartesianisme
Amsterdam: Noord-Hollandse Uitgevers, 1954
New ed., with bibl., by Th. Verbeek: Utrecht: Hes, 1989.

Todd, Margo
Christian Humanism and the Puritan Social Order.
Cambridge: Cambr. U.P. (series Ideas in Context), 1987

collections:

Jed, Stephanie H.
Chaste Thinking:
The Rape of Lucretia and the Birth of Humanism.
Bloomington: Indiana Univ. Press, 1989

B7.6   The Psychoanalytical Tradition
see also Aesthetics: Visual Arts; Social Philosophy:
Home, Family Work; Freud; Specialized Bibliographies

Baker Miller, Jane
Psychoanalysis and Women: Contributions to New Theory
and Therapy.
New York: Brunner/Mazel, 1973

Bulhof, Ilse N.
Freud en Nederland: de interpretatie en invloed van
zijn ideeën.
Baarn: Ambo, 1983

Gallop, Jane
The Daughter's Seduction, Feminism and Psychoanalysis.
London, etc.: Macmillan, 1982

Mitchell, Juliet
   Psychoanalysis and Feminism: Freud, Reich, Lang and
   Women. New York: Vintage Books, 1975
Roudinesco, Elisabeth
   Jacques Lacan & Co. A History of Psychoanalysis in
   France, 1925-1985.
   Chicago: The Univ. of Chicago Press, 1990?
Torkle, Sherry
   Psychoanalytic Politics: Freud's French Revolution.
   New York: Basic Books, 1978

Name Index

A

Aamodt Sveen, Sissel 177
Abbiero, Marcella d' 177
Abbott, Pamela 131
Abir-Am, Pnina G. 154
Adam, Barbara 39, 86
Adams, Carol J. 114
Adams, Marilyn McCord 104, 207
Adams, Parveen 121
Adams, Robert Merrihew 104
Addelson, Kathryn Pyne 69
Adelsten, Karola 165
Adornato, Ferdinando 124
Aebi, Magdalena 149
Agacinski, Sylviane 91
Agnesi, Maria 14
Agonito, Rosemary 141
Airaghi, Maria Adelia 199
Aisenberg, Nadya 96
Aitchinson, Jean 71
Aken, Carol G. van 98
Akhmanova, Olga Sergeevna 51-52,
    54
al-Hibri, Azizah 121
Alanen, Lilli 28, 145
Albertazzi, Liliana 190
Albistur, Maïté 209
Albrecht, Lisa 117
Alic, Margaret 153
Allart de Meritens, Hortense 41
Allen, Anita A. 114
Allen, Jeffner 210
Allen, Polly Wynn 133
Allen, Prudence 142
Almond, Brenda 69, 100, 104, 107
Alscher, Helga 55
Amado Levy-Valensi, Eliane 38
Ambrose, Alice 16, 207
Andersen, Margaret 24
Anderson, Barbara 184
Andia, Ysabel de 178
Andolson, Barbara Hilkert 104
Andreas-Grisebach, Manon 96, 98, 100
Andreas-Salomé, Lou 18, 193
Andree, Josephine 59

Andree, Richard 59
Andrei, Marga 48
Andrès, Mireille 185
Angier, Natalie 155
Anglemyer, Mary 99
Annas, Julia 49, 137, 160, 196
Anscombe, G.E.M. 14, 16, 71, 74, 100
Apel, Roberta J. 106
Appignanesi, Lisa 162
Aragona, Tullia d' 27
Arber, Agnes 30
Arbib, Michael A. 17
Arcari, Paola Maria 137
Archer, Margaret S. 94
Ardener, Shirley 21
Arditti, Rita 29
Arendt, Hannah 72, 115, 158, 160,
    164, 182, 187
Arens, Katherine 145
Armegaud, Françoise 53
Armogathe, Daniel 209
Arnold, Carroll C. 53
Aronowicz, Anette 187
Arroyo, Anita 169
Ascher, Carol 162
Ashworth, E.J. 147-148
Asmis, Elizabeth 172
Asperen, G.M. van 104, 108, 129, 165
Assiter, Alison 129, 158
Astell, Mary 45, 57, 81, 84, 124, 128
Astington, Janet W. 73
Atherton, Margaret 165
Atkins, Dorothy 171
Attwood, Elspeth 112
Aufenanger, Stefan 16
Augspurg, Anita 100
Austermann, Maria 164
Avramides, Anita 49
Ayres, Edith 65

B

Baas, Ludolf C. 109
Babcock, Barbara A. 94
Bachelard, Suzanne 150
Bachstütz, Laura 149

M

Maag, Regula 202
Mac Coll, Sylvia Hazelton 41
Macaulay-Graham, Catherine 33
Macauley-Graham, Catharine
 Sawbridge 180
MacCannell, Juliet Flower 185
Macciocchi, Maria Antonietta 119,
 176
MacCormack, Carol 96
Macdonald, Cynthia 74
MacDonald, Margaret 17
Macho, Thomas 19
MacIntyre, Alasdair 40
Mackenzie, Mary Margaret 197
MacKinnon, Catharine A. 111, 120
Macklin, Ruth 102
Maclaren, Elizabeth 82
Macy, Joanna 84
Maddy, Penelope 68
Maher, Gerry 107
Mahowald, Mary Briody 27, 49, 144
Maier, Anneliese 149, 156
Maitre, Doreen 36
Major-Poetzl, Pamela 173
Makai, Maria 103
Makau, Josina M. 60
Makin, Bathsua Pell 33
Malmgreen, Gail 209
Malmström, Anna-Karin 108
Manferdini, Tina 205
Mannheim, Karl 26
Mannlicher, Gertrud 48
Mannoni, Maud 107
Mansbridge, Jane J. 118
Mansfield, Sue 191
Mansion, Suzanne 147
Mappes, Thomas A. 107
Marcelli, Maria Antonietta 205
Marcialis, Maria Teresa 173
Marcil-Lacoste, Louise 19, 198
Marcus, Jane 208
Marcus, Judith 188
Marecek, Jeanne 39
Maren-Grisebach, Manon 96
Maria, Amalia de 33, 186, 189
Mariaux, Veronika 28
Marinella, Lucretia 26
Markova, Ivana 47

Marks, Elaine 163, 210
Martens, J. L. 65
Martienssen, Heather 91
Martin, Gottfried 157
Martin, Jane Roland 33
Martineau, Harriet 32, 82, 168
Martinez, Lauro 142
Masham, Damaris Cudworth 81, 82,
 126
Mason, Sheila M. 192
Massey, Barbara Delp 66
Massey, Marilyn Chapin 26
Mattfeld, Jacquelyn A. 98
Matthews, Jill Julius 143
Maurman, B. 179
Maus, Ingeborg 113
Mayberry, Katherine J. 42, 60
Mayer-Hillebrand, Franziska 166
Mayntz, Renate 40
Mc Dermott, Agnes Charlene Senape
 148
McAlister, Linda 166
McCall, Catherine 19
McCall, Dorothy 201
McCloskey, Mary 183
McCorduck, Pamela 74, 99
McCormach, R. 156
McDonagh, Enda 103
McFague, Sallie 82
McGinn, Marie 49
McGowan, Margaret 192
McLean, Sheila 107
McMillan, Carol 27
Mechanic, Janevive Jean 57
Mechthild of Magdeburg 76
Meese, Elizabeth 19
Meiches, J. 15
Meichsner, Irene 60
Meier, Olga 190
Meijsing, Monica 74
Meinwald, Constance C. 197
Mendelssohn, Everett 31
Mendus, Susan 122, 144, 152
Menzer, Ursula 96
Menzies, Lucy 150
Merchant, Carolyn 99
Mercier-Josa, Solange 177
Merleker, Margarete 181
Mernissi, Fatima 116
Merrill, Susan 129